Reteaching and Practice

Workbook

Grade 6

Scott Foresman·Addison Wesley

enVisionMATH®
Common Core

PEARSON

Glenview, Illinois • Boston Massachusetts • Chandler, Arizona • Upper Saddle River, New Jersey

ISBN-13: 978-0-328-69781-6

ISBN-10: 0-328-69781-8

1 2 3 4 5 6 7 8 9 10 V016 20 19 18 17 16 15 14 13 12 11

Contents

Place Value

A parsec is a unit of measurement equal to 30,860,000,000,000 kilometers. Each digit in the number 30,860,000,000,000 has a place value. The 3 in the number is in the ten-trillions place, and the value is 30,000,000,000,000. A comma separates the number into periods.

Trillions			Billions			Millions			Thousands			Ones		
Hundred trillions	Ten trillions	Trillions	Hundred billions	Ten billions	Billions	Hundred millions	Ten millions	Millions	Hundred thousands	Ten thousands	Thousands	Hundreds	Tens	Ones
3	0	8	6	0	0	0	0	0	0	0	0	0	0	

The number 30,860,000,000,000 can be written in different ways.

Standard form: 30,860,000,000,000

Word form: Thirty trillion, eight hundred sixty billion

Expanded form: 30,000,000,000,000 + 800,000,000,000 + 60,000,000,000

Strategy Practice For **1–3**, write each number in the place-value chart above. Then write the place and the value of the underlined digit.

1. 1,23<u>4</u>,567,890   _____

2. 5<u>6</u>8,103,528,492   _____

3. <u>1</u>2,400,221,000,445   _____

4. Write 4,200,060,000 in word form. Use the place-value chart for help.

_____

5. Write fifteen trillion, four hundred thousand in standard form.

_____

6. Lake Argyle normally holds about two hundred billion, four hundred million cubic feet of water. Write this number in expanded form.

_____

R 1·1

Place Value

For **1–4**, write the place and the value of the underlined digit.

1. 205,300,005,001 _____

2. 680,525,917,143 _____

3. 102,105,000,071,000 _____

4. 40,400,040,000,444 _____

5. Write the number 100,050,000,982 in expanded form using only addition.

_____

_____

6. What is 23,000,400,000,158 in word form?

 A Twenty-three million, four hundred thousand, one hundred fifty-eight

 B Twenty-three billion, four hundred million, one hundred fifty-eight

 C Twenty-three trillion, four hundred million, one hundred fifty-eight

 D Two trillion, three billion, four million, one hundred fifty-eight

7. **Algebra** A megabyte holds about 1,000,000 characters of data. A gigabyte holds about 1,000 times more data than a megabyte. About how many characters of data does the gigabyte hold?

 A One trillion

 B One billion

 C One million

 D One thousand

8. **Writing to Explain** How are the labels in each period alike? How are they different?

_____

_____

_____

_____

Comparing and Ordering Whole Numbers

Three whales weigh 112,290 pounds, 112,238 pounds, and 112,336 pounds. You can use a place-value chart to order the weights from greatest to least.

Write the numbers in the place-value chart.

	Trillions				Billions			Millions			Thousands			Ones	
Hundred trillions	Ten trillions	Trillions	Hundred billions	Ten billions	Billions	Hundred millions	Ten millions	Millions	Hundred thousands	Ten thousands	Thousands	Hundreds	Tens	Ones	

Start with the greatest place. Find the first place where the digits are different. That is the hundreds place. Since 3 is greater than 2 112,336 is the greatest weight. Compare the tens place for the other two weights. The weights in order are: 112,336; 112,290; 112,238.

Use < or > to compare.

1. 7,210 ◯ 7,201   **2.** 18,336 ◯ 23,214   **3.** 46,177 ◯ 46,195

4. 326,251 ◯ 316,622   **5.** 982,315 ◯ 1,200,551   **6.** 6,832,525 ◯ 8,832,114

For **7** and **8,** order the numbers from least to greatest.

7. 36,352; 42,177; 36,890

_____

8. 472,315,000; 471,278,000; 477,515,000

_____

9. Number Sense If you compare a 4-digit whole number and a 5-digit whole number, which number is greater?

_____

Comparing and Ordering Whole Numbers

Use < or > to compare.

1. 9,035 ◯ 9,062   **2.** 362,286 ◯ 360,055   **3.** 7,261,005 ◯ 7,266,500

For **4** and **5,** order the numbers from least to greatest.

4. 75,321; 72,369; 72,752; 57,575

_____

5. 6,074,232; 6,234,921; 6,243,219

_____

For **6** and **7,** order from greatest to least.

6. 300 thousand; 300 billion; 3 trillion; 30 million

_____

7. 4,810,414; 4,767,894; 4,562,626; 4,909,000

_____

8. Writing to Explain Tell how you would decide if 9,899,989 is greater than or less than 9,898,998.

_____

_____

9. Number Sense If you plot these numbers on a number line, which one will be in the middle? 105,394; 150,494; 115,054

_____

10. Geometry Which of these figures has the greatest perimeter?

   A A square with sides 109 meters long

   B A hexagon with sides 65 meters long

   C A rectangle with length 24 meters and width 46 meters

   D A pentagon with sides 72 meters long

Exponents and Place Value

base $\longrightarrow 5^4 \longleftarrow$ exponent

The number 5 is the **base**. The base is the factor that is being multiplied.

The number 4 is the **exponent**. The exponent tells how many times the base is used as a factor.

$$5^4 = 5 \times 5 \times 5 \times 5 = 625$$

The base (5) is used as a factor the exponent (4) number of times.

To write a product in exponential form: $4 \times 4 \times 4 \times 4 \times 4 \times 4 \times 4$ First write the base: **4** Count the number of times the base is used as a factor. This is the exponent. 4^7	To evaluate an exponential number: 6^3 Write the base as a factor the number of times shown by the exponent. $6^3 = 6 \times 6 \times 6 = 216$

To write the expanded form of a number using exponents:

Write the number in expanded form.

$52,965 = (5 \times 10,000) + (2 \times 1,000) + (9 \times 100) + (6 \times 10) + (5 \times 1)$

Write the place values as powers of 10.

$52,965 = (5 \times 10^4) + (2 \times 10^3) + (9 \times 10^2) + (6 \times 10^1) + (5 \times 10^0)$

Tip: Any number raised to the first power equals that number. $8^1 = 8$

Write each power as a product and evaluate the expression.

1. 9^4 _____

2. 4^5 _____

Write each product in exponential form.

3. $3 \times 3 \times 3 \times 3 \times 3$ _____

4. $7 \times 7 \times 7 \times 7 \times 7 \times 7 \times 7 \times 7$ _____

Write the number in expanded form using exponents.

5. $74,271 =$ _____ + _____ + _____ + _____ + _____

6. Number Sense Explain the difference between 4^6 and 6^4.

_____

_____

_____

Exponents and Place Value

Write each expression in exponential form.

1. $5 \times 5 \times 5 \times 5 \times 5 \times 5$ _____

2. $2 \times 2 \times 2 \times 2 \times 2 \times 2 \times 2$ _____

3. $3 \times 3 \times 3$ _____

4. 9 _____

Write each number in expanded form using exponents.

5. 53,806 _____

6. 527,519 _____

Evaluate.

7. 6^2 _____

8. 5^3 _____

9. 3^6 _____

10. 2^8 _____

11. **Reasoning** Zach invested $50 and was able to triple his money in two years. Kayla also began with $50 in investments, and was able to cube her money in two years. Who had more money after two years? Explain.

_____

_____

_____

12. **Writing to Explain** In 1968, the estimated population of the world was 3,559,028,982 people. When this number is written in expanded form using exponents, one power of 10 would not be represented. Which power of 10? Why?

_____

_____

13. **Number Sense** Which is **NOT** equal to 1?

A 10^0

B 4^1

C 1×10^0

D 1^4

Decimal Place Value

A decimal is a number that uses a decimal point. Each digit in a decimal number has a place and value. You can use a place-value chart to determine a digit's place and value. The decimal point is read "and".

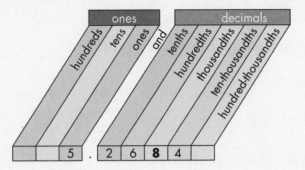

The 8 is in the thousandths place. Its value is 8 thousandths, or 0.008.

The standard form of the number is 5.2684. The word form is five and two thousand, six hundred eighty-four ten-thousandths.

The expanded form is: _____ + 0.2 + 0.06 + _____ + 0.0004.

Write the place and value of the underlined digit.

1. 2.19<u>5</u>   _____

2. 6.2<u>3</u>94   _____

3. 34.326<u>2</u>   _____

Write the number given in the form indicated.

4. 2.346 in short-word form   _____

5. 13 and 223 thousandths in standard form   _____

6. 281.1025 in word form   _____

_____

7. Number Sense Write a decimal that has 3 in the tenths place and 1 in the ten-thousandths place. _____

8. Writing to Explain Explain how you know that 17 thousandths has more than two places to the right of the decimal point.

_____

_____

Decimal Place Value

Write the place and value of the underlined digit.

1. 56.3<u>8</u>9 _____

2. 9.643<u>7</u>2 _____

Write the number given in the form indicated.

3. 8.7204 in expanded form _____

4. 43 and 962 ten thousandths in standard form _____

What is the whole number portion of the decimal?

5. 5.024 _____   **6.** 418.0972 _____

What is the decimal portion of the decimal?

7. 176.261 _____   **8.** 91.0213 _____

The slowest growing tree is a White Cedar in Canada. It grew about
0.0658 centimeters per year in 155 years. Use this information to answer **9** and **10**.

9. To what decimal place value is the yearly growth measured?

_____

10. How would you write this number in word form?

_____

11. Number Sense Write a decimal that has 6 in the
hundredths place and the ten-thousandths place. _____

12. Writing to Explain How would you write a
decimal that is less than 5 ten-thousandths? _____

_____

_____

13. Which shows the short-word form for 16.011?

A 16 and 11 thousandths   **B** 16 and 11 ten-thousandths

C 16 and 11 hundredths   **D** 16 and 11 tenths

P 1·4

Multiplying and Dividing by 10, 100, and 1,000

You can use place value and patterns to multiply and divide by 10, 100, and 1,000.

Multiplying by 10, 100, and 1,000

Move the decimal point the same number of places to the **right** as there are zeros. Annex zeros if you need to.

$1.12 \times 10 = 11.2$	The decimal point moves 1 place to the right.
$0.2 \times 100 = 20$	The decimal point moves 2 places to the right.
$0.006 \times 1,000 = 6$	The decimal point moves 3 places to the right.

Dividing by 10, 100, and 1,000

Move the decimal point the same number of places to the **left** as there are zeros. Annex zeros if you need to.

$0.2 \div 10 = 0.02$	The decimal point moves 1 place to the left.
$1.08 \div 100 = 0.0108$	The decimal point moves 2 places to the left.
$170 \div 1,000 = 0.17$	The decimal point moves 3 places to the left.

Find each product or quotient.

1. $0.31 \times 10 =$ _____

2. $1.51 \times 100 =$ _____

3. $4.061 \times 1,000 =$ _____

4. $2.6 \div 10 =$ _____

5. $142.1 \div 100 =$ _____

6. $50.5 \div 1,000 =$ _____

7. $0.01 \times 100 =$ _____

8. $30.63 \div 10 =$ _____

9. $321.2 \div 1,000 =$ _____

10. $4.59 \times 10 =$ _____

11. $0.62 \times 1,000 =$ _____

12. $0.8 \div 100 =$ _____

13. **Number Sense** Without dividing, will the quotient be greater than or less than the dividend when you divide 0.34 by 10? Explain.

_____

_____

Multiplying and Dividing by 10, 100, and 1,000

Find each product or quotient.

1. $0.006 \times 10 =$ _____

2. $0.64 \div 10 =$ _____

3. $123.3 \div 100 =$ _____

4. $8.7 \times 100 =$ _____

5. $0.145 \times 1{,}000 =$ _____

6. $542.3 \div 1{,}000 =$ _____

7. $0.91 \times 100 =$ _____

8. $0.1 \div 10 =$ _____

9. $100 \div 1{,}000 =$ _____

10. $2 \div 100 =$ _____

11. $0.302 \times 1{,}000 =$ _____

12. $1.397 \times 100 =$ _____

13. $0.038 \div 10 =$ _____

14. $0.0115 \times 10 =$ _____

15. Reasoning What number do you need to multiply by 100 to get the same result as $16.2 \div 10$? Explain.

_____

_____

16. Number Sense An alligator hatchling grew to 72.5 inches after six years. This length is 10 times its hatchling length. If you want to know its hatchling length, should you multiply or divide 72.5 by 10? Explain.

_____

_____

17. What is the quotient of $12.12 \div 100$?

A 0.1212

B 1.212

C 121.2

D 1,212

18. Writing to Explain Casey said that $0.03 \times 1{,}000$ is 3. Explain why Casey's answer is not correct. What mistake do you think he made?

_____

_____

Comparing and Ordering Decimals

| Compare decimals by place value. | 6.241
6.2**8**5
↑ | The digit in the hundredths place shows which is greater.
6.285 > 6.241 |

Order decimals on a number line.

Order 3.572, 3.746, and 3.719 from least to greatest.

```
        3.572                      3.719      3.746
◄───●──────●──────────●──────●──────●──────●───►
   3.5    3.6        3.7        3.8
```

Order decimals by place value.

Order 5.337, 6.278, 5.185, and 5.319 from least to greatest.

Order by ones:	**5**.337	**5**.185	**5**.319	(**6**.278)
Order by tenths.	(5.**1**85)	5.**3**37	5.**3**19	6.278
Order by hundredths.	5.185	(5.3**1**9)	(5.3**3**7)	6.278

5.185 < 5.319 < 5.337 < 6.278

Use >, <, or = to compare each pair of numbers.

1. 0.57 ◯ 0.75

2. 2.382 ◯ 2.283

3. 4.8693 ◯ 4.8963

4. 3.6720 ◯ 3.0672

Order from least to greatest.

5. 1.943   1.869   1.895   _____

6. 6.584   6.579   6.568   _____

7. 4.704   4.74   4.074   _____

8. 3.5603   3.5063   3.0563   _____

9. Writing to Explain Explain how you know which number is larger 2.094 or 2.904.

_____

_____

_____

Comparing and Ordering Decimals

Use >, <, or = to compare each pair of numbers.

1. 656.07 $\bigcirc$ 656.23

2. 73.42 $\bigcirc$ 72.56

3. 0.01 $\bigcirc$ 0.10

4. 7.999 $\bigcirc$ 7.998

Order from least to greatest.

5. 639.087, 639.078, 639.088

_____

6. 0.0909, 0.0989, 0.0999

_____

7. Geometry Which circle has the greatest diameter? (The diameter is the line through the center of a circle.)

4.25 in.

A

4.246 in.

B

4.308 in.

C

_____

8. Writing to Explain How would you find a number between 3.2 and 3.26?

_____

_____

9. Which decimal is greater than 3.33 but less than 3.34?

A 2.3349

B 3.305

C 3.329

D 3.336

Problem Solving: Make an Organized List

Jose, Sumi, and Tina need to stand in a straight line in the school cafeteria. In how many different ways can they stand in the line?

Read and Understand

Step 1: What do you know?

Jose, Sumi, and Tina need to be in a straight line.

Step 2: What are you trying to find?

How many different ways can the three friends stand in the line?

Plan and Solve

Step 3: Make an organized list to find the different ways Jose, Sumi, and Tina can stand in the line.

Jose First	Sumi First	Tina First
Jose, Sumi, Tina	Sumi, Jose, Tina	Tina, Jose, Sumi
Jose, Tina, Sumi	Sumi, Tina, Jose	Tina, Sumi, Jose

Answer: Jose, Sumi, and Tina can stand in the line in 6 different ways.

Solve by making an organized list. The lists have been started for you. Finish the lists.

1. Brandon is using the digits 2, 3, 6, and 9 for his locker. How many *different* combinations can he make using the four digits?

2	3	6	9
2369	3269	6239	9236
2396	3296	6293	9263
2___93	3692	6392	9326
263___	3629	6329	9362
2936	3962	6923	9623
2963	3926	6932	9632

_____

_____

2. How many *different* pairs of markers can be formed if you have one yellow, one red, one green, one blue, and one purple marker?

Yellow	Red	Green	Blue	Purple
Y, R	R, G	G, B	B, P	
Y, G	R, B	G, P		
Y, ___	R, P			
Y, ___				

_____

_____

Problem Solving: Make an Organized List

Solve by making an organized list. The lists have been started for you.
Complete the lists and answer the questions.

1. A balloon game at the county fair gives 1,000 points, 500 points,
and 250 points for each balloon that you pop. If Stewart buys 2
darts, how many possible points can he score?

1,000	500	250	Total
✓ ✓			2,000
✓	✓		1,500
✓		✓	1,250

_____

2. How many different 3-letter combinations can you make with the
letters, L, G, and F?

L	G	F
LGF		
LFG		

_____

3. In a chess tournament, Miguel, Rebecca, Kyle, Ana, and Josh will
play each other once. How many games will they play?

M	R	K	A	J
MR				
MK				
MA				
MJ				

_____

4. Tanya has to wear a cap and T-shirt for her job at the amusement
park. She can wear a red, blue, or yellow cap and a red or green
shirt. How many different cap and shirt pairs can Tanya wear?

A 5   **B** 6   **C** 9   **D** 10

5. Writing to Explain How could you find the number of different combinations of 6
letters in a computer password?

Using Variables to Write Expressions

A variable represents a quantity that can change. To use a variable to write an algebraic expression for a situation, you need to decide which operation is appropriate for the situation. To help you, some words and phrases are listed below.

Word phrase	Variable	Operation	Algebraic Expression
ten **more than** a number b	b	Addition	$b + 10$
the **sum** of 8 and a number c	c		$8 + c$
five **less than** a number d	d	Subtraction	$d - 5$
15 **decreased by** a number e	e		$15 - e$
the **product** of 8 and a number f	f	Multiplication	$8f$
19 **times** a number g	g		$19g$
the quotient of a number h **divided by** 2	h	Division	$h \div 2$
a number i **divided into** 50	i		$50 \div i$

Write each algebraic expression.

1. a number j **divided by** 5

   Identify the operation. _____   Write the expression. _____

2. the **sum** of 2 and a number k _____

3. 6 **times** a number m _____

4. a number n **divided into** 9 _____

5. 4 **less than** a number p _____

6. q fewer limes than 10 _____

7. r tickets at $7 each _____

8. A field goal scores 3 points. Write an algebraic expression to represent the number of points the Raiders will score from field goals.

   Identify the operation _____   Write the expression. _____

9. **Writing to Explain** Write an algebraic expression to represent the situation below. Explain how the expression relates to the situation.

   Some children share 5 apples equally among themselves.

   _____

   _____

R 2·1

Using Variables to Write Expressions

Write each algebraic expression.

1. 6 more than a number c _____

2. twice a number b _____

3. 25 less than a number d _____

4. the product of 7 and a number e _____

5. 50 divided by a number f _____

6. the sum of a number g and 2 _____

7. 8 more stripes than a number h _____

8. 12 fewer hats than four times a number i _____

9. Alexander has $10. He buys a snack. Which expression shows how much money Alexander has left?

   A $s + 10$

   B $10 - s$

   C $10s$

   D $s \div 10$

10. A diner has booths and counter seating. Each booth can seat 4 people. Another 15 people can sit at the counter. Which expression shows how many customers can be seated in the diner?

   A $15b - 4$

   B $15b + 4$

   C $4b - 15$

   D $4b + 15$

11. **Reasonableness** Linnia bought some flats of flowers. Each flat holds 9 flowers. Linnia has planted 10 flowers. Is $9x + 10$ a reasonable way to represent the number of flowers that Linnia has left to plant? Explain your answer.

_____

_____

_____

Properties of Operations

Commutative Properties	Associative Properties
You can add or multiply numbers in any order and the sum or product will be the same.	You can group numbers differently. It will not affect the sum or product.
Examples: $10 + 5 + 3 = 5 + 3 + 10 = 18$ $7 \times 5 = 5 \times 7 = 35$	**Examples:** $2 + (7 + 6) = (2 + 7) + 6 = 15$ $(4 \times 5) \times 8 = 4 \times (5 \times 8) = 160$
Identity Properties You can add zero to a number or multiply it by 1 and not change the value of the number.	**Multiplication Property of Zero** If you multiply a number by zero, the product will always be zero.
Examples: $17 + 0 = 17$ $\qquad 45 \times 1 = 45$	**Example:** $12 \times 0 = 0$

Find each missing number. Tell what property or properties are shown.

1. $9 \times 5 = 5 \times$ _____

_____

2. _____ $\times 89 = 89$

_____

3. $(3 + 4) + 19 = 3 + ($ _____ $+ 19)$

_____

4. $128 +$ _____ $= 128$

_____

5. _____ $+ 18 = 18 + 12$

_____

6. Reasoning What is the product of any number, x, multiplied by 1? Explain how you know.

_____

_____

Properties of Operations

Find each missing number. Tell what property or properties are shown.

1. (32 + _____) + 2 + 7 = 32 + (14 + 2) + 7

_____

2. 8 + 6 + 12 = _____ + 12 + 6

_____

3. (8 × _____) × 7 = 8 × (9 × 7)

_____

4. _____ + 0 = 34

_____

5. 12 × 3 = 3 × _____

_____

6. 1 × _____ = 288

_____

7. Reasoning Write a number sentence that shows why the associative property does not work with subtraction.

_____

8. Which property is shown in (23 × 5) × 13 × 7 = 23 × (5 × 13) × 7?

  A Commutative Property of Multiplication   **B** Identity Property of Multiplication

  C Associative Property of Multiplication   **D** Associative Property of Addition

9. Writing to Explain Explain why you do not have to do any computing to solve 15 × 0 × (13 + 7).

_____

_____

Order of Operations

Order of operations is a set of rules that mathematicians use when computing numbers. Here is how order of operations is used to solve the following problem: $7 + (5 \times 4) \times 3$.

Order of Operations

First, compute all numbers inside parentheses.	$7 + (5 \times 4) \times 3$ $7 + \quad 20 \quad \times 3$
Next, evaluate terms with exponents. If there are no exponents, go to the next step.	$7 + 20 \times 3$
Then, multiply and divide the numbers from left to right.	$7 + 60$
Finally, add and subtract the numbers from left to right.	67

How to use parentheses to make each sentence true:	$6 + 2 \times 9 = 72$
Using order of operations, $6 + 2 \times 9 = 24$, not 72.	
Place parentheses around $6 + 2$ so that this operation is done first:	$(6 + 2) \times 9 = 72$ $8 \times 9 = 72$

Evaluate each expression.

1. $8 + 7 \times 5 =$ _____

2. $18 - 3 \times 2 =$ _____

3. $3 \times 7 + 3 \times 5 =$ _____

4. $40 \div (2 \times 4) =$ _____

5. $6 \times 3 - 6 \times 2 =$ _____

6. $9 + 2^3 =$ _____

7. $7 + 12 \times 3 - 2 =$ _____

8. $4 \times (5 + 5) \div 20 + 6 =$ _____

9. $4^2 - (3 \times 5) =$ _____

10. $(3 \times 2) + 3^2 =$ _____

11. Reasoning Which operation should be performed *last* in this problem: $3^2 + 7 \times 4$? Why?

_____

Use parentheses to make each sentence true.

12. $0 \times 6 + 9 = 9$ _____

13. $3^2 + 2 \times 2 = 13$ _____

R 2·3

Order of Operations

Evaluate each expression.

1. $3 + 4 \times 7$

_____

2. $88 - 6 \times 6$

_____

3. $8 \times 2 + 7 \times 3$

_____

4. $(5 + 9) + 3 \times 8$

_____

5. $(6 + 3^2) + 5$

_____

6. $9^2 - (7 \times 5) + 3$

_____

7. $48 \div 2 + 6$

_____

8. $26 \div (5 + 8) + 1$

_____

9. $18 + 3 \times (6 \div 2)$

_____

10. Reasoning What operation would you perform *last*
in this problem: $(2 \times 3) + (7 \times 2)$?

_____

Use parentheses to make each number sentence true.

11. $10 + 5 \times 4^2 \div 2^3 = 20$

12. $124 - 6 \times 0 + 15 = 34$

13. $10^2 - 10 + 3 = 93$

14. $7 + 5 \times 3 \div 3 = 12$

15. Mr. Miller's sixth-grade class went on a field trip to hear the
symphony perform. Their seats were grouped in the following
ways: 2 groups of 3 seats; 3 groups of 4 seats, 4 groups of
2 seats, and 1 seat (for Mr. Miller). Write a number sentence to
calculate how many students went on the field trip.

_____

_____

16. Evaluate the expression $(4^2 - 4) + 6 \div 2$.

A 4 **B** 9 **C** 12 **D** 15

17. Writing to Explain Suppose you had to evaluate $9^2 + 5 \times 4$.
Tell the order in which you would compute these numbers.

_____

_____

The Distributive Property

You can use the distributive property to multiply mentally.

Example A. Evaluate 7 × 53.   7 × 53

Break 53 apart into 50 + 3.   7 × (50 + 3)

Then distribute the 7 to each part.   (7 × 50) + (7 × 3)

Multiply.   350 + 21

Add the products.   371

Example B. Evaluate 5(42) − 5(2). Remember 5(42) means 5 × 42.

Use the distributive property in reverse.   5(42) − 5(2)

Join 42 and 2 using the minus sign.   5 (42 − 2)

Subtract.   5 × 40

Multiply the difference by 5.   200

Find each missing number.

1. 8 × (30 + 2) = (8 × _____) + (8 × 2)   **2.** (6 × _____) − (6 × 7) = 6 × (37 − 7)

3. 8(28) = 8 (20) + 8 (_____)   **4.** 3(22) + 3(4) = 3(_____) + 3(6)

Use the distributive property and mental math to evaluate.

5. 6(24)   _____   **6.** 4(13) − 4(3)   _____

7. 7(24 + 6)   _____   **8.** 2(72)   _____

9. 9(12) + 9(3) _____   **10.** 5(24 − 3)   _____

11. Number Sense What are two other ways to write 9(46)?

_____

R 2·4

The Distributive Property

Find each missing number.

1. $8 \times (30 + 2) = (8 \times$ _____$) + (8 \times 2)$ **2.** $8(94) = 8($_____$) + 8(4)$

3. $5(45 + 5) = 5($_____$)$ **4.** $9(42) - 9(4) = 9(30) + 9($_____$)$

Use the distributive property and mental math to evaluate.

5. $3(58 - 8)$ _____   **6.** $7(31 + 19)$ _____

7. $9(72)$ _____   **8.** $4(26) - 4(16)$ _____

9. $8(41) + 8(5)$ _____   **10.** $5(22 - 5)$ _____

11. Writing to Explain Describe the mental math steps you would use to find $7(42)$.

_____

_____

12. Number Sense Use mental math to evaluate the expression $6(31) + 6(4) - 6(15)$.

_____

13. Geometry Write an expression for the area of this rectangle. Evaluate your expression to find the area.

```
              20 cm        4 cm
        ┌──────────────┬──────┐
  8 cm  │              │      │
        └──────────────┴──────┘
```

_____

14. Algebra Which expression is equal to $12m + 12n$?

   A $12mn$

   B $12m + n$

   C $12m - 12n$

   D $12 (m + n)$

Mental Math

Use the properties of operations and mental strategies to compute.

> **Commutative Property:** The order in which numbers are added or multiplied does not affect the sum or product.
>
> **Associative Property:** The way in which numbers are grouped to be added or multiplied does not affect the sum or product.

Break apart the numbers:	**Look for multiples of 10 or 100.**
Add the tens, add the ones, then add the sums together.	Multiply numbers having a product of 10 or 100 first. Then multiply the other number.

Break apart the numbers:

$47 + 83$
$(40 + 7) + (80 + 3)$
$(40 + 80) + (7 + 3)$
$120 + 10$
130

Look for multiples:

$20 \times 6 \times 5$
$(20 \times 5) \times 6$
100×6
600

> **Use compensation.**
> Add to make a round number, then subtract that number from the sum.
>
> $537 + 295$
> $\quad\quad (295 + ⑤ = 300)$
> $537 + 300 = 837$
> $837 - ⑤ = 832$
>
> Be sure to add and subtract the same number

Compute mentally.

1. $64 + 86 =$ _____

2. $6 \times 40 \times 5 =$ _____

3. $2 \times 8 \times 50 =$ _____

4. $65 - 22 =$ _____

5. $94 + 53 =$ _____

6. $7 + 34 + 16 =$ _____

7. $125 + 14 + 75 =$ _____

8. $4 \times 9 \times 25 =$ _____

9. $579 - 295 =$ _____

10. $380 + 20 + 105 =$ _____

11. $7 \times 25 \times 4 =$ _____

12. $801 - 187 =$ _____

13. Strategy Practice Explain the steps you can use to find $7 \times 2 \times 50$ mentally.

_____

_____

Mental Math

Compute mentally.

1. $8 \times 15 \times 50 =$ _____

2. $634 - 519 =$ _____

3. $78 + 89 =$ _____

4. $37 + 66 + 24 =$ _____

5. $4,922 - 301 =$ _____

6. $7 \times 20 \times 4 =$ _____

7. $34 + 45 + 84 =$ _____

8. $8 \times 8 \times 50 =$ _____

9. Reasoning Explain the steps you can use to find $2 \times 36 \times 50$ mentally.

_____

_____

An apartment complex needs to purchase several new appliances. They have made a price list showing the cost of a few of these appliances. Compute mentally.

Appliance	Price
Refrigerator/freezer	$938
Washing machine	$465
Dryer	$386

10. Find the cost of a washing machine and a dryer.

_____

11. How much more does a refrigerator/ freezer cost than a dryer? _____

12. Find the total cost for 3 refrigerator/freezers. _____

13. Compute mentally: $450 - 280$.

A 120   **B** 140   **C** 170   **D** 190

14. Writing to Explain Explain in your own words why $204 \times 6 = (6 \times 200) + (6 \times 4)$.

_____

_____

_____

Evaluating Expressions

To evaluate an expression, follow these steps:

1. Substitute or replace the variable with the value given in the problem.
2. Perform the operation or operations.
3. If there is more than one operation, use the order of operations.

Evaluate $4 + 2n$ for 3.

Replace n with 3.	$4 + 2(3)$
Multiply first.	$4 + 6$
Then add.	10

The value of the expression is 10.

Evaluate $g^2 - 3(3) + g \div 2$; $g = 4$.

Replace g with 4.	$4^2 - 3(3) + 4 \div 2$
Evaluate terms with exponents.	$16 - 3(3) + 4 \div 2$
Then multiply and divide.	$16 - 9 + 2$
Then subtract and add.	9

The value of the expression is 9.

Apply the substitutions and evaluate.

1. $12n$; $n = 3$ 　　　　**2.** $2t - 4$; $t = 6$ 　　　　**3.** $r + 48 \div r$; $r = 8$

_____   _____   _____

For **4–7,** evaluate each expression for 3, 6, and 8.

4. $7x$ ____, ____, ____ 　　**5.** $6x + 4$ ____, ____, ____

6. $14 + x \div 2$ ____, ____, ____ 　　**7.** $x + 2x$ ____, ____, ____

8. Katie rented a bicycle at the beach for $3 an hour plus a $5 fee. Write an expression that shows how much it will cost Katie to rent the bicycle. Then solve the expression for 4 hours.

_____

9. Writing to Explain Timothy is solving the problem $50 + 108x \div 4$. What order of operations should he follow?

_____

Evaluating Expressions

Apply the substitutions and evaluate.

1. $7x - 4$; $x = 9$ **2.** $3d + (5 - d)$; $d = 4$ **3.** $8 + 2g - g \div 2$; $g = 6$

_____   _____   _____

For **7–10**, evaluate each expression for 2, 6, and 8.

4. $5x$ _____, _____, _____   **5.** $x + 12$ _____, _____, _____

6. $96 \div x$ _____, _____, _____   **7.** $x^2 - x$ _____, _____, _____

8. Evaluate the expression for the values of h.

h	6	18	24	42	54
$(h - 6) + h \div 6$					

9. The table shows how much Tia charges for pet sitting. Write an expression to show how much Tia will earn for sitting two dogs for a day and two cats per hour. Then solve for sitting two dogs for the day and one cat for 6 hours.

Number of Pets	Per Day	Per Hour
One dog	$20	$7
Two dogs	$25	$9
One or two cats	$15	$6

_____

10. Writing to Explain Tia wrote $20 + 7x$ to find how much she earned for one pet sitting job and $15x$ for another job. Explain the difference between the expressions.

_____

_____

_____

_____

11. Evaluate the expression $6 + 8f$ for $f = 4$.

   A 8

   B 18

   C 38

   D 56

Using Expressions to Describe Patterns

You can write an expression to describe the pattern in an input/output table.

Look at the first input and output values in the table.

Ask Yourself: What do I need to do to the input 11 to get the output 5?

You might need to add, subtract, multiply, divide, or perform more than one operation.

In this table, you can subtract 6 from 11 to get 5.

Check the input and output values for 12 and 13.

$12 - 6 = 6$

$13 - 6 = 7$

The pattern is true for all of the values in the table. So, the pattern is subtract 6.

You can write the expression $x - 6$ to describe the pattern.

Substitute input values for the variable x to get the output values.

Find the output values for 15 and 20. _____

INPUT	OUTPUT
11	5
12	6
13	7
15	★
20	★

The input/output table shows how much Jake pays for toys. Use the input/output table for **1–4.**

1. If Jake buys 12 toys, what is the cost? _____

2. If Jake pays $45, how many toys did he buy? _____

3. Write an expression to describe the output pattern if the input is the variable t. _____

4. What inputs and outputs should be added to the table for 20 toys? _____

INPUT	OUTPUT
6	18
7	21
8	24
9	27

5. **Writing to Explain** Jessie says that the expression 2x describes the input/output table. Explain why Jessie's expression is correct or incorrect.

INPUT	2	3	4	5
OUTPUT	4	5	6	7

_____

_____

Using Expressions to Describe Patterns

Use this table for **1–4.**

Total Cups in Boxes	18	36	54	66	72	84
Total Number of Boxes	3	6	9	□	□	□

1. How many boxes are needed for 66, 72, and 84 cups?

   _____

2. How many cups will be in 20 boxes?

   _____

3. Write an algebraic expression that explains the relationship between the input (total cups in boxes) and output values (total number of boxes) if the variable *c* is the input.

   _____

4. **Writing to Explain** Jason thinks he needs 25 boxes to pack 144 cups. Is Jason correct? Explain.

   _____

   _____

5. **Make a Table** Lily is using seashells to make necklaces. Each necklace has 7 shells. Make an input/output table that shows the number of shells used for 10, 15, 20, and 25 necklaces. Write an algebraic expression that explains the relationship between the input and output values.

Use this table for **6** and **7.**

Large White Butterfly Wing Beats					
Number of seconds	1	2	3	4	5
Number of beats	12	24	36	48	60

6. **Critical Thinking** What algebraic expression shows the number of wing beats for a chosen number of seconds?

   A $60 + x$ **B** $x \div 12$ **C** $12 \div x$ **D** $12x$

7. How many times will a large white butterfly beat its wings in 12 seconds?

   A 144   **B** 120   **C** 84   **D** 72

Problem Solving: Make a Table

You can make a table using the information given in a problem. A table organizes the information and helps you solve the problem.

Angie has $30 to spend at a carnival. Tickets for rides cost $1.25 each. Write an expression to show how much Angie has left after buying x tickets at the carnival. Make a table to show how much Angie has left after buying $x = 3$ tickets, $x = 8$ tickets, and $x = 15$ tickets.

Write an Expression

x = number of tickets

Spending Money		Price of Tickets		Number of Tickets
↓		↓		↓
30	−	1.25	×	x

The expression $30 - 1.25x$ represents the situation.

Make a Table

Use x as a label for one column.
Use $30 - 1.25x$ for the other column.

Enter the values for x: 3, 8, and 15.

Solve the expression for each x-value and enter into the table.

x	$30 - 1.25x$
3	26.25
8	20
15	11.25

So, Angie has $26.25 left after she buys 3 tickets, $20 left after she buys 8 tickets, and $11.25 left after she buys $15 tickets.

---

1. Arturo works at a horse ranch. He makes $50 each week for cleaning out stalls and $12 for each horse that he grooms. Write an expression that describes Arturo's weekly earnings after grooming x horses.

   _____

2. Using your answer for Exercise 1, complete the table to find how much Arturo earns in a week if he grooms 5 horses, 9 horses, and 12 horses.

x	
5	
9	
12	

3. Gina sells bracelets at a fair for $6 each. Complete the table to show how much she earns for $x = 12$ bracelets, $x = 35$ bracelets, and $x = 56$ bracelets.

x	$6x$
12	
35	
56	

Problem Solving: Make a Table

1. Selena earns $8.75 per hour working at her job. It costs $3.50 to ride the bus to and from work. Write an expression that describes how much Selena has each day after x hours of work and paying her bus fare.

_____

2. Complete the table to find how much Selena earns each day if she works 3 hours, 5 hours, or 8 hours.

x	
3	
5	
8	

3. A health food store sells protein powder online. A 10-lb carton of protein powder costs $27.25. It costs $4.95 to ship the powder whether you buy 1 or more cartons. Write an expression to show the cost including shipping of x cartons of protein powder.

_____

4. Complete the table to find how much it costs to have 2, 5, and 9 cartons of protein powder shipped.

x	
2	
5	
9	

5. **Critical Thinking** Lee earns 3 points for every dollar he spends at the pet store. Which value completes this table?

x	$3x$
27	?

A 9   **B** 24   **C** 30   **D** 81

6. **Writing to Explain** A wildlife park charges $18 for each admission ticket x. Explain the labels you would use to make a table to find the cost of 4 tickets, 9 tickets, and 12 tickets.

_____

_____

Estimating Sums and Differences

Estimate: 7.382 + 4.97
1. Round each number to the nearest whole number.

$$7.383 + 4.97$$
$$\downarrow \qquad \downarrow$$
$$7 + 5$$

2. Add to estimate:
$$7 + 5 = 12$$
$$7.382 + 4.97 \approx 12$$

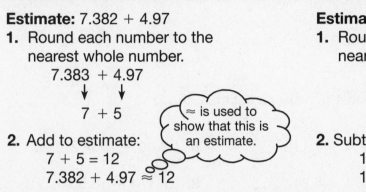

$\approx$ is used to show that this is an estimate.

Estimate: 12.57 – 6.806
1. Round each number to the nearest whole number.

$$12.57 - 6.806$$
$$\downarrow \qquad \downarrow$$
$$13 - 7$$

2. Subtract to estimate.
$$13 - 7 = 6$$
$$12.57 - 6.806 \approx 6$$

You can also round the numbers to any decimal place.
Estimate the sum. Round to the nearest tenth.

$$3.947 + 11.286$$
$$\downarrow \qquad \downarrow$$
$$3.9 \quad + 11.3 = 15.2, \text{ so } 3.947 + 11.286 \approx 15.2$$

Round each number to the nearest whole number to estimate the answer.

1. 4.38 + 9.179 _____   **2.** 62.873 – 12.7 _____   **3.** 52.83 + 97.288 _____

4. 131.049 – 82.604 _____   **5.** 79.14 + 32.546 _____   **6.** 48.468 + 63.029 _____

7. 112.658 – 81.903 _____   **8.** 586.735 – 204.63 _____   **9.** 107.139 + 90.621 _____

Round each number to the nearest tenth to estimate the answer.

10. 17.058 – 8.623 _____   **11.** 38.8314 + 15.62 _____   **12.** 26.429 – 6.703 _____

13. 238.562 – 104.387 _____   **14.** 400.628 + 291.037 _____   **15.** 76.451 – 68.399 _____

16. Geometry The area of the Davis's living room is 18.087 square yards, and their bedroom has an area of 15.78 square yards. Round to the nearest tenth and estimate the amount of carpet they need to buy.

_____

17. Explain It Angela has a $5-bill, two $10-bills, and a $20-bill. She wants to buy a DVD for $17.89, a pin for $5.12, and shoes for $12.99. Estimate the sum to the nearest dollar. Tell which bills she should hand to the cashier.

_____

_____

R 3·1

Estimating Sums and Differences

Fill in the blanks to complete the estimate.

1. 4.36 − 2.971 =

_____ − 3 = _____

2. 9.384 + 7.713 =

9 + _____ = _____

3. 8.81 + 2.78 =

8.8 + _____ = _____

Round each number to the nearest whole number to estimate the answer.

4. 15.63 − 8.497 _____

5. 3.504 + 7.118 _____

6. 13.09 − 10.902 _____

7. 14.52 + 11.118 _____

8. 9.573 − 4.817 _____

9. 22.174 + 18.561 _____

10. 37.624 − 14.826 _____

11. 15.938 + 7.627 _____

12. 19.394 − 6.943 _____

Round each number to the nearest tenth to estimate the answer.

13. 7.349 + 8.192 _____

14. 14.087 − 5.418 _____

15. 8.991 + 3.475 _____

16. 25.183 − 13.984 _____

17. 11.004 + 5.391 _____

18. 31.038 − 12.861 _____

19. Geometry Estimate the perimeter of the figure to the nearest whole number. _____

2.14 in.

1.7 in.

5.3 in.

10.676 in.

20. Four runners ran the relay. Bill ran his lap in 22.738 seconds, Tory ran in 21.874 seconds, Grace ran in 20.32 seconds, and Jessica ran in 19.047 seconds. Estimate the team's total time to the nearest tenth of a second.

_____

21. LuWanda bought a jar of mustard, a half-gallon of ice cream, and two boxes of popcorn. She gave the clerk a $20 bill. Estimate how many dollars she received in change.

On Sale Today
Mustard $1.58
Ice cream . . . $3.27
Popcorn $2.19

A $4   **B** $9   **C** $11   **D** $14

22. Writing to Explain The digit 5 is usually rounded up, but it can also be rounded down. How would you round the numbers in the equation 9.5 + 4.7 + 3.2 + 7.5 = x to the nearest whole number without getting an overestimate or an underestimate?

_____

_____

_____

Adding and Subtracting

Find 1.093 + 41.6.

Estimate: Round 1.093 to 1 and 41.6 to 42.
        1 + 42 = 43

Write the numbers, lining up the decimal points. Annex zeros so all numbers have the same number of decimal places.

$$\begin{array}{r} 1.093 \\ +41.600 \\ \hline 42.693 \end{array}$$ ← Annex 2 zeros.

Add the numbers. Regroup if necessary. Write the decimal point in your answer.

42.693 is close to 43, so the answer is reasonable.

Find 18.5 − 7.82.

Estimate: Round 7.82 to 8.
        18.5 − 8 = 10.5

Write the numbers, lining up the decimal points. Annex zeros so all numbers have the same number of decimal places.

$$\begin{array}{r} 7\ \ 4\ 10 \\ 18.5\cancel{0} \\ -\ 7.82 \\ \hline 10.68 \end{array}$$ ← Annex a zero.

Subtract. Regroup if necessary. Write the decimal point in your answer.

10.68 is close to 10.5, so the answer is reasonable.

Find each sum or difference.

1. 45.6 + 26.3

2. 14.25 − 5.14

3. 17.2 + 6.08

4. 24.84 − 22.7

5. 13.64 − 8.3

6. 0.214 + 15.9

7. 3.652 − 1.41

8. 18.06 + 9.798

9. 8.006 − 6.38

10. Reasonableness Jaime wrote 4.4 − 0.33 = 1.1. Is his answer reasonable? Why or why not?

_____

_____

Adding and Subtracting

Find each sum or difference.

1. $10.21 - 4.6$

_____

2. $0.03 + 1.85$

_____

3. $5.011 + 1.23$

_____

4. $22.9 - 0.61$

_____

5. $9.834 - 1.26$

_____

6. $24 + 7.45$

_____

7. Complete the sequence of numbers. 4.25, 5, 5.75, _____ , _____

8. Number Sense How does the cost for 1 tube of glue compare to the cost for 1 roll of tape?

_____

9. What is the difference in cost between 2 packs of markers and 4 sheets of poster board?

_____

Craft Supplies	
Poster board	$1.29/sheet
Markers	$4.50/pack
Tape	$1.99/roll
Glue	$2.39/tube
Construction paper	$3.79/pack

10. In a long jump competition, Khaila jumped 3.9 meters. Alicia jumped 3.08 meters. How much farther did Khaila jump?

A 0.01 meters

B 0.82 meters

C 0.98 meters

D 1.01 meters

11. Writing to Explain Trey wrote $9.009 - 0.01 = 9.008$. Is his answer correct? Why or why not?

_____

_____

Estimating Products and Quotients

You can use rounding or compatible numbers to estimate products and quotients.

Rounding:

Round each factor to the nearest whole number and multiply.

$$4.287 \longrightarrow 4$$
$$\times 2.804 \longrightarrow \times 3$$
$$\qquad\qquad\quad 12 \text{ so, } 4.287 \times 2.804 \approx 12$$

Compatible Numbers:

Find compatible numbers and divide.

$$16.173 \div 2.45$$
$$\quad \downarrow \qquad\quad \downarrow$$
$$\quad 15 \div \quad 3 = 5 \text{ so } 16.173 \div 2.45 \approx 5$$

Use rounding to estimate each answer.

1. 3.73×8.16 **2.** $35.518 \div 9.272$ **3.** 7.349×5.62

_____   _____   _____

4. 4.178×12.513 **5.** 8.498×5.602 **6.** $24.534 \div 7.96$

_____   _____   _____

7. $41.01 \div 4.88$ **8.** 15.812×9.47 **9.** 2.81×17.638

_____   _____   _____

Use compatible numbers to estimate each answer.

10. $55.93 \div 8.34$ **11.** $61.438 \div 8.72$ **12.** $122.899 \div 5.36$

_____   _____   _____

13. $16.954 \div 3.5$ **14.** 17.158×8.99 **15.** $38.753 \div 8.461$

_____   _____   _____

16. $73.724 \div 16.1$ **17.** $79.48 \div 8.512$ **18.** $43.518 \div 8.043$

_____   _____   _____

19. Writing to Explain Elena used rounding to estimate $7.864 \times 3.29 \approx 24$. Peter used rounding to estimate $7.864 \times 3.29 \approx 32$. Which student is correct? What mistake was made?

_____

_____

Name _____

Estimating Products and Quotients

Estimate each answer using rounding.

1. 3.48×9.673 _____

2. 5.702×4.26 _____

3. 9.734×6.8 _____

4. 8.37×2.501 _____

5. 7.936×2.491 _____

6. 5.092×3.774 _____

7. 12.123×4.802 _____

8. 6.98×8.502 _____

9. 1.948×3.728 _____

Estimate each answer using compatible numbers.

10. $19.18 \div 3.7$

11. $14.9 \div 8.432$

12. $31.047 \div 4.492$

_____

_____

_____

13. $16.07 \div 4.989$

14. $46.614 \div 9.01$

15. $61.503 \div 8.041$

_____

_____

_____

16. $73.196 \div 11.513$

17. $123.82 \div 25.937$

18. $86.431 \div 6.722$

_____

_____

_____

19. Number Sense An airliner is 9.34 feet wide. The airline wants to install 5 seats in each row. The seats are each 1.46 feet wide. Rounded to the nearest tenth, about how much space would be left for the aisle? _____

20. Geometry Estimate the area of the rectangle. _____

7.278 ft | 13.713 ft

21. Writing to Explain The library has a bookshelf 46.725 inches wide for their new encyclopedia. When the encyclopedia arrived, the librarian found that each of the 24 volumes was 1.65 inches wide. Estimate if the 24 books will fit on the shelf. How does your rounding affect the answer?

_____

_____

_____

22. Algebra Dominick wants to buy 2 CDs for $14.95 each, 3 DVDs for $19.99 each, and a video game for $36.79. Which equation could you use to estimate how much money he needs?

A $15 + 20 + 26 = x$

C $2(15) + 3(20) + 37 = x$

B $2(14) + 3(20) + 36 = x$

D $2(15) + 3(19) + 36 = x$

Multiplying Decimals

Use the same strategy to multiply a decimal by a whole number or to multiply a decimal by a decimal.

Multiply 0.72 × 23.

Ignore the decimal points. Multiply as you would with two whole numbers.

Count the number of decimal places in both factors. Use that number of decimal places to write the answer.

$$
\begin{array}{r}
0.72 \\
\times\ 23 \\
\hline
216 \\
144 \\
\hline
1656 \\
\\
16.56
\end{array}
$$

0.72 → 2 decimal places

Multiply 0.45 × 0.8.

Ignore the decimal points. Multiply as you would with two whole numbers.

Count the number of decimal places in both factors. Use that number of decimal places to write the answer.

$$
\begin{array}{r}
0.45 \\
\times\ 0.8 \\
\hline
360 \\
\\
0.360
\end{array}
$$

0.45 → 2 + 1 = 3 decimal places

Place the decimal point in each product.

1. 1.2 × 3.6 = 432

2. 5.5 × 3.77 = 20735

3. 4.4 × 2.333 = 102652

_____   _____   _____

Find the product.

4. 7 × 0.5 _____

5. 12 × 0.08 _____

6. 24 × 0.17 _____

7. 0.4 × 0.17 _____

8. 1.9 × 0.46 _____

9. 3.42 × 5.15 _____

10. Writing to Explain If you multiply two decimals less than 1, can you predict whether the product will be less than or greater than either of the factors? Explain.

_____

_____

11. Number Sense Two factors are multiplied and their product is 34.44. One factor is a whole number. How many decimal places are in the other factor?

_____

R 3·4

Multiplying Decimals

Place the decimal point in each product.

1. $3 \times 6.892 = 20676$ _____

2. $0.3 \times 4.57 = 1371$ _____

Find each product.

3. $14.3 \times 2.1 \times 8.9 =$ _____

4. $0.45 \times 0.01 =$ _____

5. $67.1 \times 0.3 \times 0.4 =$ _____

6. $582.1 \times 4.2 =$ _____

7. Reasoning Show how to find the product of 16.2×4 using addition.

_____

8. Which activity is 6 times faster than the fastest rowing speed?

_____

9. The fastest speed a table tennis ball has been hit is 21.12 times faster than the speed for the fastest swimmer. What is the speed for the table tennis ball?

_____

10. How fast would 1.5 times the fastest rowing speed be?

_____

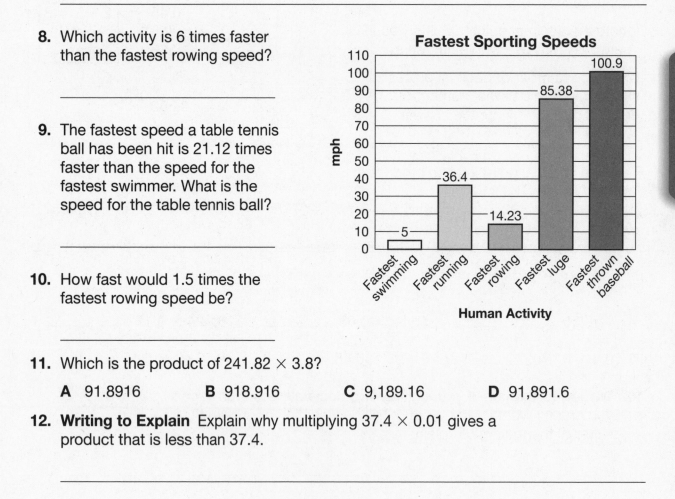

Fastest Sporting Speeds

11. Which is the product of 241.82×3.8?

A 91.8916   **B** 918.916   **C** 9,189.16   **D** 91,891.6

12. Writing to Explain Explain why multiplying 37.4×0.01 gives a product that is less than 37.4.

_____

_____

_____

Dividing Whole Numbers

Find 362 ÷ 5.

Step 1: To decide where to place the first digit in the quotient, compare the first digit of the dividend with the divisor. 3 < 5, so the first digit in the quotient will not go in the hundreds place. Now, compare the first two digits of the dividend with the divisor. 36 > 5, so the first digit in the quotient will go in the tens place.	**Step 2:** Divide the tens. Use multiplication facts and compatible numbers. Think 5 × ? = 35. Write 7 in the tens place of the quotient. Multiply. 5 × 7 = 35 7 5)3 6 2 −3 5 1 Subtract. 36 − 35 = 1 Compare. 1 < 5 Bring down the ones.	**Step 3:** Divide the ones. Use multiplication facts and compatible numbers. Think 5 × ? = 10. Write 2 in the ones place of the quotient. Multiply. 5 × 2 = 10 7 2 R2 5)3 6 2 −3 5 ↓ 1 2 −1 0 2 Subtract. 12 − 10 = 2 Compare. 2 < 5 There are no more digits to bring down, so 2 is the remainder.	**Step 4:** Check by multiplying and then adding. 5 × 72 = 360 360 + 2 = 362

In **1** through **6** find each quotient. Check your answers.

1. 8)863

2. 7)249

3. 5)365

4. 8)448

5. 2)499

6. 6)396

7. **Number Sense** How can you tell before you divide 425 by 9 that the first digit of the quotient is in the tens place?

_____

Dividing Whole Numbers

In **1** through **8**, find each quotient. Check your answers.

1. 2)586　　　**2.** 3)565　　　**3.** 5)718　　　**4.** 4)599

5. 5)642　　　**6.** 6)354　　　**7.** 9)210　　　**8.** 8)927

The Paez family lives in Louisville, Kentucky, and has decided to take a road trip for their summer vacation.

9. How many miles will the Paez family drive each day if they decide to take 5 days to drive 865 miles to Dallas?　_____

10. The Paez family decides they want to drive 996 miles to Boston in 6 days. How many miles will they drive each day?　_____

11. **Reasonableness** If a staff of 9 people had to clean a hotel with 198 rooms, how many rooms would each person have to clean if each person cleans the same number of rooms?

　A 29　　　**B** 25　　　**C** 23　　　**D** 22

12. Explain how to check the quotient from a division problem.

_____

_____

_____

Name _____

Dividing by a Whole Number

Find 196 ÷ 32.

Step 1

Put the decimal point in the dividend. Divide. Put the decimal in the quotient right above the decimal in the dividend. Subtract.

```
      6.
32 ) 196.
    -192
      4
```

Step 2

Add a zero after the decimal point in the dividend. Bring down the zero. Divide. Subtract.

```
      6.1
32 ) 196.0
    -192 ↓
       4 0
      -3 2
         8
```

Step 3

Repeat Step 2 until there is no remainder.

```
        6.125
32 ) 196.000
    -192 ↓
       4 0
      -3 2 ↓
         80
        -64 ↓
          160
         -160
            0
```

Remember, you can use estimation to see if your answer is reasonable: 180 ÷ 30 = 6. You can check your answer using multiplication: 32 × 6.125 = 196

Find the quotient.

1.
```
      2.
9 ) 20.7
  -18
    2
```
_____

2.
```
      3.
7 ) 22.61
  -21
```
_____

3.
```
     $ 3.
12 ) $44.40
   - 36
      8
```
_____

4. 11) 93.5

5. 30) 1.56

6. 8) 412

_____   _____   _____

7. Writing to Explain Destiny said that 0.6 ÷ 2 = 0.3. Is she correct? Explain why or why not.

_____

_____

_____

R 3·6

Dividing by a Whole Number

Find the quotient.

1. $42.78 ÷ 3

2. 85.5 ÷ 6

3. 3.4 ÷ 10

_____

_____

_____

4. 9 ÷ 900

5. 59.6 ÷ 8

6. 188.4 ÷ 60

_____

_____

_____

7. $1.24 ÷ 4

8. 231 ÷ 42

9. 11.2 ÷ 25

_____

_____

_____

10. Yolanda bought 8 tickets to a concert for $214. What was the cost
of each ticket?

_____

11. Algebra Tony bought a 72-ounce box of dog biscuits.
How many pounds of dog biscuits did he buy?
(Remember: 1 pound = 16 ounces.)

A 4 pounds

B 4.5 pounds

C 90 pounds

D 4,320 pounds

12. Number Sense Vicky uses 42 beads for each necklace she
makes. She bought a bag of 500 beads. How many necklaces can
she make?

_____

13. Writing to Explain In what place is the first digit of the quotient for
12.88 ÷ 4? Tell how you know.

_____

_____

Dividing Decimals

When you divide by a decimal, you need to rewrite the dividend and the divisor so that you are dividing by a whole number.

Find 2.48 ÷ 0.8.

Step 1: Estimate. Use compatible numbers.

Step 2: Make the divisor a whole number. Multiply the divisor AND the dividend by the same power of 10.

Place the decimal in the quotient.

Step 3: Divide as you would with whole numbers. Remember that sometimes you may need to annex zeros to complete your division.

Step 4: Compare the quotient with your estimate.

240 ÷ 80 = 3

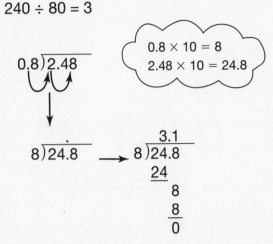

Since 3.1 is close to 3, the answer checks.

Find each quotient.

1. $0.2\overline{)1.5}$

Estimate: _____

Multiply dividend and divisor by what power of 10? _____

Place the decimal point in the quotient.

Divide. How many zeros do you need to annex? _____

Compare the quotient to your estimate. Is the answer reasonable? _____

2. $0.6\overline{)0.36}$

3. $0.4\overline{)9.6}$

4. $0.75\overline{)0.3}$

5. **Draw a Picture** Fernando used tenths grids to draw this picture showing 1.6 ÷ 0.4 = 4. Draw a picture to show 1.8 ÷ 0.6. Write the quotient.

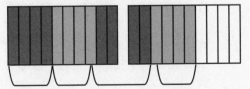

Name _____

Dividing Decimals

Find each quotient.

1. $8.4 \div 0.3 =$ _____

2. $66.15 \div 0.63 =$ _____

3. $10.5 \div 1.5 =$ _____

4. $86 \div 0.4 =$ _____

5. $72.8 \div 1.4 =$ _____

6. $14.36 \div 0.4 =$ _____

7. $2.87 \div 0.01 =$ _____

8. $78.32 \div 0.22 =$ _____

9. Reasoning Why would multiplying both the dividend and the divisor by 10 sometimes make a problem easier to solve?

_____

_____

For each item, find how many times greater the 2002 cost is than the 1960 cost. Round your answer to the nearest hundredth.

Item	1960 Cost	2002 Cost
Movie admission	$0.75	$8.50
Regular popcorn	$0.25	$3.25
Regular drink	$0.35	$2.75

10. movie admission

11. regular popcorn

12. regular drink

_____   _____   _____

13. Which item has increased the greatest amount of times from its original cost?   _____

14. Divide. Round to the nearest hundredth. $250.6 \div 1.6$

  A 156

  B 156.6

  C 156.61

  D 156.63

15. Writing to Explain Lynn and Randi got different quotients when they divided 3.60 by 0.12. Whose work is correct? Explain why.

Lynn
$$\begin{array}{r} 0.30 \\ 12\overline{)3.60} \end{array}$$

Randi
$$\begin{array}{r} 30.0 \\ 12\overline{)360.} \end{array}$$

_____

_____

Evaluating Expressions

Brackets and parentheses are both used to show groupings.
Brackets are used to avoid double parentheses: [(instead of ((.

Evaluate expressions according to the order of operations.

1. Evaluate inside parentheses, then evaluate inside brackets.		$2.3^2 + [(9 \times 0.4) + (3 \times 0.8)] \times 1.2$ $2.3^2 + [3.6 + 2.4] \times 1.2$ $2.3^2 + 6 \times 1.2$
2. Evaluate exponents.		$\mathbf{2.3^2} + 6 \times 1.2$ $5.29 + 6 \times 1.2$
3. Multiply and divide from left to right.		$5.29 + \mathbf{6 \times 1.2}$ $5.29 + 7.2$
4. Add and subtract from left to right.		$\mathbf{5.29 + 7.2}$ 12.49

Evaluate each expression.

1. $(7.8 \div 2) \times 12$

_____

2. $5.6 + (3 \times 9.6 - 4.8)$

_____

3. $[(4.2 \times 3.4) - 9.28]$

_____

4. $[4 \times (9.6 \div 3)] + 8.4$

_____

5. $5 \times [(6 \times 2.3) + 0.9]$

_____

6. $2^4 \div [(3.2 \times 0.8) + 1.44]$

_____

7. $5.6 + [(3.1 \times 4) - 7.3] + 5^2$

_____

8. $4^2 - 9 \div [(0.24 \times 7) + (0.66 \times 2)]$

_____

9. Reasoning Is it possible to have an expression that uses brackets without using any parentheses? Give your reasons.

_____

10. Estimation How could you estimate to get an approximate answer for this expression: $12.3 \times [(2 \times 1.7) + 6] - 2^3$?

_____

Evaluating Expressions

1. $6^2 - (3.1 \times 5 + 2.3)$

2. $[(8 - 3.7) \times 6] + 1.5$

3. $9^2 - [(4.2 \times 3.4) - 9.28]$

_____   _____   _____

4. $3.2^2 - [(12.6 - 2^2) \times 0.6]$

5. $[(0.3 \times 8) + (1.5 \times 3)] + 6^2$

_____   _____

6. $40 \div [9.6 - (8 \times 0.2)]$

7. $3^3 + 4.2 \times 8 \div 0.2$

_____   _____

8. $8.8 + [(0.4 \times 7) + (3.1 \times 2)]$

9. $7^2 - [(6^2 - 22.4) + (8 \div 0.5)] + 3.8$

_____   _____

10. $9 + [(4.2 - 3.3) + (6.4 \div 0.8)] \times 3$

11. $41 - 3^2 + (8 \times 2.3) - 15 + (2.1 \times 4)$

_____   _____

12. $13 + 26 - [(2.8 \times 5) \div 7]$

13. $16 + 23 - [(5 + 2) \times 1.9] - 13 + 6.8$

_____   _____

14. Jessica bought a new computer for $800. She put $120 down
and got a student discount of $50. Her mother gave her $\frac{1}{2}$ of the
balance for her birthday. Which of these expressions could be
used to find the amount Jessica still owes on the computer?

A $800 - 120 + 50 \div 2$

C $800 - (120 - 50) \div 2$

B $[800 - (120 - 50) \div 2]$

D $[800 - (120 + 50)] \div 2$

15. Number Sense A printing error in a math book removed the
brackets and parentheses from the original expression of
$(7 \times 3.4) - [(2.8 \times 5) - (4.3 \times 2)] + 4^2$. Give the order of
operations a student solving this problem would have used to
evaluate the expression with the printing error, and find the value of
the incorrect expression and the correct expression.

_____

_____

16. Writing to Explain How would you add parentheses and brackets to make this
sentence true: $45 \div 2 \times 4.7 - 4.4 \times 6 = 54$

_____

Name _____

Reteaching

3-9

Solutions for Equations and Inequalities

Which of the values is a solution to the equation?

$1.5 + p = 3.5$ $p = 1, 2, 3, 4$

You can draw a model to show that $1.5 + p$ equals 3.5.

3.5	
1.5	p

Try each value of p.

$1.5 + \mathbf{1} = 2.5$ Not a solution
$1.5 + \mathbf{2} = 3.5$ Solution
$1.5 + \mathbf{3} = 4.5$ Not a solution
$1.5 + \mathbf{4} = 5.5$ Not a solution

Which numbers, when substituted for p, are solutions to

$5.6 + p \geq 8.7$ $p = 3, 4, 5$

$5.6 + \mathbf{3} \geq 8.7$ Not a solution

$5.6 + \mathbf{4} \geq 8.7$ Solution

$5.6 + \mathbf{5} \geq 8.7$ Solution

Tell which values of the variable are solutions to the equation or inequality. You can draw a model to help you.

1. $c + 4 = 8$ $c = 1, 2, 3, 4$

2. $9 - g > 6$ $g = 3, 4, 5, 6$

3. $15 \geq r - 7.1$ $r = 10, 15, 20$

4. $k - 7 < 3.5$ $k = 12.1, 10, 9, 7.2$

5. Sahil bought a book of 25 ride tickets at the carnival. So far he has used 20 of them. The table shows numbers of tickets for some carnival rides. If t equals the number of tickets per ride, which numbers, when substituted for t are solutions for $20 + t \leq 25$?

Carnival Rides	
Ride	**Number of Tickets**
Whiplash	6
Sunset Cruise	2
Up 'N Down	3
Fireball	5

_____

Solutions for Equations and Inequalities

Tell which value(s) of the variable are solutions to the equation or inequality.

1. $p - 13 = 6$ $p = 17, 18, 19, 20$

2. $3.4 + c > 6$ $c = 1.1, 2.2, 3.3, 4.4$

3. $0.2 \leq g + 4$ $g = 0.1, 0.2, 0.5, 1.3$

4. $6 \geq 12 - d$ $d = 0, 2, 3, 5$

5. $r - 0 \geq 4.9$ $r = 3.4, 4.6, 7.7, 9$

6. $45 - 19.6 = b$ $b = 25.4, 64.6, 70$

7. $5 + q > 7.2$ $q = 0, 3, 5$

8. $18.2 + c < 18.2$ $c = 0, 3, 6, 9$

9. $7.6 + a = 9.7$ $a = 0.7, 1.1, 1.9, 21$

10. $x - 5 < 74$ $x = 85, 82, 80, 75$

11. $3.4 - y \leq 1.4$ $y = 3.3, 2.6, 1, 0$

12. $n + 10 \geq 41.2$ $n = 22, 28, 30, 31.1$

13. $9.6 - y \leq 4.3$ $y = 3.3, 3.6, 4.4, 5.5$

14. $0.6 + a = 1.3$ $a = 0.5, 06, 0.7, 0.8$

15. $\$7.26 - b = \$3.01$ $b = \$6.25, \$6.24, \$5.25, \$4.25$

16. Carole has spent $14.65 of a $20.00 gift card on a new T-shirt. Can she purchase $4.55 worth of merchandise with the balance on the card? If $x = \$4.55$, use $\$14.65 + x \leq \$20.00$ to decide.

_____

_____

17. Algebra Which number when substituted for y is a solution to the following inequality?

$y + 0.5 \geq 5$

A 4.9 **B** 3.6 **C** 2.2 **D** 0.5

18. Writing to Explain Andre is running in a 5-kilometer race. He just passed the 3.2-kilometer mark and thinks that he has only 0.8 kilometer more to run. Use the equation $3.2 + d = 5$ to explain whether or not Andre is correct.

_____

_____

Problem Solving: Multiple-Step Problems

Multiple-step problems often contain hidden questions. Sometimes you cannot answer the problem until you have answered these hidden questions.

James and Raul designed and printed T-shirts for school spirit week. James had 35 T-shirts printed and Raul had 3 times that number printed. It costs $3.25 each to print the T-shirts. How much did it cost altogether for James and Raul to print the T-shirts?

Hidden question: How many T-shirts did Raul have printed?
     35 T-shirt × 3 = 105 T-shirts

Solve the problem:
     35 + 105 = 140
     140 × $3.25 = $455

Answer: It cost $455 to print the T-shirts.

---

1. The school store offers a discount for purchases made during lunchtime. The usual price of pencils is $0.25. The discount price is $0.15. How much can you save by buying 5 pencils during lunchtime?

   _____

2. Janine practiced piano for 1.25 hours each day Monday through Friday. Her sister Emily practiced twice as long as Janine on Wednesday, Thursday, and Friday. Who practiced more hours during the week?

   _____

3. During a week-long dry spell, the water level in a pond decreased by 4 in. per day, except for two days when it decreased by half that amount. How much did the water level decrease in the pond in one week?

   _____

4. **Critical Thinking** What hidden questions did you have to answer to solve the above problem?

   _____

   _____

   _____

R 3·10

Problem Solving:
Multiple-Step Problems

1. At a school concert, the orchestra plays 8 songs that are 4.25 min long and 3 songs that are twice as long as each of the others. How long is the concert?

_____

2. A shoe store sold 53 pairs of shoes on Monday and 35 pairs on Tuesday. On Wednesday, the store sold as many pairs of shoes as they sold on Monday and Tuesday combined. They sold half as many on Thursday as Wednesday. How many pairs of shoes did the shoe store sell Monday through Thursday?

_____

3. **Write a Problem** Use a real-life situation to create a problem in which there is a hidden question. Then identify the hidden question and the answer.

_____

_____

_____

_____

4. **Critical Thinking** Jackson is writing a report on California missions. He spent 2 hours researching missions on the Internet and three times as long writing the report. What is the hidden question if you want to find how many total hours Jackson spent on the report?

   A How many hours did he spend researching and writing the report?

   B How many hours did he spend researching the report?

   C How much longer did it take to write the report than research it?

   D How many hours did he spend writing the report?

5. **Writing to Explain** Explain how you can find the hidden questions in problem 2.

_____

_____

_____

Properties of Equality

To keep an equation balanced, you must do the same thing to each side.

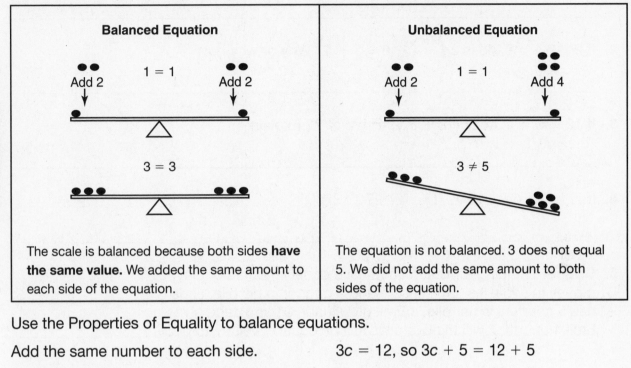

Balanced Equation	**Unbalanced Equation**
The scale is balanced because both sides **have the same value.** We added the same amount to each side of the equation.	The equation is not balanced. 3 does not equal 5. We did not add the same amount to both sides of the equation.

Use the Properties of Equality to balance equations.

Add the same number to each side. $3c = 12$, so $3c + 5 = 12 + 5$

Subtract the same number from each side. $3c = 12$, so $3c - 3 = 12 - 3$

Multiply each side by the same number. $3c = 12$, so $3c \times 2 = 12 \times 2$

Divide each side by the same number. $3c = 12$, so $3c \div 4 = 12 \div 4$

Evaluate the equations.

1. If $16 + 5 = 21$, does $16 + 5 - 4 = 21 - 4$? Why or why not?

_____

2. If $3p = 27$, does $3p \times 2 = 27 \times 3$? Why or why not?

_____

3. If $4s - 6 = 18$, does $(4s - 6) \div 2 = 18 \div 2$? Why or why not?

_____

4. Reasoning A pan balance shows $x + 2 = 10$. If you add 5 units to one side, can you balance the scale by adding x units to the other side? Explain.

_____

Properties of Equality

1. If $16 + 4 = 20$, does $16 + 4 - 4 = 20 - 4$? Why or why not?

_____

2. If $2d \div 4 = 5$, does $2d \div 4 + 6 = 5 + 4$? Why or why not?

_____

3. If $12 - 8 = 4$, does $(12 - 8) \div 2 = 4 \times 2$? Explain.

_____

4. If $7t = 70$, does $12 \times 7t = 12 \times 70$? Explain.

_____

5. Critical Thinking Emil and Jade have equal amounts of play money in two piles. Emil has $1 and a quarter in his pile. Jade has 5 quarters in her pile. If Emil gives Jade $1 and Jade gives Emil 4 quarters, will the two piles still be equal in value? Explain.

_____

_____

_____

6. Which equation shows the Multiplication Property of Equality if $n + 4 = 11$?

A $(n + 4) \times 2 = 11$ **B** $(n + 4) \times 2 = 11 \div 2$

C $(n + 4) \times 2 = 11 \times 4$ **D** $(n + 4) \times 2 = 11 \times 2$

7. Writing to Explain Bobbie wrote $y + 6 = 15$. Then she wrote $(y + 6) \div 3 = 15$. Explain why the second equation is not balanced and how to balance it.

_____

_____

_____

Solving Addition and Subtraction Equations

You can use inverse relationships and the properties of equality to get the variable alone to solve an equation. Remember that you need to do the same thing to both sides of the equation to keep the equation equal.

Solve the equation $5 + c = 15$.	Solve the equation $x - 20 = 16$.
To get c alone, undo adding 5 by subtracting 5 from both sides.	To get x alone, undo subtracting 20 by adding 20 to both sides.

$$5 + c = 15$$
$$5 + c - \mathbf{5} = 15 - \mathbf{5}$$
$$c = 10$$

$$x - 20 = 16$$
$$x - 20 + \mathbf{20} = 16 + \mathbf{20}$$
$$x = 36$$

Check your solution by substituting 10 for c in the equation.

Check your solution by substituting 36 for x in the equation.

$$5 + c = 15$$
$$5 + 10 = 15$$
$$15 = 15 \quad \text{It checks.}$$

$$x - 20 = 16$$
$$36 - 20 = 16$$
$$16 = 16 \quad \text{It checks.}$$

Explain how to get the variable alone in each equation.

1. $x + 13 = 25$
$x + 13 - \mathbf{13} = 25 - \mathbf{13}$

2. $n - 30 = 10$
$n - 30 + \mathbf{30} = 10 + \underline{\mathbf{?}}$

_____   _____

Solve each equation and check your answer. Show your work.

3. $g - 100 = 150$

$g - 100 + \underline{\hspace{1cm}} = 150 + \underline{\hspace{1cm}}$

$g = \underline{\hspace{4cm}}$

4. $y + 56 = 63$

_____

5. The Olympic triathlon is 51.5 km. A contestant has completed two of the three legs of the race and has traveled 41.5 km. Solve $41.5 + d = 51.5$ to find the distance of the third leg.

_____

Solving Addition and Subtraction Equations

Explain how to get the variable alone in each equation.

1. $n + 10 = 100$
$n + 10 - 10 = 100 - 10$

2. $x - 75 = 49$
$x - 75 + \underline{} = 49 + \underline{}$

_____   _____

Solve each equation and check your answer.

3. $g - 8 = 25$

4. $25 + y = 42$

5. $r + 82 = 97$

_____   _____   _____

6. $30 = m - 18$

7. $150 = e + 42$

8. $a - 51 = 12$

_____   _____   _____

9. Jo loaned Al $15. She had $15 left. Solve the equation $15 = s - 15$ to find how much money Jo had before she made the loan.

   A $0

   B $15

   C $30

   D $60

10. Critical Thinking If $n + 10 = 40$, then what is the value of the expression $n - 25$?

   A 5

   B 25

   C 30

   D 50

11. Writing to Explain Explain how to solve the equation $35 + p = 92$. Then solve.

_____

Problem Solving: Draw a Picture and Write an Equation

> Tico spent $37.51 at the computer store. Now he has $29.86 left. How much did Tico have before he went to the computer store?

What do you know?	Tico has $29.86 now.
	He spent $37.51
What do you need to find out?	How much Tico had before.
1. Assign a variable.	b = how much Tico had before
2. Draw a picture.	

$$b$$

$29.86	$37.51

3. Write and solve an equation.	$29.86 + $37.51 = b
	$67.37 = b
4. Answer the question.	Tico had $67.37 before he went to the store.

Draw a picture and write an equation to solve each problem.

1. Gina's book has 349 fewer pages than Terri's. If Gina's book has 597 pages, how many pages does Terri's book have?

2. Peter played a video game. Before dinner, he had collected 24,729 gold coins. At the end of the game he had collected 97,304 gold coins. How many coins did he collect after dinner?

3. SaveMart can store 840 cases of canned food in the big warehouse. This is 394 cases more than the number that can be displayed on the shelves. How many cases can be displayed?

Problem Solving: Draw a Picture and Write an Equation

Draw a picture and write an equation to solve each problem.

1. Mike has already driven 176 laps. The race is 250 laps long. How many more laps does he have to drive to finish the race?

   _____

2. Antonio found 133 golf balls in the water. He picked up a total of 527 lost golf balls. How many golf balls did he find in the weeds and bushes?

   _____

3. A lumber company plants 840 trees. If the company cuts down 560 trees, how many more trees did it plant than it cut down?

   _____

4. **Writing to Explain** What operation would you use to solve this problem? Why?

   > Erik wants to buy a new stereo for $359. He has $288 saved already. How much more will he have to save to buy the stereo?

   _____

   _____

5. **Reasonableness** Write an estimate that will show if 77 is a reasonable solution to the equation $14 + m = 91$.

   _____

6. Juan brought 87 pounds of recyclables to the recycling center. He brought 54 pounds of glass, and the rest was plastic. Which equation could be used to find p, the number of pounds of plastic Juan recycled?

   A $87 + p = 54$

   B $54 + p = 87$

   C $p - 54 = 87$

   D $p + 87 = 54$

Solving Multiplication and Division Equations

To solve an equation, make the two sides of the equation equal with the variable alone on one side. You can use inverse operations and properties of equality.

Remember: Inverse operations "undo" each other. **Properties of Equality** say that you can multiply or divide both sides of an equation by the same number and the two sides of the equation remain equal.

Use division to "undo" multiplication.

Use multiplication to "undo" division.

With numbers:
$3 \times 6 = 18$
$3 \times 6 \div \mathbf{6} = 18 \div \mathbf{6}$
$3 = 3$

With numbers:
$24 \div 2 = 12$
$24 \div 2 \times \mathbf{2} = 12 \times \mathbf{2}$
$24 = 24$

In algebra:
$m \times 9 = 54$
$m \times 9 \div \mathbf{9} = 54 \div \mathbf{9}$
$m = 6$

In algebra:
$p \div 8 = 7$
$p \div 8 \times \mathbf{8} = 7 \times \mathbf{8}$
$p = 56$

For **1** through **3**, name the inverse operation you will use to get the variable alone on one side of the equation. In **2** and **3**, also fill in the blanks.

1. $5p = 50$
$5p \div 5 = 50 \div 5$

2. $n \div 16 = 4$
$n \div 16 \times 16 = 4 \times$ ___

3. $15 = r \times 3$
$15 \div$ ___ $= r \times 3 \div$ ___

_____   _____   _____

For **4** through **6** solve the equation.

4. $w \div 5 = 8$

5. $20y = 100$

6. $3 = s \div 10$

_____   _____   _____

7. Writing to Explain Jason solved the equation $r \div 14 = 19$. He got 266. Is his answer correct? Explain how you know.

_____

_____

Solving Multiplication and Division Equations

For **1** through **3**, explain how to get the variable alone in each equation.

1. $r \times 7 = 42$
$r \times 7 \div 7 = 42 \div 7$

2. $m \div 6 = 12$
$m \div 6 \times \_\_ = 12 \times \_\_$

3. $44 = 2k$

_____

_____

_____

For **4** through **9**, solve the equation. Check your answer.

4. $9n = 72$

5. $y \times 5 = 60$

6. $v \div 13 = 2$

_____

_____

_____

7. $w \div 7 = 15$

8. $216 = 36p$

9. $17 = t \div 3$

_____

_____

_____

10. Writing to Explain Tell how you would get the variable m alone on one side of the equation $15m = 45$.

_____

_____

11. Write a Problem Write a problem that can be solved with the equation $r \div 6 = 14$.

_____

_____

12. Number Sense Which equation can you use to solve this problem?

There are 12 muffins in a package. Will bought 84 muffins. How many packages did he buy?

A $12 \times p = 84$

B $84 \times 12 = p$

C $12 \div p = 84$

D $84 = 12 + p$

Problem Solving: Draw a Picture and Write an Equation

Zoo keepers divided some land into 4 sections for the monkeys at the zoo. Each section has 23 monkeys. How many monkeys are at the zoo?

Read and Understand

Choose a variable for the unknown. The unknown is the total number of monkeys at the zoo.

Let m = the total number of monkeys.

Draw a picture to show that the total number of monkeys is divided into 4 equal sections of 23 monkeys.

	m		
23	23	23	23

Plan and Solve
Write an equation using the variable and the picture.

$m \div 4 = 23$ ← Use division.

Solve the equation.

$$m \div 4 = 23$$
$$m \div 4 \times 4 = 23 \times 4$$
$$m = 92$$

There are 92 monkeys at the zoo.

Write an equation for **1**. Solve each problem.

1. Juan has 6 times as many basketball cards as Nick. If Juan has 192 basketball cards, how many does Nick have?

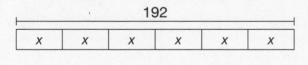

_____

2. Several sixth grade classes are going on a field trip to a planetarium. The teachers divided the classes into 19 groups. There are 7 students in each group. How many students are going to the planetarium? Use the equation $c \div 19 = 7$.

_____

3. Each bus for a field trip can carry 27 students. If 216 students are going on the field trip, how many buses are needed? Use the equation $27n = 216$.

Problem Solving: Draw a Picture and Write an Equation

Draw a picture and write an equation to solve each problem.

1. Mr. Conover bought 6 boxes of pastels for his art class. He paid $4.50 for each box. What was the total cost of the boxes?

   _____

2. A company charters boats for whale watching. The company chartered 13 boats. There were a total of 325 passengers on the boats. What was the average number of passengers per boat?

   _____

3. A store sells 5-gallon bottles of water for $8. The store made $288 on Monday selling the water. How many bottles were sold?

   _____

4. A sign at a recycling center states that 118 pounds of recycled newspapers saves one tree. How many pounds of newspapers will save 3 trees?

   _____

5. **Algebra** Students mailed invitations to a play to 414 parents. Each student mailed 18 invitations. If s equals the number of students who mailed invitations, which equation best shows the number of invitations that were mailed?

   A $s + 18 = 414$ **C** $18 \div s = 414$

   B $s \div 18 = 414$ **D** $18s = 414$

Factors, Multiples, and Divisibility

You can use these divisibility rules to determine if a number is divisible by another number.

A whole number is divisible by	Examples
2 if the ones digit is 0, 2, 4, 6, or 8.	2, 8, 24, 96, 300
3 if the sum of the digits of the number is divisible by 3.	144 $1 + 4 + 4 = 9$ $9 \div 3 = 3$
4 if the last two digits of the number are divisible by 4.	124 Last two digits are 24. $24 \div 4 = 6$
5 if the ones digit is 0 or 5.	205; 300; 1,005; 270
6 if the number is divisible by both 2 and 3.	522 Divisible by 2 because ones digit is 2 Divisible by 3 because $5 + 2 + 2 = 9$ $9 \div 3 = 3$
9 if the sum of the digits of the number is divisible by 9.	3,123 $3 + 1 + 2 + 3 = 9$ $9 \div 9 = 1$
10 if the ones digit is 0.	20; 40; 150; 2,570

Tell whether each number is divisible by 2, 3, 4, 5, 6, 9, or 10.

1. 25 _____

2. 32 _____

3. 124 _____

Tell whether the first number is a multiple of the second.

4. 45; 2 _____

5. 155; 5 _____

6. 240; 6 _____

7. 320; 10 _____

8. Number Sense Name 3 factors of 40. _____

There are 100 members in the U.S. Senate. There are 435 members in the U.S. House of Representatives.

9. Is the total number of U.S. senators divisible by 2, 3, 4, 5, 6, 9, or 10?

_____

10. Could the members of the U.S. House of Representatives be evenly divided into committees with 3 members on each? 5 members on each? 8 members on each?

Factors, Multiples, and Divisibility

Tell whether each number is divisible by 2, 3, 4, 5, 6, 9, or 10.

1. 27 _____

2. 86 _____

3. 348 _____

4. 954 _____

Tell whether each number is a multiple of the second.

5. 78; 2 _____

6. 535; 3 _____

7. Number Sense Name 3 numbers that are factors of both 15 and 30.

_____

The sixth graders at Washington Middle School researched the history of their city. The students then gave a presentation to the other students at the school.

8. If there were 64 sixth graders, list all of the ways they could have been divided equally into groups of 10 or fewer students.

_____

_____

9. Only 60 sixth graders were present. Of the 60, 14 were needed to run the light and sound equipment during the presentation. How could the remaining students be divided into equal groups of 6 or fewer students to read the presentation?

_____

10. The 60 students were transported in vans to the high school to share their presentation. If the vans carry a maximum of 7 students each, what was the minimum number of vans required to carry the students to the high school?

_____

11. Which of the following numbers is divisible by both 9 and 4?

A 24,815 **B** 18,324 **C** 9,140 **D** 9,126

12. Writing in Math If a number is divisible by both 2 and 6, is it always divisible by 12? Use examples in your answer.

_____

Prime Factorization

A prime number has exactly two factors, 1 and itself.

> Example: 17 is prime. Its factors are 1 and 17.

A composite number has more than two factors.

> Example: 10 is composite. Its factors are 1, 2, 5, and 10.

One way to find the prime factors of a composite number is to divide by prime numbers.

$84 \div 2 = 42$	84 is even. Divide by 2.
$42 \div 2 = 21$	Divide by 2 until the quotient is odd.
$21 \div 3 = 7$	3 is a prime factor of 21, divide by 3.
$7 \div 7 = 1$	7 is prime. You have found the prime factors.

Write the prime factors from least to greatest: $84 = 2 \times 2 \times 3 \times 7$.

Then write the factors in exponential form: $2^2 \times 3 \times 7$.

For **1** through **12**, if a number is prime, write *prime.* If the number is composite, write the prime factorization.

1. 28 _____

2. 36 _____

3. 29 _____

4. 70 _____

5. 55 _____

6. 81 _____

7. 84 _____

8. 99 _____

9. 75 _____

10. 43 _____

11. 45 _____

12. 64 _____

13. Writing to Explain Explain how you can check to see if your prime factorization is correct.

_____

14. Strategy Practice How can you tell that 342 is divisible by 3?

_____

Prime Factorization

For **1** through **10** if the number is prime, write *prime.* If the number is composite, write the prime factorization.

1. 24 _____

2. 43 _____

3. 51 _____

4. 66 _____

5. 61 _____

6. 96 _____

7. 144 _____

8. 243 _____

9. 270 _____

10. 124 _____

11. Writing to Explain Find the first ten prime numbers. Tell how you do it.

_____

_____

12. Reasoning How many even prime numbers are there?

A 0

B 1

C 2

D 3

13. Critical Thinking Which answer completes the sentence below?

The number 1 is _____.

A prime.

B composite.

C neither prime nor composite.

D both prime and composite.

Greatest Common Factor

The greatest number that divides into two numbers is the greatest common factor (GCF) of the two numbers. Here are two ways to find the GCF of 12 and 40.

List the Factors

Step 1: List the factors of each number.

12: 1, 2, 3, 4, 6, 12

40: 1, 2, 4, 5, 8, 10, 20, 40

Step 2: Circle the factors that are common to both numbers.

12: 1, ②, 3, ④, 6, 12

40: 1, ②, ④, 5, 8, 10, 20, 40

Step 3: Choose the greatest factor that is common to both numbers. Both 2 and 4 are common factors, but 4 is greater.

The GCF is 4.

Use Prime Factorization

Step 1: Write the prime factorization of each number.

12: $2 \times 2 \times 3$

40: $2 \times 2 \times 2 \times 5$

Step 2: Circle the prime factors that the numbers have in common.

12: ②$\times$②$\times 3$

40: ②$\times$②$\times 2 \times 5$

Step 3: Multiply the common factors.

$2 \times 2 = 4$ The GCF is 4.

Find the GCF for each set of numbers.

1. 10, 70 _____

2. 4, 20 _____

3. 18, 24 _____

4. 18, 63 _____

5. 36, 42 _____

6. 14, 28 _____

7. Number Sense Name two numbers that have a greatest common factor of 8.

_____

8. Geometry Al's garden is 18 feet long and 30 feet wide. He wants to put fence posts the same distance apart along both the length and width of the fence. What is the greatest distance apart he can put the fence posts?

_____

Greatest Common Factor

Find the GCF for each set of numbers.

1. 12, 48 _____   **2.** 20, 24 _____   **3.** 21, 84 _____

4. 24, 100 _____   **5.** 18, 130 _____   **6.** 200, 205 _____

7. Number Sense Name three pairs of numbers
that have 5 as their greatest common factor.
Use each number only once in your answer.

_____

8. The bake-sale committee divided each type of item
evenly onto plates, so that every plate contained
only one type of item and every plate had exactly the
same number of items with no leftovers. What is the
maximum number of items that could have been
placed on each plate?

Bake Sale Donations	
Muffins	96
Bread sticks	48
Rolls	84

_____

9. Using this system, how many plates of rolls could the
bake-sale committee make?   _____

10. Using this system, how many plates of muffins could
the bake-sale committee make?   _____

11. Which of the following pairs of numbers is correctly listed with its
greatest common factor?

A 20, 24; GCF: 4

B 50, 100; GCF: 25

C 4, 6; GCF: 24

D 15, 20; GCF: 10

12. Writing to Explain Explain one method of finding the greatest
common factor of 48 and 84.

_____

_____

_____

_____

Understanding Fractions

Fractions are used to show part of a set.

The fraction of the shapes that are stars can be written as:

$$\frac{\text{Number of stars}}{\text{Total number of shapes}} = \frac{3}{7}$$

Fractions are used to show part of 1 whole.

The length between 0 and 1 is divided into 4 equal sections. The fraction for the shaded section can be written as:

$$\frac{\text{Number of shaded sections}}{\text{Total number of sections}} = \frac{3}{4}$$

Write the fraction that represents the shaded portion.

1.

$$\frac{\text{Number of shaded parts}}{\text{Total number of parts}} = \frac{4}{\blacksquare}$$

_____

2.

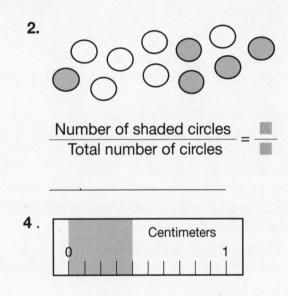

$$\frac{\text{Number of shaded circles}}{\text{Total number of circles}} = \frac{\blacksquare}{\blacksquare}$$

_____

3.

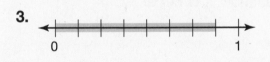

_____

4.

Centimeters

_____

Draw models of fractions.

5. Draw a set and shade $\frac{2}{5}$.

6. Draw a whole and shade $\frac{3}{4}$.

7. Number Sense If you shade $\frac{1}{3}$ of a set, what fraction of the set is not shaded?

_____

Understanding Fractions

Write the fraction that represents the shaded portion.

1.

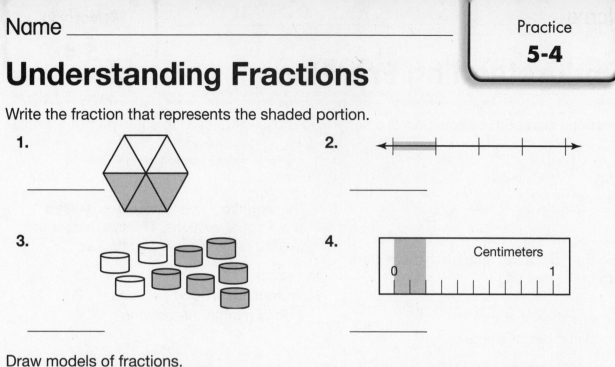

_____

2.

_____

3.

_____

4.

_____

Draw models of fractions.

5. Draw a set to represent $\frac{4}{10}$.

6. Draw a number line to represent $\frac{1}{6}$.

7. Write a Problem Write a fraction problem that can be solved using this model.

_____

8. Writing to Explain Sharon drew this drawing to show $\frac{3}{5}$. Is her drawing correct? Explain why or why not.

_____

9. Estimation Which is the best estimate of how full the cup is?

A $\frac{3}{4}$ full

B $\frac{1}{2}$ full

C $\frac{1}{3}$ full

D $\frac{1}{8}$ full

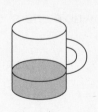

Equivalent Fractions

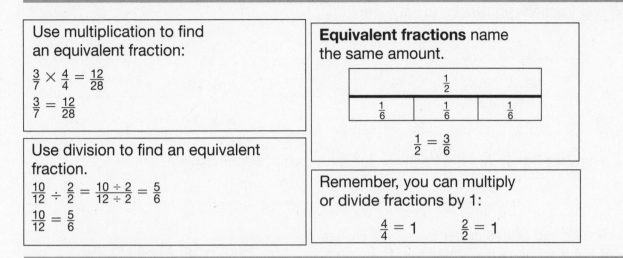

Use multiplication to find an equivalent fraction:

$\frac{3}{7} \times \frac{4}{4} = \frac{12}{28}$

$\frac{3}{7} = \frac{12}{28}$

Use division to find an equivalent fraction.

$\frac{10}{12} \div \frac{2}{2} = \frac{10 \div 2}{12 \div 2} = \frac{5}{6}$

$\frac{10}{12} = \frac{5}{6}$

Equivalent fractions name the same amount.

	$\frac{1}{2}$	
$\frac{1}{6}$	$\frac{1}{6}$	$\frac{1}{6}$

$\frac{1}{2} = \frac{3}{6}$

Remember, you can multiply or divide fractions by 1:

$\frac{4}{4} = 1 \qquad \frac{2}{2} = 1$

Use multiplication to find an equivalent fraction.

1. $\frac{3}{8}$ _____   **2.** $\frac{1}{3}$ _____   **3.** $\frac{4}{7}$ _____

4. $\frac{1}{2}$ _____   **5.** $\frac{5}{9}$ _____   **6.** $\frac{3}{10}$ _____

7. $\frac{8}{11}$ _____   **8.** $\frac{7}{16}$ _____   **9.** $\frac{11}{12}$ _____

Use division to find an equivalent fraction.

10. $\frac{9}{12}$ _____   **11.** $\frac{4}{18}$ _____   **12.** $\frac{15}{60}$ _____

13. $\frac{16}{20}$ _____   **14.** $\frac{80}{100}$ _____   **15.** $\frac{35}{45}$ _____

16. $\frac{25}{75}$ _____   **17.** $\frac{32}{48}$ _____   **18.** $\frac{18}{32}$ _____

Find two equivalent fractions for each given fraction.

19. $\frac{2}{4}$ _____   **20.** $\frac{3}{9}$ _____   **21.** $\frac{10}{12}$ _____

22. $\frac{75}{100}$ _____   **23.** $\frac{1}{2}$ _____   **24.** $\frac{7}{12}$ _____

25. $\frac{36}{48}$ _____   **26.** $\frac{5}{6}$ _____   **27.** $\frac{1}{8}$ _____

28. Number Sense Why do you have to multiply or divide both the numerator and denominator of a fraction to find an equivalent fraction?

_____

_____

_____

R 5·5

Equivalent Fractions

Find two fractions equivalent to each fraction.

1. $\frac{5}{6}$ _____

2. $\frac{15}{30}$ _____

3. $\frac{45}{60}$ _____

4. $\frac{7}{8}$ _____

5. $\frac{20}{8}$ _____

6. $\frac{16}{32}$ _____

7. $\frac{36}{60}$ _____

8. $\frac{32}{96}$ _____

9. $\frac{2}{3}$ _____

10. **Number Sense** Are the fractions $\frac{1}{5}$, $\frac{5}{5}$, and $\frac{5}{1}$ equivalent? Explain.

_____

11. The United States currently has 50 states. What fraction of the states had become a part of the United States by 1795? Write your answer as two equivalent fractions.

_____

Number of States in the United States

Year	Number of States
1795	15
1848	30
1900	45
1915	48
1960	50

12. In what year was the total number of states in the United States $\frac{3}{5}$ the number it was in 1960?

_____

13. The United States currently has 50 states. Write two fractions that describe the number of states that had become part of the United States in 1915?

_____

14. Which of the following pairs of fractions are equivalent?

A $\frac{1}{10}, \frac{3}{33}$

B $\frac{9}{5}, \frac{5}{9}$

C $\frac{5}{45}, \frac{1}{9}$

D $\frac{6}{8}, \frac{34}{48}$

15. **Writing to Explain** In what situation can you use only multiplication to find equivalent fractions to a given fraction? Give an example.

_____

_____

Fractions in Simplest Form

Remember:

> A fraction is in simplest form if the numerator and denominator have no common factors except 1.

Divide the numerator and denominator by the same number. Divide until you cannot divide evenly.	$\frac{42}{48} \div \frac{2}{2} = \frac{42 \div 2}{48 \div 2} = \frac{21}{24}$ $\frac{21}{24} \div \frac{3}{3} = \frac{21 \div 3}{24 \div 3} = \frac{7}{8}$

Find the GCF (greatest common factor). Divide both the numerator and denominator by the GCF.	Factors of 42:
	     1, 2, 3, 6, 7, 14, 21, 42
	 Factors of 48:
	     1, 2, 3, 4, 6, 8, 12, 16, 24, 48
	
	 The GCF is 6.
	
	 $\frac{42}{48} \div \frac{6}{6} = \frac{42 \div 6}{48 \div 6} = \frac{7}{8}$

Use division to write each fraction in simplest form.

1. $\frac{8}{10}$ _____

2. $\frac{14}{20}$ _____

3. $\frac{6}{9}$ _____

4. $\frac{20}{35}$ _____

5. $\frac{16}{24}$ _____

6. $\frac{12}{18}$ _____

7. $\frac{36}{96}$ _____

8. $\frac{45}{60}$ _____

9. $\frac{91}{156}$ _____

10. $\frac{6}{20}$ _____

11. $\frac{21}{105}$ _____

12. $\frac{75}{90}$ _____

Find the GCF of the numerator and denominator.

13. $\frac{6}{16}$ _____

14. $\frac{35}{50}$ _____

15. $\frac{24}{40}$ _____

16. $\frac{28}{32}$ _____

17. $\frac{18}{24}$ _____

18. $\frac{33}{36}$ _____

Use the GCF to write each fraction in simplest form.

19. $\frac{32}{48}$ _____

20. $\frac{21}{56}$ _____

21. $\frac{9}{54}$ _____

22. $\frac{30}{54}$ _____

23. $\frac{21}{36}$ _____

24. $\frac{18}{42}$ _____

25. Reasoning Under what circumstances would the GCF be equal to the numerator of a fraction before simplifying?

_____

_____

Fractions in Simplest Form

Write each fraction in simplest form.

1. $\frac{8}{16}$ _____

2. $\frac{15}{20}$ _____

3. $\frac{10}{12}$ _____

4. $\frac{20}{35}$ _____

5. $\frac{16}{48}$ _____

6. $\frac{45}{100}$ _____

7. $\frac{60}{96}$ _____

8. $\frac{72}{75}$ _____

9. $\frac{32}{36}$ _____

10. $\frac{8}{28}$ _____

11. $\frac{21}{56}$ _____

12. $\frac{63}{81}$ _____

13. **Number Sense** How can you check to see if a fraction is written in simplest form?

_____

_____

14. **Writing to Explain** What is the GCF and how is it used to find the simplest form of a fraction?

_____

_____

_____

Find the GCF of the numerator and denominator of the fraction.

15. $\frac{8}{26}$ _____

16. $\frac{30}{75}$ _____

17. $\frac{48}{72}$ _____

Use the GCF to write each fraction in simplest form.

18. $\frac{12}{16}$ _____

19. $\frac{12}{20}$ _____

20. $\frac{30}{36}$ _____

21. $\frac{35}{56}$ _____

22. $\frac{28}{63}$ _____

23. $\frac{42}{72}$ _____

24. What is the simplest form of the fraction $\frac{81}{108}$?

A $\frac{28}{36}$

B $\frac{3}{4}$

C $\frac{2}{3}$

D $\frac{4}{5}$

Problem Solving:
Make and Test Conjectures

Remember — A **conjecture** is a generalization that you think is true.

Make a conjecture.

The sum of two prime numbers is never a prime number.

Find and test several examples.
3 + 5 = 8

Prime numbers: 2, 3, 5, 7, 11, 13, 17, 19, 23, 29
5 + 7 = 12   2 + 3 = 5

Do the examples show your conjecture is reasonable or not reasonable?

The sum may be prime.
The conjecture is not reasonable.

Test these conjectures. Give three examples. Explain whether the conjectures are *reasonable* or *not reasonable*.

1. All multiples of 5 are even numbers.

    _____

2. All odd numbers are prime numbers.

    _____

    _____

3. The difference of two even numbers is always an even number.

    _____

4. Write a conjecture about the sum of two negative integers. Then test your conjecture.

    _____

    _____

5. **Critical Thinking** After testing, why is a conjecture considered reasonable, but not proven?

    _____

    _____

    _____

Problem Solving: Make and Test Conjectures

Test these conjectures. Give three examples. Explain if the conjecture is *reasonable* or *not reasonable*.

1. If a number is divisible by 4, it is always an even number.

   _____

2. The product of two whole numbers is always greater than 1.

   _____

3. If a number has a 9 in the ones place, it is always divisible by 3.

   _____

4. The least common denominator of two fractions is always greater than the denominators of the fractions.

   _____

5. Write a conjecture about the product of two odd numbers. Then test your conjecture.

   _____

   _____

6. Write a conjecture about the sum of two fractions. Then test your conjecture.

   _____

   _____

7. **Reasoning** How is testing a conjecture like finding a statement true or false? How is it different?

   _____

   _____

   _____

   _____

Fractions and Division

You can think of fractions as division: The numerator is the same as the dividend and the denominator is the same as the divisor.

Write $\frac{5}{8}$ as a division expression.

Think: $\frac{1}{8}$ of 5 wholes.

Shortcut: The numerator is 5, so the dividend is 5. The denominator is 8, so the divisor is 8.

So $\frac{5}{8} = 5 \div 8$.

Write $3 \div 8$ as a fraction.

Think: 3 wholes divided into 8 equal parts. Each part is equal to $\frac{3}{8}$.

Shortcut: The dividend is 3, so the numerator is 3. The divisor is 8, so the denominator is 8.

So $3 \div 8 = \frac{3}{8}$.

Write a division expression for each fraction.

1. $\frac{1}{4}$ _____

2. $\frac{2}{5}$ _____   3. $\frac{7}{8}$ _____   4. $\frac{3}{10}$ _____

5. $\frac{5}{7}$ _____   6. $\frac{4}{15}$ _____   7. $\frac{10}{13}$ _____

Write each division expression as a fraction.

8. $4 \div 5$ _____   9. $2 \div 3$ _____   10. $2 \div 9$ _____

11. $1 \div 6$ _____   12. $9 \div 10$ _____   13. $11 \div 12$ _____

14. **Writing to Explain** Explain how to write *seventeen divided by twenty* as a division expression and as a fraction.

_____

_____

_____

_____

R 6·1

Fractions and Division

Write a division expression for each fraction.

1. $\frac{4}{10}$ _____   **2.** $\frac{1}{6}$ _____   **3.** $\frac{2}{7}$ _____

4. $\frac{3}{8}$ _____   **5.** $\frac{5}{12}$ _____   **6.** $\frac{3}{17}$ _____

7. $\frac{7}{9}$ _____   **8.** $\frac{18}{25}$ _____   **9.** $\frac{99}{100}$ _____

Write each division expression as a fraction.

10. $7 \div 12$ _____   **11.** $2 \div 5$ _____   **12.** $8 \div 11$ _____

13. $1 \div 8$ _____   **14.** $7 \div 10$ _____   **15.** $6 \div 13$ _____

16. $5 \div 9$ _____   **17.** $11 \div 21$ _____   **18.** $13 \div 100$ _____

19. Zane was telling his mother that he learned about rational numbers in school. Which is the definition of a rational number?

A Any number that can be shown as the quotient of two integers

B Any number that can be shown as the product of two integers

C Any number that can be written as an integer

D Any integer that can be written as a decimal

20. Tanisha used the division expression $2 \div 5$ to equally divide two same-size pizzas among five people. Which fraction represents each person's share of the pizza?

A $\frac{5}{2}$

B $\frac{2}{5}$

C $\frac{2}{7}$

D $\frac{5}{7}$

21. Writing to Explain Can the division expression $-4 \div 15$ be shown as a fraction? If yes, write the fraction. Explain why or why not.

_____

_____

Fractions and Decimals

A fraction and a decimal can both be used to represent the same value.

Write 0.35 as a fraction.

Write the decimal as a fraction with a denominator of 10, 100, 1000, or another power of ten.

$0.35 = 35$ hundredths $= \frac{35}{100}$

Then write the fraction in simplest form.

$\frac{35}{100} = \frac{35 \div 5}{100 \div 5} = \frac{7}{20}$

So $0.35 = \frac{7}{20}$.

Write $\frac{3}{25}$ as a decimal.

Method 1: Write an equivalent fraction with a denominator of 10, 100, 1000, or another power of ten. Then write the decimal.

$\frac{3}{25} = \frac{3 \times 4}{25 \times 4} = \frac{12}{100} = 0.12$

Method 2: Divide the numerator by the denominator.

$$\begin{array}{r} 0.12 \\ 25\overline{)3.00} \\ -25 \\ \hline 50 \\ -50 \\ \hline 0 \end{array}$$

So $\frac{3}{25} = 0.12$.

Write a decimal and a fraction in simplest form for each shaded portion.

1.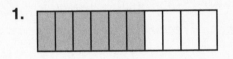

2.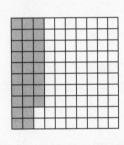

_____   _____

Write each decimal as a fraction in simplest form.

3. 0.5 _____   **4.** 0.8 _____   **5.** 0.36 _____

6. 0.25 _____   **7.** 0.125 _____   **8.** 0.070 _____

Convert each fraction to a decimal.

9. $\frac{93}{100}$ _____   **10.** $\frac{7}{10}$ _____   **11.** $\frac{11}{20}$ _____

12. $\frac{14}{25}$ _____   **13.** $\frac{7}{40}$ _____   **14.** $\frac{6}{100}$ _____

15. Geometry Draw eight congruent figures. Shade some of the figures to make a color pattern. Write a decimal and a fraction in simplest form to represent the shaded part of the set.

Fractions and Decimals

Write a decimal and a fraction in simplest form for each shaded portion.

1.    **2.**

_____   _____

Write each decimal as a fraction in simplest form.

3. 0.15 _____ **4.** 0.31 _____ **5.** 0.82 _____

6. 0.27 _____ **7.** 0.375 _____ **8.** 0.920 _____

Convert each fraction to a decimal.

9. $\frac{56}{100}$ _____ **10.** $\frac{90}{200}$ _____ **11.** $\frac{9}{25}$ _____

12. $\frac{8}{50}$ _____ **13.** $\frac{57}{60}$ _____ **14.** $\frac{7}{8}$ _____

15. Draw a Picture Show $\frac{46}{200}$ on the hundredths grid. Then write the fraction as a decimal.

_____

16. About $\frac{2}{5}$ of the students in the after school program have a cell phone. Which decimal is equivalent to $\frac{2}{5}$?

    A 0.2

    B 0.25

    C 0.4

    D 0.5

17. Writing to Explain Solve the problem. Then explain how you found the answer. In Tori's favorite class, $\frac{12}{25}$ of the students are girls. Write a decimal that represents the number of boys in the class.

_____

_____

Improper Fractions and Mixed Numbers

A mixed number combines a whole number with a fraction. It is greater than one.

An improper fraction has a numerator that is larger than its denominator.

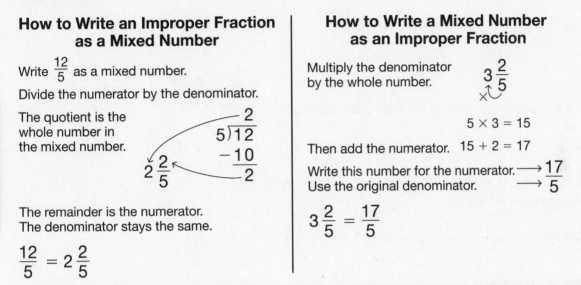

How to Write an Improper Fraction as a Mixed Number

Write $\frac{12}{5}$ as a mixed number.

Divide the numerator by the denominator.

The quotient is the whole number in the mixed number.

$$5\overline{)12}$$
$$\underline{-10}$$
$$2$$

$$2\frac{2}{5}$$

The remainder is the numerator. The denominator stays the same.

$$\frac{12}{5} = 2\frac{2}{5}$$

How to Write a Mixed Number as an Improper Fraction

Multiply the denominator by the whole number.

$$3\frac{2}{5}$$

$$5 \times 3 = 15$$

Then add the numerator. $15 + 2 = 17$

Write this number for the numerator. $\longrightarrow \frac{17}{5}$
Use the original denominator. $\longrightarrow$

$$3\frac{2}{5} = \frac{17}{5}$$

---

1. Draw a picture to show $4\frac{2}{3}$.

Write each improper fraction as a whole number or mixed number in simplest form.

2. $\frac{60}{40}$ _____

3. $\frac{33}{10}$ _____

4. $\frac{12}{7}$ _____

Write each mixed number as an improper fraction.

5. $4\frac{1}{3}$ _____

6. $1\frac{20}{50}$ _____

7. $8\frac{7}{8}$ _____

8. Reasoning Write 6 as an improper fraction with a denominator of 10. _____

Improper Fractions and Mixed Numbers

1. Draw a picture to show $\frac{9}{7}$.

2. Draw a picture to show $3\frac{4}{5}$.

Write each improper fraction as a whole number or mixed number in simplest form.

3. $\frac{25}{5}$ _____

4. $\frac{47}{9}$ _____

5. $\frac{52}{7}$ _____

Write each mixed number as an improper fraction.

6. $4\frac{4}{5}$ _____

7. $13\frac{3}{4}$ _____

8. $9\frac{5}{8}$ _____

9. Reasoning Write 8 as an improper fraction with a denominator of 4.

_____

Which letter on the number line corresponds to each number?

10. $5\frac{2}{5}$ _____

11. $4\frac{7}{10}$ _____

12. $\frac{23}{5}$ _____

13. Which number does the picture show?

A $\frac{12}{8}$

B $2\frac{1}{8}$

C $2\frac{1}{4}$

D $\frac{20}{8}$

14. Writing to Explain Can you express $\frac{9}{9}$ as a mixed number? Why or why not?

_____

_____

Decimal Forms of Fractions And Mixed Numbers

How to Convert Fractions to Decimals

Write $\frac{5}{9}$ as a decimal.

Divide the numerator by the denominator. Annex zeros if necessary.

$$
\begin{array}{r}
0.555 \\
9\overline{)5.000} \\
-45 \\
\hline
50 \\
-45 \\
\hline
50 \\
-45 \\
\hline
5
\end{array}
$$

The decimal 0.555 is a repeating decimal. Place a bar over the repeating digit.

So, $\frac{5}{9} = 0.\overline{5}$.

How to Convert Decimals to Fractions

Write 0.65 as a fraction.

$0.65 = 65$ hundredths $= \frac{65}{100}$

Write $\frac{65}{100}$ in simplest form.

$\frac{65}{100} = \frac{65 \div 5}{100 \div 5} = \frac{13}{20}$

So, $0.65 = \frac{13}{20}$

Write 3.375 as a mixed number.

$3.375 = 3 + 0.375$

$0.375 = 375$ thousandths $= \frac{375}{1,000}$

$\frac{375}{1,000} = \frac{375 \div 125}{1000 \div 125} = \frac{3}{8}$

$3 + \frac{3}{8} = 3\frac{3}{8}$

So, $3.375 = 3\frac{3}{8}$.

Write each fraction or mixed number as a decimal.

1. $\frac{1}{3}$ _____

2. $\frac{20}{100}$ _____

3. $\frac{6}{10}$ _____

4. $2\frac{1}{4}$ _____

5. $5\frac{1}{8}$ _____

6. $1\frac{4}{9}$ _____

Write each decimal as a fraction or a mixed number in simplest form.

7. 0.4 _____

8. 0.625 _____

9. 0.45 _____

10. 3.2 _____

11. 2.18 _____

12. 4.68 _____

13. **Number Sense** The Lady Bug trail in Sequoia National Forest is 5.1 miles long. How does it compare to a trail that is $5\frac{2}{5}$ miles long?

_____

_____

Decimal Forms of Fractions and Mixed Numbers

Write each fraction or mixed number as a decimal.

1. $\frac{33}{100}$ _____ **2.** $\frac{2}{5}$ _____ **3.** $\frac{1}{6}$ _____

4. $1\frac{3}{16}$ _____ **5.** $4\frac{7}{9}$ _____ **6.** $6\frac{5}{11}$ _____

Write each decimal as a fraction or a mixed number in simplest form.

7. 0.08 _____ **8.** 0.24 _____ **9.** 0.325 _____

10. 4.75 _____ **11.** 1.06 _____ **12.** 5.15 _____

13. The label on a cosmetic bottle says 0.04 oz. What is the fraction equivalent for this amount? _____

14. The scale at a deli counter shows 2.54 lb. What is the mixed number equivalent for the number shown? _____

15. Reasoning What is a situation in which you would use fractions to express a number less than one? What is a situation in which decimals seem to work better?

_____

_____

16. Which decimal is equivalent to $4\frac{4}{5}$?

  A 4.4

  B 4.45

  C $4.\overline{5}$

  D 4.8

17. Writing to Explain How do you know where to place the bar when a decimal is a repeating decimal?

_____

_____

Problem Solving: Draw a Picture

Sometimes you need to draw a picture to solve a problem.

Jasmine is making a charm bracelet. She wants to put a charm every 0.5 inch on the bracelet. The bracelet is 6 inches long. Use a ruler and the number line below to mark and label the place for each charm.

0   2   6

inches

Read and Understand

You know the length of the bracelet and where to place each charm. You know the length of the number line.

You need to mark and label each 0.5 unit on the number line.

Plan and Solve

Divide the line from 0 to 2 into fourths to show 0.5, 1, and 1.5.

Use each unit of 0.5 to mark and label the rest of the number line.

bracelet = 6 inches
charm = every 0.5 inches
number line = labels at 0, 2, and 6

Measure the number line to divide it into equal units of 0.5.

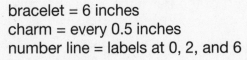

0   2

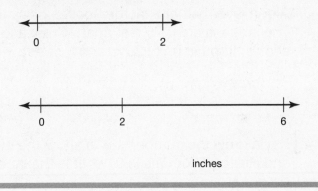

0   2   6

inches

Draw a picture to solve the problems.

1. A neighborhood has speed bumps every 0.25 miles along the main road. Use your ruler and the number line to mark and label the place of each speed bump.

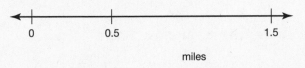

0   0.5   1.5

miles

2. A path between neighborhoods is 0.7 miles long. Mark and label the end of the path on the number line below.

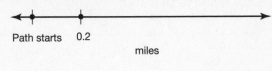

Path starts   0.2

miles

R 6·5

Problem Solving: Draw a Picture

1. A community swimming pool places buoys every 1.5 feet across the pool to mark off swimming areas. Use your ruler and the number line to show where each buoy is placed.

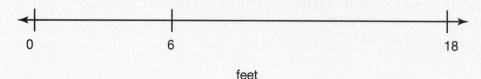

feet

2. A trail is marked every 0.6 mile. Use the number line below to show the start of the trail if the trail is 5.4 miles long.

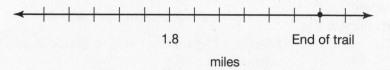

miles

3. A conveyer belt at a factory moves parts from station to station. The stations are 0.75 feet apart. Draw and label a number line that shows stops at 0.75, 2.25, and 4.5 feet.

4. Kayla drew the number line to show the distance between Fontana and Rialto. If Fontana is 0, what is the label at Rialto?

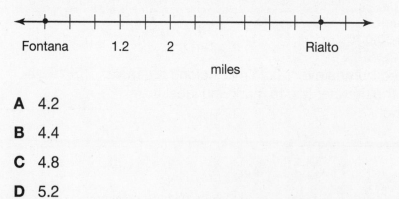

miles

A 4.2

B 4.4

C 4.8

D 5.2

5. Writing to Explain Maggie is planting bushes every 1.5 feet along the side of a fence. The fence is 22.5 feet long. Explain how Maggie can draw a picture to show where each bush is planted.

_____

_____

Adding and Subtracting: Like Denominators

How to find sums or differences of fractions with like denominators:

Find $\frac{2}{14} + \frac{6}{14}$.	The fractions have like denominators, so you can just add the numerators.
$\frac{2}{14} + \frac{6}{14} = \frac{8}{14}$	Write the sum over the common denominator.
$\frac{8}{14} = \frac{4}{7}$	Simplify if possible.

Find $\frac{5}{7} - \frac{2}{7}$.	The denominators are the same, so you can subtract the numerators.
$\frac{5}{7} - \frac{2}{7} = \frac{3}{7}$	$\frac{3}{7}$ cannot be simplified, so
	$\frac{5}{7} - \frac{2}{7} = \frac{3}{7}$

Find each sum or difference. Simplify your answer.

1. $\frac{1}{6} + \frac{3}{6} =$ _____

2. $\frac{9}{11} - \frac{4}{11} =$ _____

3. $\frac{6}{7} - \frac{2}{7} =$ _____

4. $\frac{3}{12} + \frac{8}{12} =$ _____

5. $\frac{8}{9} - \frac{5}{9} =$ _____

6. $\frac{1}{10} + \frac{8}{10} =$ _____

7. $\frac{4}{15} + \frac{11}{15} =$ _____

8. $\frac{16}{20} - \frac{9}{20} =$ _____

9. Number Sense Give an example of two fractions whose sum can be simplified to $\frac{1}{2}$.

_____

_____

10. A quarter has a diameter of $\frac{15}{16}$ in. A dime has a diameter of $\frac{11}{16}$ in., and a nickel has a diameter of $\frac{13}{16}$ in. If you put each coin side by side, what is the combined width of the three coins?

_____

R 7·1

Adding and Subtracting: Like Denominators

Find each sum or difference. Use a number line. Simplify your answers.

1. $\frac{7}{8} - \frac{3}{8}$ _____

$0 \ \frac{1}{8} \ \frac{2}{8} \ \frac{3}{8} \ \frac{4}{8} \ \frac{5}{8} \ \frac{6}{8} \ \frac{7}{8} \ 1$

2. $\frac{3}{5} + \frac{4}{5}$ _____

$0 \ \frac{1}{5} \ \frac{2}{5} \ \frac{3}{5} \ \frac{4}{5} \ 1 \ 1\frac{1}{5} \ 1\frac{2}{5} \ 1\frac{3}{5} \ 1\frac{4}{5} \ 2$

Find each sum or difference. Simplify your answers.

3. $\frac{6}{7} + \frac{1}{7}$ _____

4. $\frac{9}{10} - \frac{4}{10}$ _____

5. $\frac{8}{15} - \frac{5}{15}$ _____

6. $\frac{1}{11} + \frac{3}{11} + \frac{4}{11}$ _____

7. $\frac{1}{6} + \frac{2}{6} + \frac{5}{6}$ _____

8. $\frac{2}{20} + \frac{5}{20} + \frac{7}{20}$ _____

Evaluate **9** through **11** for $x = \frac{2}{9}$.

9. $\frac{8}{9} + x$ _____

10. $\frac{5}{9} - x$ _____

11. $\left(\frac{7}{9} - x\right) + \frac{1}{9}$ _____

12. Use the table to answer the questions.

a. What is the total amount of seafood in the soup?

_____

b. How much more shrimp than cod is in the soup?

Seafood for Soup	
Cod	$\frac{5}{8}$ lb
Scallops	$\frac{2}{8}$ lb
Shrimp	$\frac{7}{8}$ lb

13. Critical Thinking Max has 12 pairs of socks. Of them, 6 pairs are blue, 3 pairs are brown, and 2 pairs are white. Max wants to know what fraction of the socks are blue or brown. How can he find the numerator?

A Add $6 + 3 + 2$.

B Add $6 + 3$.

C Subtract 11 from 12.

D Subtract 9 from 12.

14. Writing to Explain Explain how you can add two fractions with denominators of 10 and end up with a sum whose denominator is 5.

_____

_____

Least Common Multiple

There are different ways to find the least common multiple (LCM) of two numbers. Here are two ways of finding the LCM of 4 and 5:

List Multiples	**Use Prime Factors**

List Multiples

Step 1: List multiples of each number.

4: 4, 8, 12, 16, 20, 24, 28, 32, 36, 40, 44, 48…

5: 5, 10, 15, 20, 25, 30, 35, 40, 45, 50…

Step 2: Check the multiples the numbers have in common.

4: 4, 8, 12, 16,⟨20⟩ 24, 28, 32, 36,⟨40⟩ 44, 48…

5: 5, 10, 15,⟨20⟩ 25, 30, 35,⟨40⟩ 45, 50…

Step 3: Determine which of the common multiples is the least.

20 and 40 are both common multiples, but 20 is the least.

The LCM of 4 and 5 is 20.

Use Prime Factors

Step 1: List the prime factors of each number.

4: 2 × 2

5: 5

Step 2: Circle the greatest number of times each different factor appears.

4:⟨2 × 2⟩

5:⟨5⟩

Step 3: Find the product of the factors you circled.

2 × 2 × 5 = 20

The LCM of 4 and 5 is 20.

Find the LCM of each set of numbers.

1. 6, 7 _____

2. 4, 5 _____

3. 10, 15 _____

4. 2, 5, 10 _____

5. 6, 21 _____

6. 8, 10 _____

7. 12, 20 _____

8. 5, 10, 25 _____

9. 7, 8 _____

10. Number Sense If you know the LCM of 4 and 5, how could you find the LCM of 40 and 50?

_____

_____

11. Writing to Explain Peter says the least common multiple of 4, 6, and 12 is 24. Do you agree or disagree? Explain.

_____

_____

_____

Least Common Multiple

Find the LCM of each set of numbers.

1. 15, 20 _____

2. 4, 50 _____

3. 8, 12 _____

4. 14, 42 _____

5. 21, 30 _____

6. 3, 7, 10 _____

7. 6, 7, 8 _____

8. 16, 20 _____

9. 12, 16 _____

10. At what times of the day between 10:00 A.M. and 5:00 P.M. do the chemistry presentation and the recycling presentation start at the same time?

_____

_____

Science Museum
— Show Schedule —
Chemistry — Every 30 minutes
Electricity — Every 20 minutes
Recycling — Every 40 minutes
Fossils — Every 45 minutes
The first showing for all shows is at 10:00 A.M.

11. The museum does shows in schools every Monday and shows in public libraries every fifth day (on both weekdays and weekends). If the museum did both a school show and a library show on Monday, how many days will it be until it does both shows on the same day again?

_____

12. Which of the following pairs of numbers is correctly listed with its LCM?

A 5, 15; LCM: 30

B 20, 30; LCM: 60

C 24, 36; LCM: 12

D 7, 9; LCM: 21

13. Writing to Explain What method would you use to find the LCM of a group of four numbers? Explain and give an example.

_____

_____

_____

_____

Adding and Subtracting: Unlike Denominators

If you are adding or subtracting fractions and the denominators are not the same, the first thing to do is find a common denominator. The best common denominator to use is the least common multiple of the two denominators.

Step 1:
Use the LCM to find a common denominator.

Find $\frac{2}{6} + \frac{1}{2}$.
The LCM of 2 and 6 is 6. The least common denominator (LCD) is 6.

Find $\frac{3}{4} - \frac{1}{3}$.
The LCD of 3 and 4 is 12.

Step 2:
Write equivalent fractions.

$$\frac{2}{6} = \frac{2}{6}$$
$$+\frac{1}{2} = +\frac{3}{6}$$

$$\frac{3}{4} = \frac{9}{12}$$
$$-\frac{1}{3} = -\frac{4}{12}$$

Step 3:
Add or subtract. Simplify if possible.

$$\frac{2}{6} = \frac{2}{6}$$
$$+\frac{1}{2} = +\frac{3}{6}$$
$$\frac{5}{6}$$

$$\frac{3}{4} = \frac{9}{12}$$
$$-\frac{1}{3} = -\frac{4}{12}$$
$$\frac{5}{12}$$

Find each sum or difference. Simplify your answer.

1. $\frac{3}{4} + \frac{5}{2} =$ _____

2. $\frac{11}{12} - \frac{1}{3} =$ _____

3. $\frac{4}{15} + \frac{4}{5} =$ _____

4. $\frac{5}{6} - \frac{4}{9} =$ _____

5. $\frac{2}{3} + \frac{7}{10} =$ _____

6. $\frac{2}{5} + \frac{2}{3} - \frac{6}{30} =$ _____

7. Number Sense The least common denominator for the sum $\frac{3}{8} + \frac{5}{12}$ is 24. Name another common denominator that you could use.

_____

8. A recipe calls for $\frac{1}{2}$ cup of milk and $\frac{1}{3}$ cup of water. What is the total amount of liquid in the recipe?

_____

Adding and Subtracting: Unlike Denominators

Find each sum or difference. Simplify your answer.

1. $\frac{5}{6} + \frac{4}{12} =$ _____

2. $\frac{4}{5} - \frac{1}{10} =$ _____

3. $\frac{5}{12} + \frac{2}{3} =$ _____

4. $\frac{9}{20} + \frac{3}{5} =$ _____

5. $\frac{6}{16} - \frac{1}{4} =$ _____

6. $\frac{19}{21} - \frac{2}{7} =$ _____

7. $\frac{2}{5} + \frac{5}{20} =$ _____

8. $\frac{8}{9} - \frac{5}{12} =$ _____

9. $\frac{7}{8} + \frac{11}{24} - \frac{5}{6} =$ _____

10. Number Sense Is $\frac{7}{8}$ or $\frac{11}{10}$ closer to 1? How did you decide?

_____

_____

Emma has a small garden. Emma's garden is $\frac{1}{5}$ beans, $\frac{1}{8}$ peas, and $\frac{1}{2}$ corn. The rest is planted with flowers.

11. What fraction of Emma's garden is planted with vegetables?

_____

_____

12. Are there more flowers or peas in Emma's garden?

_____

_____

13. To solve the subtraction sentence $\frac{17}{10} - \frac{2}{5} = ?$, which common denominator is the best choice?

    A 10

    B 15

    C 20

    D 50

14. Writing to Explain To find the sum of $\frac{4}{9}$ and $\frac{7}{12}$, Mario rewrites the fractions as $\frac{8}{36}$ and $\frac{21}{36}$. His answer is $\frac{29}{36}$. Is Mario right? If not, show his error and correct it.

_____

_____

Estimating Sums and Differences of Mixed Numbers

You can use rounding to estimate sums and differences of fractions and mixed numbers.

How to round fractions:

If the fractional part is greater than or equal to $\frac{1}{2}$, round up to the next whole number.

Example: Round $3\frac{5}{7}$ to the nearest whole number.

$\frac{5}{7}$ is greater than $\frac{1}{2}$, so $3\frac{5}{7}$ rounds up to 4.

If the fractional part is less than $\frac{1}{2}$, drop the fraction and use the whole number you already have.

Example: Round $6\frac{1}{3}$ to the nearest whole number.

$\frac{1}{3}$ is less than $\frac{1}{2}$, so drop $\frac{1}{3}$ and round down to 6.

How to estimate sums and differences of fractions and mixed numbers:

Round both numbers to the nearest whole number. Then add or subtract.

Example: Estimate $4\frac{1}{8} + 7\frac{2}{3}$.

$4\frac{1}{8}$ rounds down to 4.

$7\frac{2}{3}$ rounds up to 8.

$4 + 8 = 12$

So, $4\frac{1}{8} + 7\frac{2}{3}$ is about 12.

Round to the nearest whole number.

1. $8\frac{6}{7}$ _____

2. $14\frac{2}{9}$ _____

3. $42\frac{4}{7}$ _____

4. $6\frac{51}{100}$ _____

5. $29\frac{4}{5}$ _____

6. $88\frac{2}{4}$ _____

7. $19\frac{3}{34}$ _____

8. $63\frac{41}{49}$ _____

Estimate each sum or difference.

9. $7\frac{2}{5} + 8\frac{1}{9}$ _____

10. $13\frac{5}{8} - 2\frac{7}{10}$ _____

11. $2\frac{1}{4} + 5\frac{1}{2} + 10\frac{3}{4}$ _____

12. $11\frac{3}{5} - 4\frac{1}{12}$ _____

13. $8 + 4\frac{11}{14} + 5\frac{1}{9}$ _____

14. $15\frac{6}{7} - 12\frac{2}{10}$ _____

Estimating Sums and Differences of Mixed Numbers

Round to the nearest whole number.

1. $3\frac{4}{9}$ _____

2. $5\frac{6}{7}$ _____

3. $2\frac{2}{5}$ _____

4. $11\frac{12}{15}$ _____

Estimate each sum or difference.

5. $2\frac{1}{4} + 3\frac{5}{6}$ _____

6. $5\frac{6}{9} - 1\frac{3}{4}$ _____

7. $8\frac{5}{13} + 5\frac{3}{5}$ _____

8. $11 - 6\frac{3}{7} + 2\frac{2}{5}$ _____

Rodrigo and Mel are competing in a track meet. The table at the right shows the results of their events.

9. Rodrigo claims his best jump was about 1 ft longer than Mel's best jump. Is he correct?

_____

_____

Participant	Event	Results/Distance
Rodrigo	Long jump	1. $6\frac{3}{8}$ ft 2. $5\frac{5}{6}$ ft
	Softball throw	$62\frac{1}{5}$ ft
Mel	Long jump	1. $4\frac{7}{10}$ ft 2. $4\frac{3}{4}$ ft
	Softball throw	$71\frac{7}{8}$ ft

10. Use the table above. If the school record for the softball throw is 78 ft, about how much farther must Rodrigo throw the ball to match the record?

A 15 ft   **B** 16 ft   **C** 18 ft   **D** 20 ft

11. **Writing to Explain** Consider the sum of $\frac{3}{5} + \frac{3}{4}$. Round each fraction and estimate the sum. Add the two fractions using a common denominator and then round the result. Which estimate is closest to the actual answer?

_____

_____

_____

_____

Adding Mixed Numbers

You can add to find the total weight of these two packages of cheese.

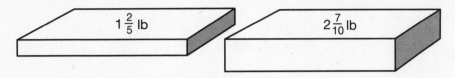

$1\frac{2}{5}$ lb $2\frac{7}{10}$ lb

Write the fractions so they both have the same denominator. Add the whole numbers. Add the fractions.

$$1\frac{2}{5} = 1\frac{4}{10}$$
$$+ 2\frac{7}{10} = + 2\frac{7}{10}$$
$$\overline{\phantom{+ 2\frac{7}{10}}} \overline{3\frac{11}{10}}$$

Write the improper fraction as a mixed number. Add the whole numbers. Write the fraction in simplest form.

$$= 3 + 1\frac{1}{10} = 4\frac{1}{10}.$$

The total weight of the cheese is $4\frac{1}{10}$ pounds.

Find each sum. Simplify your answer.

1. $5\frac{2}{3} = 5\frac{4}{6}$

    $+ 3\frac{1}{6} = + 3\frac{1}{6}$

    _____

2. $7\frac{4}{5} = 7\frac{}{20}$

    $+ 6\frac{1}{4} = + 6\frac{}{20}$

    _____

3. $8\frac{7}{11} + 14\frac{6}{11} =$ _____

4. $6\frac{1}{4} + 9\frac{7}{8} =$ _____

5. $3\frac{5}{8} + 12\frac{1}{6} =$ _____

6. $14 + 13\frac{5}{7} =$ _____

7. On Monday, $3\frac{7}{10}$ inches of snow fell during the day. Another $5\frac{1}{2}$ inches of snow fell that night. What was the total snowfall?

_____

8. **Writing to Explain** Explain how to rewrite $5\frac{7}{8} + 14\frac{1}{6}$ so the fractions have the same denominator. Find the sum.

_____

_____

_____

Adding Mixed Numbers

Find each sum. Simplify your answer.

1. $5 + 3\frac{1}{6} =$ _____

2. $4\frac{4}{5} + 8\frac{1}{10} =$ _____

3. $1\frac{5}{8} + \frac{15}{16} =$ _____

4. $6\frac{2}{3} + \frac{5}{4} =$ _____

5. $2\frac{7}{8} + 4 =$ _____

6. $7\frac{6}{10} + 1\frac{9}{20} =$ _____

7. $\frac{7}{8} + 3\frac{3}{5} + 2 =$ _____

8. $9 + 3\frac{2}{3} + \frac{5}{6} =$ _____

9. **Number Sense** Give an example of two mixed numbers whose sum is a whole number.

_____

_____

_____

10. An ostrich egg is $6\frac{4}{5}$ in. long. A California condor's egg is $4\frac{3}{10}$ in. long, and an albatross egg is $5\frac{7}{10}$ in. long. If the three eggs are placed end to end, what is the total length in inches?

_____

11. Shanda can travel 10 mi on her electric scooter before she has to recharge the batteries. If it is $4\frac{5}{8}$ mi to the library and $5\frac{2}{5}$ mi to her friend's house, can she make both trips before she needs to recharge the batteries?

_____

_____

12. Which is the fractional portion of the solution to $5\frac{3}{8} + 2\frac{3}{12}$?

   A $\frac{6}{12}$

   B $\frac{5}{8}$

   C $\frac{6}{8}$

   D $\frac{15}{8}$

13. **Writing to Explain** Explain the steps to adding mixed numbers. What must you do first?

_____

_____

Name _____

Subtracting Mixed Numbers

To subtract mixed numbers, the fractional parts must have the same denominator. Use one of these methods:

Step 1	Step 2	Step 3	Step 4
Find $8\frac{1}{3} - 5\frac{4}{5}$ Estimate: $8 - 6 = 2$	Use the LCD to write equivalent fractions. $8\frac{1}{3} = 8\frac{5}{15}$ $5\frac{4}{5} = 5\frac{12}{15}$	Rename $8\frac{5}{15}$ to show more fifteenths so you can subtract. $8\frac{5}{15}$ $7\frac{5}{15} + \frac{15}{15}$ $7\frac{20}{15}$	Subtract and simplify if possible. $7\frac{20}{15} - 5\frac{12}{15} = 2\frac{8}{15}$
Find $3\frac{1}{2} - 1\frac{5}{8}$ Estimate: $4 - 2 = 2$	Write each mixed number as an improper fraction. $3\frac{1}{2} = \frac{7}{2}$ $1\frac{5}{8} = \frac{13}{8}$	Use the LCD to rewrite the improper fractions with the same denominator. $\frac{7}{2} = \frac{28}{8}$ $\frac{13}{8}$	Subtract and simplify if possible. $\frac{28}{8} - \frac{13}{8} =$ $\frac{15}{8} =$ $1\frac{7}{8}$

Use this method when the mixed numbers are small.

Find each difference. Simplify if possible.

1. $5\frac{9}{10} - 2\frac{3}{5} =$ _____

2. $11\frac{7}{16} - 8\frac{3}{8} =$ _____

3. $9\frac{2}{3} - 9\frac{1}{6} =$ _____

4. $4\frac{2}{3} - 2 =$ _____

5. $4\frac{1}{4} - \frac{7}{12} =$ _____

6. $5\frac{6}{7} - 2\frac{13}{14} =$ _____

7. $6\frac{5}{16} - 3\frac{3}{4} =$ _____

8. $8 - 4\frac{7}{10} =$ _____

9. $2\frac{1}{5} - \frac{13}{15} =$ _____

10. $7\frac{7}{8} - 2\frac{3}{4} =$ _____

11. $3\frac{1}{3} - 1\frac{7}{9} =$ _____

12. $12\frac{3}{8} - 5\frac{1}{8} =$ _____

13. $7\frac{3}{4} - 2\frac{7}{8} =$ _____

14. $3\frac{7}{9} - 1\frac{1}{3} =$ _____

15. $12\frac{1}{8} - 5\frac{3}{8} =$ _____

16. Number Sense How do you know if you need to rename the first number in a subtraction problem involving mixed numbers?

_____

_____

_____

Name _____

Subtracting Mixed Numbers

Find each difference. Simplify if possible.

1. $2\frac{3}{5} - 1\frac{1}{5} =$ _____

2. $1\frac{4}{9} - \frac{8}{9} =$ _____

3. $5\frac{5}{8} - 1\frac{9}{16} =$ _____

4. $12 - 4\frac{5}{6} =$ _____

5. $6\frac{15}{16} - 4 =$ _____

6. $3\frac{7}{12} - 2\frac{3}{4} =$ _____

7. $9 - 7\frac{5}{8} =$ _____

8. $15\frac{1}{6} - 8\frac{2}{3} =$ _____

9. $6\frac{8}{9} - 1\frac{2}{3} =$ _____

10. $2\frac{3}{7} - 1\frac{5}{14} =$ _____

11. In which of the exercises above do you have to rename the first mixed number to show more fractional parts before subtracting?

_____

The table at the right shows the lengths of various carpentry nails.

12. How much longer is a 30d nail than a 5d nail?

_____

13. How much longer is a 12d nail than a 9d nail?

_____

Carpentry Nails

Size	Length (inches)
5d	$1\frac{3}{4}$
9d	$2\frac{3}{4}$
12d	$3\frac{1}{4}$
30d	$4\frac{1}{2}$

14. To subtract $4\frac{5}{6}$ from $10\frac{1}{3}$, which of the following must the mixed number $10\frac{1}{3}$ first be renamed as?

A $9\frac{2}{3}$

B $9\frac{4}{6}$

C $9\frac{8}{6}$

D $10\frac{2}{6}$

15. Writing to Explain Jack says that once you have a common denominator you are ready to subtract two mixed numbers. What other step might be necessary before you can subtract? Give an example.

_____

_____

Problem Solving:
Make a Table

Mario plans to walk $\frac{3}{4}$ mile today. Tomorrow he will walk $\frac{1}{2}$ mile more, then $\frac{1}{2}$ mile more every day after that. How long will it take before Mario walks 3 miles in one day?

Make a table showing each day and the distance he walks every day.

Day	1	2	3	4	5	6
Distance (mi)	$\frac{3}{4}$	$1\frac{1}{4}$	$1\frac{3}{4}$	$2\frac{1}{4}$	$2\frac{3}{4}$	$3\frac{1}{4}$

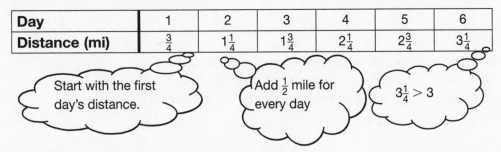

Start with the first day's distance.

Add $\frac{1}{2}$ mile for every day

$3\frac{1}{4} > 3$

Mario will walk at least 3 miles on Day 6.

Make tables to solve. Write each answer in a complete sentence.

1. The phone company charges 10¢ to connect a call for one minute and 8¢ per minute after that. How long could you talk on the phone for $1?

   _____

2. A plumber charges $30 for a house call and $20 per $\frac{1}{2}$ hour of work. How much will the plumber charge for $4\frac{1}{2}$ hours of work at Mrs. DiMarco's house?

   _____

3. **Geometry** The angles of a triangle have a sum of 180°. The angles of a rectangle have a sum of 360°. The angles of a pentagon have a sum of 540°. Continue this pattern to find the sum of the angles of an octagon.

   _____

4. **Writing to Explain** Write a problem based on the information in the table. Extend the table if necessary.

Day	1	2	3	4	5
Pages Read	23	58	93	128	☐

_____

Problem Solving:
Make a Table

Make tables to solve. Write each answer in a complete sentence.

1. A train has 3 engines, 52 boxcars, and 1 caboose. At every stop, it picks up 8 more boxcars. How many total cars (engines, cars, and cabooses) will the train have after 5 stops?

_____

2. Eileen likes to keep scrapbooks. She already has 4 scrapbooks filled with 40 pages each. If she fills 5 pages every month, how many months will it take her to fill up 2 more 40-page scrapbooks?

_____

3. Phil's Garage charges $50 for towing and $40 per hour to fix a car. Cliff's Cars charges $60 for towing and $38 per hour to fix a car. After how many hours of working on a car will the cost of towing and fixing a car be the same at the two repair shops?

_____

4. Dominic got a new video game. The first time he played the game he scored 80 points. After that, each time he played he increased his score by 60 points. How many times will he have to play before he scores 500 points?

_____

5. A scientist is studying certain germs. She places 3 germs in a special solution that will help the germs grow. The number of germs doubles every hour. How many germs will there be after 8 hours?

A 24   **B** 384   **C** 768   **D** 786

6. Writing to Explain Ed saved $50 one week. For the next 6 weeks, he saved $25 more than he saved the week before. How much did he save in all? One student solved this problem using the expression $50 + 6($25) = $200. What error was made? What is the correct answer?

_____

_____

_____

Multiplying a Fraction and a Whole Number

Find $12 \times \frac{1}{4}$.

$12 \times \frac{1}{4}$ is the same as dividing

12 by 4.

$12 \div 4 = 3$

$12 \times \frac{1}{4} = 3$

Find $\frac{3}{5}$ of 15, or $\frac{3}{5} \times 15$.

$15 \div 5 = 3$, so $\frac{1}{5} \times 15 = 3$

Since $\frac{3}{5}$ is 3 times $\frac{1}{5}$,

$\frac{3}{5} \times 15 = 3 \times \left(\frac{1}{5} \times 15\right) = 3 \times 3 = 9$.

$\frac{3}{5} \times 15 = 9$

Find each product.

1. $\frac{4}{5} \times 20 =$ _____

2. $\frac{6}{7}$ of $14 =$ _____

3. $24 \times \frac{3}{4} =$ _____

4. $\frac{2}{5}$ of $15 =$ _____

5. $400 \times \frac{3}{8} =$ _____

6. $\frac{7}{10}$ of $80 =$ _____

7. Reasoning Can you use division and mental math to find $\frac{2}{3}$ of 24? Why or why not?

_____

_____

_____

The chart shows the average high temperatures for different months in Phoenix, Arizona.

Phoenix Weather

Month	Average High
February	70°F
May	93°F
July	105°F

8. What is $\frac{4}{5}$ the average temperature in July? _____

9. What is $\frac{1}{2}$ the average temperature in February? _____

10. What is $\frac{2}{3}$ the average temperature in May? _____

R 8·1

Multiplying a Fraction and a Whole Number

Find each product.

1. $\frac{3}{4} \times 16 =$ _____

2. $\frac{5}{6} \times 30 =$ _____

3. $42 \times \frac{5}{6} =$ _____

4. $\frac{1}{8}$ of $72 =$ _____

5. $900 \times \frac{2}{3} =$ _____

6. $\frac{13}{20}$ of $100 =$ _____

7. **Reasoning** Without multiplying, tell which is greater, $\frac{5}{6}$ of 81 or $\frac{9}{10}$ of 81. Explain.

_____

Driving Distances

Departure City	Destination City	Distance
Pittsfield, Massachusetts	Providence, Rhode Island	132 mi
Reno, Nevada	Wendover, Utah	400 mi

8. Mike drove $\frac{1}{3}$ of the distance between Pittsfield, Massachusetts, and Providence, Rhode Island. How far did he drive?

_____

9. Bimal drove $\frac{3}{5}$ of the distance between Reno, Nevada, and Wendover, Utah. How far did he drive?

_____

10. **Estimation** How many more miles does Bimal have to drive to get to Wendover, Utah?

_____

11. There are 25 students in Mr. Fitch's sixth-grade class. If $\frac{3}{5}$ of the students are girls, how many girls are in Mr. Fitch's class?

   A 5 girls   **B** 10 girls   **C** 15 girls   **D** 20 girls

12. **Writing to Explain** Explain how you would find the product of 36 and $\frac{2}{3}$.

_____

_____

_____

Estimating Products

When you are working with fractions and mixed numbers, you can estimate using rounding, compatible numbers, or compatible benchmark fractions.

Estimate $\frac{3}{10} \times 21$ using a whole number that is compatible with the denominator.

$\frac{3}{10} \times 21$ Change 21 to the nearest whole number that is compatible with 10.

$\downarrow$ $\downarrow$

$\frac{3}{10} \times 20 = 6$

$\frac{3}{10} \times 21 \approx 6$ Think: $20 \div 10 = 2$.

           $3 \times 2 = 6$.

Estimate $\frac{3}{10} \times 12$ using a compatible benchmark fraction.

$\frac{3}{10} \times 12$ Round $\frac{3}{10}$ to a compatible benchmark fraction. Since $\frac{3}{10}$ is close to $\frac{1}{4}$ and 4 is a factor of twelve, use $\frac{1}{4}$.

$\downarrow$ $\downarrow$

$\frac{1}{4} \times 12 = 3$

$\frac{3}{10} \times 12 \approx 3$ Think: $12 \div 4 = 3$.

           $1 \times 3 = 3$.

Estimate each product by using compatible numbers or benchmark fractions.

1. $\frac{1}{6} \times 19 =$ _____

2. $\frac{4}{7} \times 10 =$ _____

3. $\frac{5}{8} \times 23 =$ _____

4. $31 \times \frac{2}{5} =$ _____

5. $\frac{7}{12} \times 18 =$ _____

6. $\frac{9}{16} \times 90 =$ _____

7. $43 \times \frac{2}{7} =$ _____

8. $35 \times \frac{5}{12} =$ _____

9. $16 \times \frac{4}{9} =$ _____

Estimate each product by rounding each factor to the nearest whole number.

10. $6\frac{2}{3} \times 5\frac{1}{8} \rightarrow$ Round $6\frac{2}{3}$: _____   Round $5\frac{1}{8}$: _____   Multiply: _____

11. $10\frac{2}{9} \times 4\frac{5}{6} =$ _____

12. $2\frac{7}{8} \times 3\frac{3}{4} =$ _____

13. $4\frac{1}{5} \times 2\frac{4}{10} =$ _____

14. **Reasonableness** Carlotta estimated that $\frac{3}{7} \times 20$ is about $\frac{3}{7} \times 14 = 6$. Is her estimate reasonable? Why or why not?

_____

15. **Critical Thinking** Why are the estimates of $\frac{6}{10} \times 18$ shown below different? Is one estimate better than the other?

$\frac{6}{10} \times 18 \approx \frac{6}{10} \times 20 = 12$ $\frac{6}{10} \times 18 \approx \frac{1}{2} \times 18 = 9$.

_____

_____

_____

_____

_____

© Pearson Education, Inc. 6

Estimating Products

Estimate each product.

1. $4\frac{5}{8} \times \frac{1}{3} =$ _____

2. $3 \times 2\frac{1}{5} =$ _____

3. $\frac{6}{10} \times 5\frac{3}{4} =$ _____

4. $2\frac{7}{9} \times 4\frac{2}{5} =$ _____

5. $6\frac{1}{2} \times 2\frac{1}{3} =$ _____

6. $\frac{7}{8} \times 2\frac{3}{8} =$ _____

7. $38 \times \frac{3}{8} =$ _____

8. $\frac{1}{4} \times 17 =$ _____

9. $\frac{3}{5} \times 51 =$ _____

10. $7\frac{4}{9} \times 5\frac{6}{7} =$ _____

11. $\frac{12}{25} \times 8 =$ _____

12. $11 \times \frac{1}{2} =$ _____

13. $\frac{8}{9} \times 6\frac{4}{10} =$ _____

14. $7\frac{1}{7} \times 2\frac{2}{3} =$ _____

15. $\frac{5}{12} \times 13 =$ _____

16. Show three ways to estimate $\frac{3}{5} \times 5\frac{3}{4}$. Identify each method you use.

_____

_____

17. **Explain It** Mr. Simpson lives $11\frac{3}{10}$ miles from his office. He estimates that he commutes $11 \times 2 \times 5$, or 110 miles each week. Is his estimate an overestimate or an underestimate? Explain.

_____

_____

18. Which benchmark fraction could you use to estimate the product of $38 \times \frac{7}{12}$? _____

19. **Geometry** Which is the best estimate for the area of a square with sides equal to $3\frac{1}{5}$ inches?

A   3 sq in.
B   6 sq in.
C   9 sq in.
D   16 sq in.

$3\frac{1}{5}$ in.

20. Joyce and Marianne have money jars. Joyce has 54 dimes in her jar. Marianne has $\frac{9}{10}$ as many dimes as Joyce. Estimate the number of dimes that Marianne has in her jar.

A   60 dimes
B   45 dimes
C   6 dimes
D   5 dimes

Multiplying Fractions

Find $\frac{3}{4} \times \frac{2}{5}$.
Draw a picture.
Shade the squares.
There are 20 squares in all.
6 squares have overlapping shading.
$\frac{3}{4} \times \frac{2}{5} = \frac{6}{20}$.

Simplify: $\frac{6}{20} = \frac{3}{10}$

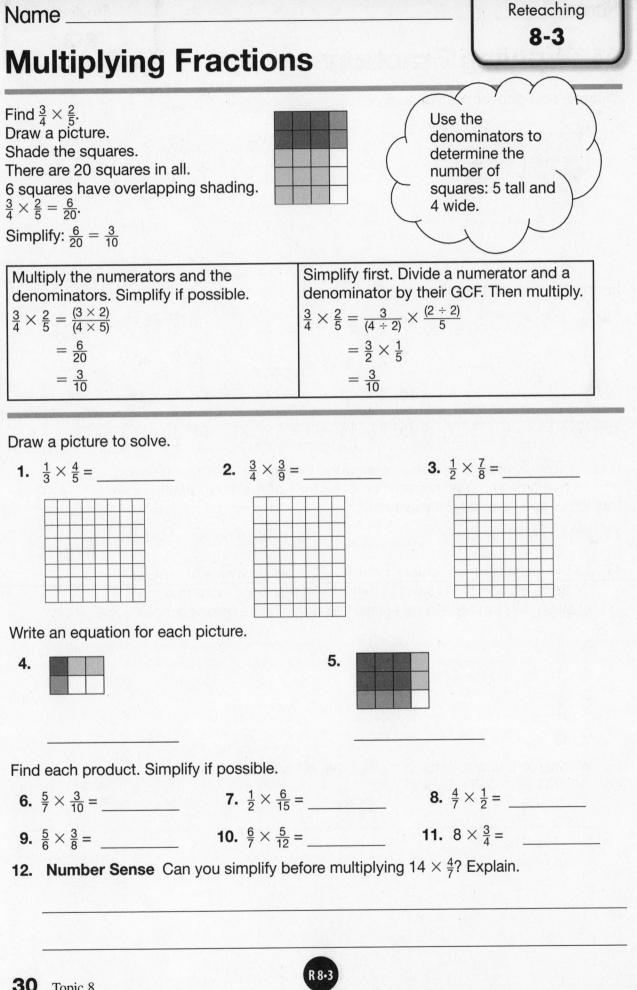

Use the denominators to determine the number of squares: 5 tall and 4 wide.

Multiply the numerators and the denominators. Simplify if possible.	Simplify first. Divide a numerator and a denominator by their GCF. Then multiply.
$\frac{3}{4} \times \frac{2}{5} = \frac{(3 \times 2)}{(4 \times 5)}$ $= \frac{6}{20}$ $= \frac{3}{10}$	$\frac{3}{4} \times \frac{2}{5} = \frac{3}{(4 \div 2)} \times \frac{(2 \div 2)}{5}$ $= \frac{3}{2} \times \frac{1}{5}$ $= \frac{3}{10}$

Draw a picture to solve.

1. $\frac{1}{3} \times \frac{4}{5} =$ _____

2. $\frac{3}{4} \times \frac{3}{9} =$ _____

3. $\frac{1}{2} \times \frac{7}{8} =$ _____

Write an equation for each picture.

4.

_____

5.

_____

Find each product. Simplify if possible.

6. $\frac{5}{7} \times \frac{3}{10} =$ _____

7. $\frac{1}{2} \times \frac{6}{15} =$ _____

8. $\frac{4}{7} \times \frac{1}{2} =$ _____

9. $\frac{5}{6} \times \frac{3}{8} =$ _____

10. $\frac{6}{7} \times \frac{5}{12} =$ _____

11. $8 \times \frac{3}{4} =$ _____

12. Number Sense Can you simplify before multiplying $14 \times \frac{4}{7}$? Explain.

_____

_____

Multiplying Fractions

Write an equation for each picture.

1.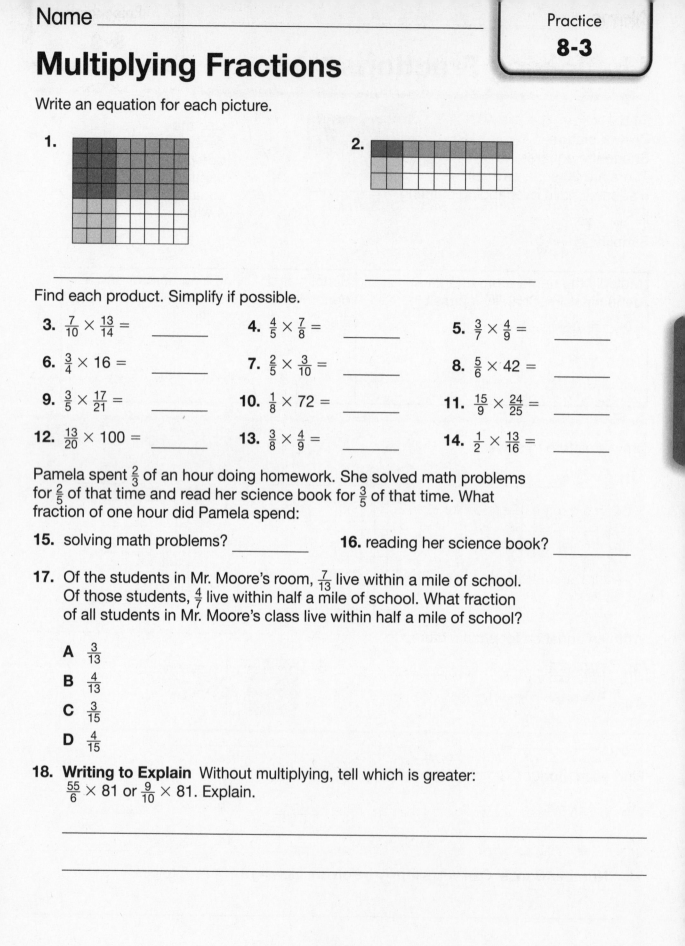

2.

_____   _____

Find each product. Simplify if possible.

3. $\frac{7}{10} \times \frac{13}{14} =$ _____

4. $\frac{4}{5} \times \frac{7}{8} =$ _____

5. $\frac{3}{7} \times \frac{4}{9} =$ _____

6. $\frac{3}{4} \times 16 =$ _____

7. $\frac{2}{5} \times \frac{3}{10} =$ _____

8. $\frac{5}{6} \times 42 =$ _____

9. $\frac{3}{5} \times \frac{17}{21} =$ _____

10. $\frac{1}{8} \times 72 =$ _____

11. $\frac{15}{9} \times \frac{24}{25} =$ _____

12. $\frac{13}{20} \times 100 =$ _____

13. $\frac{3}{8} \times \frac{4}{9} =$ _____

14. $\frac{1}{2} \times \frac{13}{16} =$ _____

Pamela spent $\frac{2}{3}$ of an hour doing homework. She solved math problems for $\frac{2}{5}$ of that time and read her science book for $\frac{3}{5}$ of that time. What fraction of one hour did Pamela spend:

15. solving math problems? _____

16. reading her science book? _____

17. Of the students in Mr. Moore's room, $\frac{7}{13}$ live within a mile of school. Of those students, $\frac{4}{7}$ live within half a mile of school. What fraction of all students in Mr. Moore's class live within half a mile of school?

A $\frac{3}{13}$

B $\frac{4}{13}$

C $\frac{3}{15}$

D $\frac{4}{15}$

18. Writing to Explain Without multiplying, tell which is greater: $\frac{55}{6} \times 81$ or $\frac{9}{10} \times 81$. Explain.

_____

_____

Name _____

Multiplying Mixed Numbers

How to find the product of two mixed numbers: Find $3\frac{2}{3} \times 4\frac{1}{2}$.

Step 1
Estimate the product by rounding.

Round $3\frac{2}{3}$ to 4 and $4\frac{1}{2}$ to 5:
$4 \times 5 = 20$

Step 2
Write each mixed number as an improper fraction.

$3\frac{2}{3} = \frac{11}{3}$ and $4\frac{1}{2} = \frac{9}{2}$

Look for common factors and simplify.

$3\frac{2}{3} \times 4\frac{1}{2} = \frac{11}{\cancel{3}_1} \times \frac{\cancel{9}^3}{2} = \frac{11}{1} \times \frac{3}{2}$

Step 3
Multiply the numerators and denominators.

$\frac{11}{1} \times \frac{3}{2} = \frac{33}{2}$

Write the product as a mixed number.

$\frac{33}{2} = 16\frac{1}{2}$

$16\frac{1}{2}$ is close to 20, so the answer is reasonable.

Find each product. Simplify if possible.

1. $2\frac{3}{4} \times 3\frac{1}{2}$ _____

2. $2\frac{1}{5} \times 2\frac{2}{3}$ _____

3. $6 \times 3\frac{1}{4}$ _____

4. $1\frac{2}{5} \times 3\frac{1}{4}$ _____

5. $4\frac{1}{2} \times 16$ _____

6. $1\frac{3}{8} \times 2\frac{1}{2}$ _____

Evaluate each expression for $K = 2\frac{1}{3}$.

7. $12K$ _____

8. $1\frac{3}{4}K$ _____

9. $2\frac{2}{3}K$ _____

10. Reasonableness What is a reasonable estimate for $7\frac{3}{4} \times 2\frac{2}{3}$? Explain.

_____

11. The cups of mushrooms in a recipe is $2\frac{1}{2}$ times the cups of onions. The cups of onions is $1\frac{1}{2}$. Solve $c = 1\frac{1}{2} \times 2\frac{1}{2}$ to find c, the cups of mushrooms.

_____

Multiplying Mixed Numbers

Find each product. Simplify if possible.

1. $3\frac{1}{2} \times 1\frac{2}{3}$ _____

2. $1\frac{1}{8} \times 2\frac{1}{3}$ _____

3. $7 \times 1\frac{1}{4}$ _____

4. $2\frac{1}{6} \times 1\frac{1}{5}$ _____

5. $3\frac{1}{6} \times 18$ _____

6. $1\frac{1}{8} \times 2\frac{1}{2}$ _____

7. $1\frac{2}{3} \times 2\frac{1}{4}$ _____

8. $10 \times 1\frac{1}{3}$ _____

9. $2\frac{4}{5} \times 3\frac{1}{3}$ _____

Evaluate each expression for $S = 1\frac{4}{5}$.

10. $2\frac{1}{3}S$ _____

11. $3\frac{3}{4}S$ _____

12. $5\frac{1}{6}S$ _____

Use the table to answer the questions.

13. If Berkeley receives $1\frac{1}{4}$ times its average January rainfall, how much rain will it receive?

_____

Average Rainfall in Berkeley, California	
January	$3\frac{7}{10}$ in.
April	$1\frac{4}{5}$ in.
October	$1\frac{1}{2}$ in.

14. How much rain will Berkeley receive if it is $2\frac{1}{3}$ times the October average?

_____

15. Which month has about twice the rainfall as April?

_____

16. Jessie stacked photographs of 6 zoo animals on top of each other to create a display. Each photo is $14\frac{1}{4}$ in. high. How high is the display?

A $84\frac{2}{3}$ in.

B $85\frac{1}{2}$ in.

C $86\frac{3}{4}$ in.

D 87 in.

17. Writing to Explain Explain how you would find $2 \times 2\frac{1}{3}$ using the Distributive Property.

_____

_____

Problem Solving: Multiple-Step Problems

Some word problems have hidden questions that must be answered before you can solve the problem.

A paved trail is 8 miles long. Rita runs $\frac{3}{8}$ of the length of the trail and walks the rest of the way. How many miles of the trail does Rita walk?

What do you know?	Rita runs $\frac{3}{8}$ of an 8-mile trail.
What are you asked to find?	How many miles of the trail that Rita walks.
How can you find the distance that Rita walks?	Subtract the distance Rita ran from the length of the trail.
What is the hidden question? The hidden question will help you find data you need to solve the problem.	How many miles did Rita run? To answer, find $\frac{3}{8} \times 8 = 3$.

Use the data to solve: $8 - 3 = 5$, so Rita walked 5 of the 8 miles.

Write and answer the hidden question(s) in each problem. Then solve the problem.

1. April surfed for $\frac{1}{3}$ of the 6 hours she was at the beach. She spent the rest of the time building a sand castle. How many hours did she spend building the castle?

    Hidden question:_____

    Solution:_____

2. Bill put gasoline in 2 of his 5-gallon cans and 4 of his 2-gallon cans. He filled all the cans to the exact capacity. How many gallons of gasoline did he buy?

    Hidden question 1:_____

    Hidden question 2:_____

    Solution:_____

3. It costs Le Stor $20 to buy a shirt. The store sells the shirt for $2\frac{1}{2}$ times its cost. What is the profit for 100 of these shirts? Hint: Profit equals sales minus cost.

    Hidden question 1:_____

    Hidden question 2:_____

    Solution:_____

Problem Solving:
Multiple-Step Problems

Write and answer the hidden question(s) in each problem. Then solve the problem.

1. Tiwa spent $1\frac{1}{2}$ hours setting up her computer. It took her 3 times as long to install the software. How long did it take Tiwa to set up the computer and install software?

   Hidden question(s):_____

   Solution:_____

2. Lon bought 40 ounces of sliced ham. He used $\frac{3}{4}$ of the ham to make sandwiches for his friends and $\frac{1}{5}$ of the ham in an omelet. How many ounces of ham were left?

   Hidden question(s):_____

   Solution:_____

3. Lionel cut off $\frac{1}{6}$ of a 48-inch piece of rope. Marsha cut off $\frac{1}{4}$ of a 36-inch piece of rope. They compared their cut pieces. Whose piece is longer? How much longer?

   Hidden question(s):_____

   Solution:_____

4. Melanie bought 3 CDs. The country music CD cost $15. The rock music CD cost $\frac{2}{3}$ as much as the country music CD. The platinum edition CD cost twice as much as the rock CD. What was the cost of the three CDs?

   Hidden question(s):_____

   Solution:_____

5. **Writing to Explain** Choose one of the problems above. Explain how you determined the hidden question and why it was necessary to answer that question in order to solve the problem.

   _____

   _____

   _____

Understanding Division of Fractions

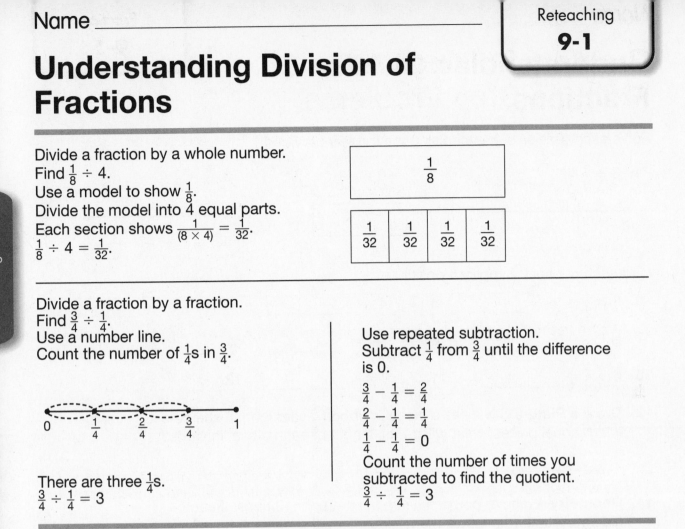

Divide a fraction by a whole number.
Find $\frac{1}{8} \div 4$.
Use a model to show $\frac{1}{8}$.
Divide the model into 4 equal parts.
Each section shows $\frac{1}{(8 \times 4)} = \frac{1}{32}$.
$\frac{1}{8} \div 4 = \frac{1}{32}$.

$\frac{1}{8}$

| $\frac{1}{32}$ | $\frac{1}{32}$ | $\frac{1}{32}$ | $\frac{1}{32}$ |

Divide a fraction by a fraction.
Find $\frac{3}{4} \div \frac{1}{4}$.
Use a number line.
Count the number of $\frac{1}{4}$s in $\frac{3}{4}$.

There are three $\frac{1}{4}$s.
$\frac{3}{4} \div \frac{1}{4} = 3$

Use repeated subtraction.
Subtract $\frac{1}{4}$ from $\frac{3}{4}$ until the difference is 0.

$\frac{3}{4} - \frac{1}{4} = \frac{2}{4}$
$\frac{2}{4} - \frac{1}{4} = \frac{1}{4}$
$\frac{1}{4} - \frac{1}{4} = 0$

Count the number of times you subtracted to find the quotient.
$\frac{3}{4} \div \frac{1}{4} = 3$

Solve each division sentence. Use a model if you wish.

1. $3 \div \frac{1}{3} =$ _____

2. $\frac{1}{5} \div 4 =$ _____

Find each quotient. Simplify if possible.

3. $3 \div \frac{1}{2} =$ _____

4. $\frac{9}{10} \div \frac{1}{10} =$ _____

5. $\frac{1}{5} \div 3 =$ _____

6. $\frac{3}{16} \div \frac{1}{16} =$ _____

7. $5 \div \frac{1}{3} =$ _____

8. $\frac{1}{2} \div 6 =$ _____

9. $8 \div \frac{1}{4} =$ _____

10. $\frac{7}{12} \div \frac{1}{12} =$ _____

11. $\frac{6}{7} \div \frac{1}{7} =$ _____

12. Draw a Picture The square dancing club meets for 3 hours. Every $\frac{3}{4}$ hour, the dancers change partners. How many different partners will each dancer have in one meeting? Draw a picture to show your solution.

_____

13. Writing to Explain Explain why the quotient of two fractions is always greater than either fraction.

_____

Understanding Division of Fractions

Solve each division sentence using the models provided.

1. $3 \div \frac{1}{3} =$ _____

2. $\frac{1}{4} \div 6 =$ _____

$$\boxed{\frac{1}{4}}$$

3. $\frac{5}{6} \div \frac{1}{6} =$ _____

Find each quotient. Simplify if possible.

4. $8 \div \frac{1}{4} =$ _____

5. $\frac{1}{7} \div 4 =$ _____

6. $5 \div \frac{1}{2} =$ _____

7. $\frac{7}{8} \div \frac{1}{8} =$ _____

8. $\frac{11}{12} \div \frac{1}{12} =$ _____

9. $\frac{1}{12} \div 3 =$ _____

10. $6 \div \frac{2}{3} =$ _____

11. $7 \div \frac{1}{3} =$ _____

12. $\frac{15}{16} \div \frac{1}{16} =$ _____

13. Draw a Picture Olivia has a piece of ribbon $\frac{1}{2}$ yard long. If she cuts it into 6 equal pieces, what will be the length of each piece, in yards?

_____

14. Geometry A regular polygon has a perimeter of 12 units. If each side measures $\frac{3}{4}$ unit, how many sides does the polygon have?

_____

15. Which division expression is shown by this model?

A $\frac{9}{10} \div \frac{1}{10}$ **B** $1 \div \frac{1}{10}$ **C** $\frac{9}{10} \div 1$ **D** $10 \div \frac{9}{10}$

16. Writing to Explain When you divide a whole number by a fraction less than 1, will the quotient be greater than or less than the whole number? Explain, and give an example.

_____

_____

_____

Dividing a Whole Number by a Fraction

To divide a whole number by a fraction, you can multiply the whole number by the reciprocal of the fraction. The reciprocal of a number has the numerator and the denominator reversed. The product of a number and its reciprocal is 1.

Number	×	Reciprocal	=	Product
3	×	$\frac{1}{3}$	=	1
$\frac{1}{8}$	×	$\frac{8}{1}$	=	1
$\frac{2}{3}$	×	$\frac{3}{2}$	=	1

Find $14 \div \frac{4}{7}$.

Step 1

Rewrite the division as multiplication using the reciprocal of the divisor.

The reciprocal of $\frac{4}{7}$ is $\frac{7}{4}$.

$14 \div \frac{4}{7} = 14 \times \frac{7}{4}$

Step 2

Divide out common factors if possible. Then multiply.

$$\frac{\overset{7}{\cancel{14}}}{1} \times \frac{7}{\underset{2}{\cancel{4}}} = \frac{49}{2}$$

Step 3

If your answer is an improper fraction, change it to a mixed number.

$\frac{49}{2} = 24\frac{1}{2}$

Find the reciprocal of each fraction or whole number.

1. $\frac{5}{7}$ _____

2. 11 _____

3. $\frac{9}{2}$ _____

Find each quotient. Simplify if possible.

4. $12 \div \frac{4}{5}$ _____

5. $2 \div \frac{1}{4}$ _____

6. $16 \div \frac{8}{10}$ _____

7. $24 \div \frac{3}{4}$ _____

8. $18 \div \frac{8}{9}$ _____

9. $25 \div \frac{10}{11}$ _____

10. $36 \div \frac{8}{9}$ _____

11. $42 \div \frac{7}{8}$ _____

12. $40 \div \frac{4}{5}$ _____

13. Karolyn makes rolls for a friend's dinner party. She uses 3 lb of butter. Each stick of butter weighs $\frac{1}{4}$ lb. How many sticks of butter does Karolyn need to make her rolls?

_____

Dividing a Whole Number by a Fraction

Find the reciprocal of each fraction or whole number.

1. $\frac{5}{9}$ _____

2. 8 _____

3. $\frac{7}{3}$ _____

Find each quotient. Simplify if possible.

4. $8 \div \frac{2}{5} =$ _____

5. $4 \div \frac{1}{6} =$ _____

6. $18 \div \frac{3}{8} =$ _____

7. $12 \div \frac{1}{2} =$ _____

8. $42 \div \frac{7}{9} =$ _____

9. $10 \div \frac{5}{6} =$ _____

10. $20 \div \frac{3}{4} =$ _____

11. $22 \div \frac{5}{6} =$ _____

12. $7 \div \frac{2}{3} =$ _____

13. $9 \div \frac{1}{8} =$ _____

14. $15 \div \frac{1}{3} =$ _____

15. $6 \div \frac{1}{5} =$ _____

16. Writing to Explain Will the quotient of $5 \div \frac{7}{8}$ be greater than or less than 5? Explain.

_____

17. Reasoning How many times will you need to fill a $\frac{1}{2}$ cup measuring cup to measure 4 cups of flour?

_____

18. Geometry The distance around a circular flower bed is 36 feet. Jasper wants to put stakes every 8 inches ($\frac{2}{3}$ of a foot) around the bed. How many stakes does he need?

_____

19. Algebra Which expression is equal to $9 \times \frac{3}{2}$?

    A $2 \div \frac{3}{9}$

    B $3 \div \frac{9}{2}$

    C $9 \div \frac{2}{3}$

    D $9 \div \frac{3}{2}$

Dividing Fractions

To divide by a fraction, you can multiply by its reciprocal. The reciprocal of a number has the numerator and the denominator reversed.

Find $\frac{4}{5} \div \frac{3}{10}$.

Step 1

Rewrite the division as multiplication using the reciprocal of the divisor.

The reciprocal of $\frac{3}{10}$ is $\frac{10}{3}$.

$\frac{4}{5} \div \frac{3}{10} = \frac{4}{5} \times \frac{10}{3}$

Step 2

Divide out common factors if possible. Then multiply.

$\frac{4}{\overset{}{\underset{1}{5}}} \times \frac{\overset{2}{10}}{3} = \frac{8}{3}$

Step 3

If your answer is an improper fraction, change it to a mixed number.

$\frac{8}{3} = 2\frac{2}{3}$

Find each quotient. Simplify if possible.

1. $\frac{1}{2} \div \frac{1}{4} = \frac{1}{2} \times$ _____ = _____

Reciprocal of $\frac{1}{4}$

2. $\frac{4}{7} \div \frac{8}{21} =$ _____ × _____ = _____

Reciprocal of $\frac{8}{21}$

3. $\frac{1}{3} \div \frac{1}{2}$ _____

4. $\frac{2}{5} \div \frac{2}{3}$ _____

5. $\frac{5}{8} \div \frac{7}{10}$ _____

6. $\frac{3}{7} \div 3$ _____

7. $\frac{1}{3} \div \frac{8}{9}$ _____

8. $\frac{5}{6} \div \frac{1}{8}$ _____

9. $\frac{5}{9} \div \frac{1}{2}$ _____

10. $\frac{3}{5} \div \frac{3}{4}$ _____

11. $\frac{3}{4} \div \frac{5}{6}$ _____

12. $\frac{9}{10} \div \frac{4}{5}$ _____

13. $\frac{1}{3} \div \frac{3}{8}$ _____

14. $\frac{4}{7} \div \frac{3}{4}$ _____

15. Aaron has $\frac{7}{8}$ gallon of bottled water. How many $\frac{3}{16}$-gallon servings can he pour?

_____

16. Draw a Picture Show how Rebecca can divide $\frac{3}{4}$ of a cake into 9 pieces. What fraction of the whole cake will each piece be?

_____

Dividing Fractions

Find each quotient. Simplify if possible.

1. $\frac{1}{3} \div \frac{5}{6} =$ _____

2. $\frac{3}{8} \div \frac{1}{2} =$ _____

3. $\frac{7}{8} \div \frac{7}{12} =$ _____

4. $\frac{5}{9} \div 5 =$ _____

5. $\frac{6}{7} \div \frac{3}{4} =$ _____

6. $\frac{2}{3} \div \frac{3}{4} =$ _____

7. $\frac{1}{2} \div \frac{3}{10} =$ _____

8. $\frac{5}{12} \div \frac{2}{3} =$ _____

9. $\frac{14}{15} \div \frac{2}{5} =$ _____

10. $\frac{1}{3} \div \frac{3}{4} =$ _____

11. $\frac{3}{8} \div 4 =$ _____

12. $\frac{9}{10} \div \frac{3}{5} =$ _____

13. **Writing to Explain** Serena said that by looking for common factors and simplifying the expression, she found that $\frac{4}{10} \div \frac{5}{8} = 1\frac{9}{16}$. Do you agree with Serena? Why or why not?

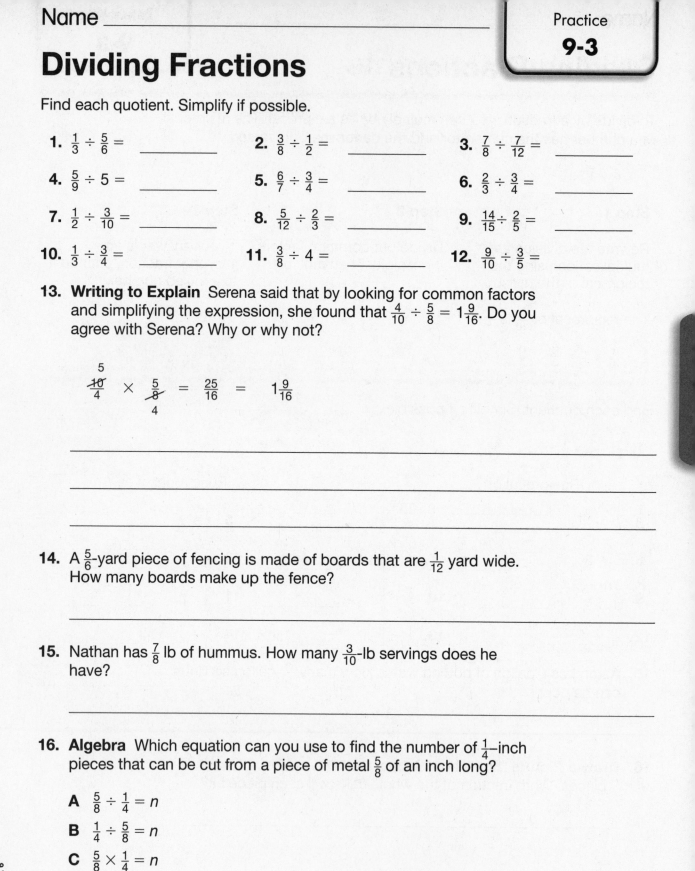

$$\frac{\overset{5}{\cancel{10}}}{4} \times \frac{5}{\underset{4}{\cancel{8}}} = \frac{25}{16} = 1\frac{9}{16}$$

_____

_____

_____

14. A $\frac{5}{6}$-yard piece of fencing is made of boards that are $\frac{1}{12}$ yard wide. How many boards make up the fence?

_____

15. Nathan has $\frac{7}{8}$ lb of hummus. How many $\frac{3}{10}$-lb servings does he have?

_____

16. **Algebra** Which equation can you use to find the number of $\frac{1}{4}$-inch pieces that can be cut from a piece of metal $\frac{5}{8}$ of an inch long?

A $\frac{5}{8} \div \frac{1}{4} = n$

B $\frac{1}{4} \div \frac{5}{8} = n$

C $\frac{5}{8} \times \frac{1}{4} = n$

D $\frac{1}{4} \times \frac{8}{5} = n$

Estimating Quotients

When you are working with fractions and mixed numbers, you can estimate using rounding and compatible numbers.

Estimate $23\frac{5}{6} \div 8\frac{3}{7}$.

$23\frac{5}{6} \div 8\frac{3}{7}$

Round each mixed number to the nearest whole number.

$24 \div 8 = 3$ Divide.

$23\frac{5}{6} \div 8\frac{3}{7} \approx 3$

Estimate $31\frac{1}{6} \div 4\frac{5}{8}$.

$31\frac{1}{6} \div 4\frac{5}{8}$

Change $31\frac{1}{6}$ and $4\frac{5}{8}$ to the nearest compatible whole numbers.

$30 \div 5 = 6$ Think: $31\frac{1}{6}$ and $4\frac{5}{8}$ are close to 30

$31\frac{1}{6} \div 4\frac{5}{8} \approx 6$ and 5.

Estimate each quotient.

1. $11\frac{1}{2} \div 6\frac{1}{4}$ _____

2. $19\frac{1}{3} \div 3\frac{2}{3}$ _____

3. $41\frac{7}{9} \div 7\frac{1}{5}$ _____

4. $35\frac{1}{8} \div 5\frac{4}{5}$ _____

5. $61\frac{3}{8} \div 8\frac{5}{9}$ _____

6. $72\frac{2}{9} \div 7\frac{7}{8}$ _____

7. $86\frac{3}{4} \div 10\frac{5}{6}$ _____

8. $26\frac{9}{10} \div 2\frac{5}{8}$ _____

9. $11\frac{2}{7} \div 3\frac{3}{5}$ _____

10. $7\frac{9}{10} \div 2\frac{3}{10}$ _____

11. $47\frac{6}{10} \div 7\frac{1}{12}$ _____

12. $60\frac{5}{12} \div 5\frac{4}{9}$ _____

13. Critical Thinking Which of these two estimates is closer to the actual quotient? How do you know?

Lisa's estimate: $55\frac{1}{2} \div 6\frac{3}{4} \approx 54 \div 6 = 9$

Hayden's estimate: $55\frac{1}{2} \div 6\frac{3}{4} \approx 56 \div 7 = 8$

_____

_____

14. Patrick uses wire to make wreaths. He has $31\frac{1}{2}$ feet of wire left on a spool. Estimate how many $3\frac{3}{4}$ pieces can he cut from the longer piece of wire.

_____

Estimating Quotients

Estimate each product.

1. $37\frac{1}{3} \div 5\frac{7}{8} =$ _____

2. $25\frac{1}{2} \div 6\frac{1}{4} =$ _____

3. $49\frac{4}{5} \div 6\frac{1}{2} =$ _____

4. $12\frac{3}{4} \div 5\frac{5}{9} =$ _____

5. $43\frac{2}{3} \div 5\frac{2}{5} =$ _____

6. $8\frac{1}{3} \div 2\frac{9}{10} =$ _____

7. $67\frac{1}{5} \div 7\frac{2}{7} =$ _____

8. $55\frac{5}{9} \div 7\frac{1}{6} =$ _____

9. $19\frac{6}{7} \div 4\frac{1}{8} =$ _____

10. $71\frac{4}{5} \div 7\frac{8}{9} =$ _____

11. $15\frac{7}{10} \div 3\frac{4}{9} =$ _____

12. $79\frac{4}{7} \div 8\frac{5}{8} =$ _____

13. $26\frac{1}{4} \div 2\frac{3}{8} =$ _____

14. $40\frac{8}{9} \div 7\frac{3}{5} =$ _____

15. $58\frac{1}{3} \div 19\frac{5}{6} =$ _____

16. Number Sense Tran wants to cut strips of paper that are $2\frac{1}{4}$ in. wide. His sheet of paper is $11\frac{1}{2}$ in. wide. He estimates that $11\frac{1}{2} \div 2\frac{1}{4} = 6$, so he can cut 6 strips from each sheet of paper. Is his estimate an overestimate or an underestimate? Explain.

_____

_____

17. Writing to Explain Eliza uses $2\frac{7}{8}$ feet of yarn in each gift basket she makes. Explain how to estimate how many baskets Eliza can make if she has 22 feet of yarn.

_____

_____

18. Geometry The area of this rectangle is $257\frac{1}{4}$ sq in. What is the best estimate of side length w?

A 66,000 in.

B 50 in.

C 25 in.

D 5 in.

$257\frac{1}{4}$ sq in. | $10\frac{1}{2}$ in.

w

19. Critical Thinking What estimation method did you use to find the length of side w in Problem 18?

_____

_____

Name _____

Dividing Mixed Numbers

You can follow these steps to find $5\frac{1}{3} \div 1\frac{1}{3}$ and $21 \div 2\frac{1}{3}$.

Step 1	Step 2	Step 3
First estimate. Then write each number as an improper fraction.	Find the reciprocal of the divisor. Rewrite as a multiplication problem.	Look for common factors. Simplify, then multiply.
Find $5\frac{1}{3} \div 1\frac{1}{3}$. Estimate $5 \div 1 = 5$. $5\frac{1}{3} \div 1\frac{1}{3} =$ $\downarrow \qquad \downarrow$ $\frac{16}{3} \div \frac{4}{3}$	$\frac{16}{3} \div \frac{4}{3} =$ $\frac{16}{3} \times \frac{3}{4}$	$\frac{16}{3} \times \frac{3}{4} =$ $\overset{4}{\underset{1}{\cancel{\frac{16}{3}}}} \times \overset{1}{\underset{1}{\cancel{\frac{3}{4}}}} = \frac{4}{1} = 4$ 4 is close to 5, so the answer is reasonable.
Find $21 \div 2\frac{1}{3}$. Estimate $21 \div 2 = 10\frac{1}{2}$. $21 \div 2\frac{1}{3}$ $\downarrow \qquad \downarrow$ $\frac{21}{1} \div \frac{7}{3}$	$\frac{21}{1} \div \frac{7}{3} =$ $\frac{21}{1} \times \frac{3}{7}$	$\frac{21}{1} \times \frac{3}{7} =$ $\overset{3}{\underset{1}{\cancel{\frac{21}{1}}}} \times \frac{3}{\cancel{7}} = \frac{9}{1} = 9$ 9 is close to $10\frac{1}{2}$, so the answer is reasonable.

Find each quotient. Simplify if possible.

1. $2\frac{2}{3} \div 3\frac{1}{4} =$ _____

2. $1\frac{3}{4} \div 4\frac{1}{8} =$ _____

3. $2\frac{1}{5} \div 2\frac{1}{3} =$ _____

4. $5\frac{1}{4} \div 3 =$ _____

5. $10 \div 3\frac{1}{4} =$ _____

6. $7\frac{1}{4} \div 2\frac{1}{8} =$ _____

7. Writing to Explain Paper needs to be cut for voting ballots. Each piece of paper is $10\frac{1}{2}$ in. long. Each ballot should be $1\frac{3}{4}$ in. long. How many ballots can be cut from one piece of paper?

_____

R 9·5

Dividing Mixed Numbers

Find each quotient. Simplify if possible.

1. $1\frac{1}{2} \div 2\frac{1}{3} =$ _____

2. $4\frac{1}{4} \div 3\frac{1}{8} =$ _____

3. $2\frac{1}{4} \div 5\frac{1}{2} =$ _____

4. $3\frac{1}{2} \div 2\frac{1}{4} =$ _____

5. $3\frac{3}{4} \div 2 =$ _____

6. $1\frac{1}{2} \div 2\frac{1}{4} =$ _____

7. $8 \div 2\frac{3}{4} =$ _____

8. $2\frac{1}{2} \div 1\frac{3}{8} =$ _____

9. $4\frac{2}{3} \div 1\frac{3}{4} =$ _____

10. Reasoning Is it possible to divide 15 by a mixed number and get a quotient that is greater than 15? Explain.

_____

_____

Room	Gallons of Paint
Kitchen	$2\frac{1}{2}$
Bedroom	$3\frac{3}{4}$
Living room	$4\frac{1}{3}$

Max is painting the inside of an apartment complex. The table shows how many gallons of paint are needed to paint each type of room.

11. How many kitchens can Max paint with 20 gal? _____

12. How many living rooms can Max paint with 26 gal? _____

13. How many bedrooms can Max paint with 60 gal? _____

14. Find $4\frac{1}{2} \div 2\frac{1}{4}$.

A 1

B 2

C 3

D 4

15. Writing to Explain Explain how you would find $4\frac{1}{5} \div 2\frac{1}{3}$.

_____

_____

_____

Solving Equations

Here is how to solve addition, subtraction, multiplication, and division equations with fractions.

Addition	**Subtraction**
Solve $n + \dfrac{3}{5} = 9$.	Solve $x - 2\dfrac{1}{3} = 6\dfrac{1}{9}$.
$n + \dfrac{3}{5} = 9$	$x - 2\dfrac{1}{3} = 6\dfrac{1}{9}$
$n + \dfrac{3}{5} - \dfrac{3}{5} = 9 - \dfrac{3}{5}$	$x - 2\dfrac{1}{3} + \mathbf{2\dfrac{1}{3}} = 6\dfrac{1}{9} + \mathbf{2\dfrac{1}{3}}$
$n = 8\dfrac{2}{5}$	$x = 6\dfrac{1}{9} + 2\dfrac{3}{9}$
	$x = 8\dfrac{4}{9}$

Multiplication	**Division**
Solve $\dfrac{5}{8}y = 1\dfrac{2}{3}$.	Solve $a \div \dfrac{1}{4} = 3\dfrac{1}{2}$.
$\dfrac{5}{8}y = 1\dfrac{2}{3}$	$a \div \dfrac{1}{4} = 3\dfrac{1}{2}$
$\left(\dfrac{8}{5}\right)\dfrac{5}{8}y = \dfrac{5}{3}\left(\dfrac{8}{5}\right)$	$a \times \dfrac{4}{1} = 3\dfrac{1}{2}$
$y = \dfrac{\overset{1}{\cancel{5}}}{3} \times \dfrac{8}{\underset{1}{\cancel{5}}}$	$a \times \dfrac{4}{1}\left(\dfrac{1}{4}\right) = \dfrac{7}{2}\left(\dfrac{1}{4}\right)$
$y = \dfrac{8}{3} = 2\dfrac{2}{3}$	$a = \dfrac{7}{8}$

Solve each equation and check your answer.

1. $z + 2\dfrac{1}{3} = 3\dfrac{1}{6}$ _____

2. $6n = \dfrac{3}{4}$ _____

3. $x - 1 = 4\dfrac{2}{3}$ _____

4. $y \div \dfrac{1}{2} = 2\dfrac{1}{8}$ _____

5. $\dfrac{3}{8} + n = 10$ _____

6. $2\dfrac{2}{9} \div 5 = x$ _____

7. Algebra The rainfall total for this month is $4\dfrac{9}{10}$ in. Yesterday it rained $2\dfrac{1}{10}$ in. Use the equation $n + 2\dfrac{1}{10} = 4\dfrac{9}{10}$ to calculate how much rainfall was received before yesterday.

_____

Solving Equations

Solve each equation and check your answer.

1. $y + 1\frac{1}{4} = 2\frac{3}{8}$ _____

2. $w - 2 = 3\frac{1}{2}$ _____

3. $z \div \frac{3}{4} = 4\frac{1}{4}$ _____

4. $\frac{1}{3} = \frac{7}{8}q$ _____

5. $6\frac{1}{2} = \frac{5}{6}b$ _____

6. $2\frac{1}{4} = p - \frac{3}{8}$ _____

7. $2\frac{1}{4} = x \div \frac{1}{2}$ _____

8. Number Sense Is the solution of $m \div \frac{2}{3} = 9$ greater than or less than the solution of $m \div \frac{1}{4} = 9$? Explain.

_____

_____

9. The bakery used $42\frac{1}{3}$ c of flour. There were $10\frac{1}{3}$ c left in the flour bin. Use the equation $x - 42\frac{1}{3} = 10\frac{1}{3}$ to find out how many cups of flour the bakery had to start with. _____

10. Alex had a ball of string. He cut the string into 26 equal pieces. Each piece measured $3\frac{1}{4}$ in. Use the equation $m \div 26 = 3\frac{1}{4}$ to find the length of the ball of string. _____

11. Solve $12y = 2\frac{1}{4}$.

A $1\frac{1}{2}$ **B** $1\frac{1}{8}$ **C** $\frac{7}{36}$ **D** $\frac{3}{16}$

12. Writing to Explain Write the steps you would use to solve the equation $z + 3\frac{1}{5} = 6\frac{3}{5}$. Solve.

_____

_____

Problem Solving:
Look for a Pattern

Sometimes you can solve a problem by identifying a pattern.
Here are two types of patterns.

Patterns in sets of numbers

$\frac{15}{4}, \frac{13}{4}, \frac{11}{4}, \frac{9}{4}, \frac{7}{4}, \frac{5}{4}, \frac{3}{4}$

Ask yourself:
Are the numbers increasing?
Are they decreasing?
Do they change by the same amount each time?
Do you add, subtract, multiply, or divide to find
the next number?

Patterns in groups of figures

Ask yourself:
How is the first figure modified to make the
second figure?
How is the second figure modified to make the
third?

Remember: Once you have identified a possible number pattern,
check at least two other consecutive numbers to make sure that the
pattern is true for all of the numbers.

Find the missing numbers. Describe the pattern.

1. $\frac{3}{4}$, 1, $1\frac{1}{4}$, $1\frac{1}{2}$, _____, _____, _____, _____, $2\frac{3}{4}$ _____

2. 89, 78, 67, _____, _____, _____, _____, 12, 1   _____

3. $\frac{1}{5}, \frac{4}{5}, \frac{7}{5}, \frac{10}{5}$, _____, _____, _____, _____, $\frac{25}{5}$ _____

4. Draw the next figure in the pattern below.

5. Number Sense The table below shows the number of cells in a
culture. How many cells will there be at 4:30?

Time	1:00	1:30	2:00	2:30	3:00
Number of Cells	1	2	4	8	16

R 9·7

Problem Solving: Look for a Pattern

Find the missing numbers. Describe the pattern.

1. $\frac{1}{8}$, $\frac{6}{8}$, $\frac{11}{8}$, $\frac{16}{8}$, _____, _____, _____, _____, $\frac{41}{8}$ _____

2. $\frac{1}{4}$, $\frac{1}{2}$, 1, _____, _____, _____, _____, 32, 64 _____

3. 1.1, 1.1, 2.2, 6.6, _____, _____, _____, _____ _____

4. $14\frac{1}{2}$, $12\frac{3}{4}$, 11, _____, _____, _____, _____, $2\frac{1}{4}$, $\frac{1}{2}$ _____

5. 27, 9, 3, 1, $\frac{1}{3}$, _____, _____, _____, _____ _____

6. 3, 5, 9, 15, _____, _____, _____, _____, 75 _____

7. **Number Sense** In the figure, the sum of each row forms a pattern. What is the sum of the seventh row?

_____

```
        1
      2   2
    3   3   3
  4   4   4   4
5   5   5   5   5
```

8. Which figure completes this pattern?

A

B

C

D

9. **Writing to Explain** How can you find the answer to **7** without finding the sum of the numbers in a row?

_____

_____

Understanding Integers

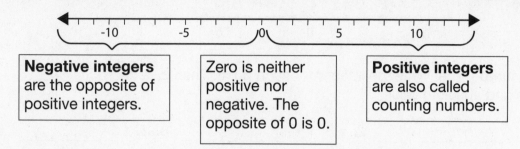

Negative integers are the opposite of positive integers.

Zero is neither positive nor negative. The opposite of 0 is 0.

Positive integers are also called counting numbers.

The **absolute value** of an integer is the distance from that integer to zero on the number line. Distance is always a positive measure, so the absolute value of any integer is positive.

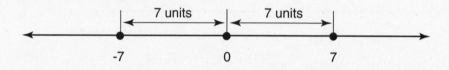

The distance from 0 to 7 is 7 units, so $|7| = 7$.

The distance from 0 to -7 is 7 units, so $|-7| = 7$.

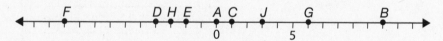

Use the number line above. Write the integer for each point. Then write its opposite and absolute value.

1. A _____

2. B _____

3. C _____

4. D _____

5. E _____

6. F _____

7. G _____

8. H _____

9. J _____

10. Number Sense John borrowed $6 from Adam. The next week John borrowed $15 more from Adam. Write an integer that represents John's total debt to Adam. _____

11. Reasoning What is the opposite of the opposite of negative nine? _____

R 10·1

Understanding Integers

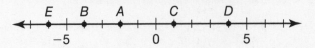

Use the number line. Write the integer for each point. Then give its opposite and absolute value.

1. *A* _____   **2.** *B* _____   **3.** *C* _____

4. *D* _____   **5.** *E* _____

6. On the number line, graph the points −8, 3, −4, 2, and −1.

The table gives the highest and lowest temperatures for some states in the United States. Use integers to describe the two temperatures for each state.

**Record Temperatures
(in degrees, relative to zero)**

State	Highest	Lowest
Alabama	112 above	27 below
Delaware	110 above	17 below
California	134 above	45 below
Colorado	118 above	61 below

7. Delaware _____

8. California _____

9. Colorado _____

10. Alabama _____

11. Which is an integer?

A −0.5

B −5

C 5.5

D $5\frac{4}{5}$

12. Writing to Explain In your own words, tell what is meant by "the absolute value of an integer."

_____

_____

_____

Comparing and Ordering Integers

When comparing two integers on a number line, the integer that is farther to the right is greater. The integer that is farther to the left is less.

-10 -9 -8 -7 -6 -5 -4 -3 -2 -1 0 1 2 3 4 5 6 7 8 9 10

Compare −6 and −10.	Compare −1 and 2.	Order −4, 0, and −7 from least to greatest.
Because −6 is farther to the right than −10, it is greater. So, −6 > −10.	Because 2 is farther to the right than −1, it is greater. So, 2 > −1.	Because −7 is the farthest to the left, it is the least. 0 is farther to the right than −4, so −4 is the next least. So, the numbers in order from least to greatest are −7, −4, and 0.

Use >, <, or = to compare.

1. −5 ◯ 3   **2.** 15 ◯ −4   **3.** 0 ◯ 27

4. 52 ◯ |−52| **5.** −9 ◯ |−9| **6.** −6 ◯ −7

7. 13 ◯ 12   **8.** −17 ◯ −15   **9.** −8 ◯ −8

Order the numbers from least to greatest.

10. 9, −1, −4, 2   **11.** 1, |−2|, −8, 6   **12.** 15, −7, −12, 0, |5|

_____   _____   _____

13. Manuel dug holes to plant an oak tree, a rosebush, lantana, and prairie grass. The table shows the depths of the holes. You can think of ground level as 0, so the holes closest to ground level are not as deep as the holes farthest from ground level. Which plant hole is closest to ground level? Which is farthest? Compare the depths of their holes.

Plant	Hole (inches)
Lantana	−8
Prairie Grass	−6
Oak Tree	−22
Rosebush	−15

_____

14. Reasoning Write 3 integers less than −27. _____

R 10-2

Name _____

Comparing and Ordering Integers

Use <, >, or = to compare.

1. 6 ◯ −8

2. −12 ◯ −11

3. 2 ◯ |−2|

4. 12 ◯ −11

5. 11 ◯ −1

6. |−3| ◯ 4

Order from least to greatest.

7. −6, 4, 7, 0, −9

_____

8. −1, −5, 5 , 7, −8

_____

9. −7, −8, −2, 6, |−11|, −11, −9, 4, 5

_____

10. Reasoning Can any negative integer be greater than a positive integer? Explain.

_____

_____

_____

Kyle kept track of the number of points he scored each time he played a video game. Sometimes the score is less than zero.

11. Order the negative plays from least to greatest.

_____

12. Order the positive plays from greatest to least.

_____

Kyle's Scores	
Play 1:	Gained 5 points
Play 2	Lost 15 points
Play 3:	Gained 32 points
Play 4:	Gained 10 points
Play 5:	Lost 12 points
Play 6:	Lost 8 points

13. Which integer is greatest?

    A 1   **B** −10   **C** 9   **D** 3

14. Writing to Explain Explain how to find the greatest integer plotted on a number line.

_____

_____

Rational Numbers on a Number Line

When comparing and ordering rational numbers on a number line, it helps to change all of the numbers to fractions and mixed numbers or to decimals.

How do you compare rational numbers?	**How do you order rational numbers?**
Compare $-1.3\overline{3}$ and $-\frac{9}{5}$.	Order 0.3, $-\frac{5}{6}$ and $\frac{5}{8}$ from least to greatest.

How do you compare rational numbers?

Compare $-1.3\overline{3}$ and $-\frac{9}{5}$.

Convert $-\frac{9}{5}$ to a decimal so that both numbers are in the same form.
$-\frac{9}{5} = -9 \div 5 = -1.8$

Place the numbers on a number line.

$-1.3\overline{3}$ is to the right of -1.8.

So, $-1.3\overline{3} > -9/5$.

How do you order rational numbers?

Order 0.3, $-\frac{5}{6}$ and $\frac{5}{8}$ from least to greatest.

Convert 0.3 to a fraction so that all of the numbers are in the same form.

$0.3 = \frac{3}{10}$

Place the numbers on a number line.

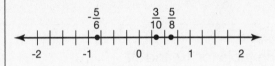

$\frac{3}{10}$ is to the right of $-\frac{5}{6}$ and $\frac{5}{8}$ is to the right of 0.3.

So, the numbers in order from least to greatest are $-\frac{5}{6}$, 0.3, $\frac{5}{8}$.

Write $<$ or $>$ in the circle.

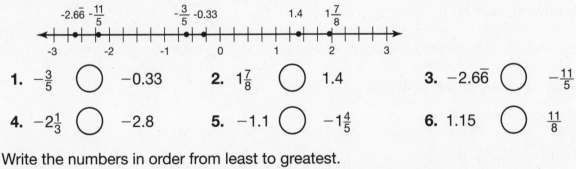

1. $-\frac{3}{5}$ ◯ -0.33 **2.** $1\frac{7}{8}$ ◯ 1.4 **3.** $-2.6\overline{6}$ ◯ $-\frac{11}{5}$

4. $-2\frac{1}{3}$ ◯ -2.8 **5.** -1.1 ◯ $-1\frac{4}{5}$ **6.** 1.15 ◯ $\frac{11}{8}$

Write the numbers in order from least to greatest.

7. 0.15, $-\frac{2}{3}$, -0.1 **8.** $-\frac{11}{5}$, -2.5, $-2\frac{2}{3}$ **9.** 1.6, $\frac{15}{8}$, $1\frac{2}{5}$

_____   _____   _____

10. Reasoning The rainfall in a city was $-\frac{3}{8}$ in. below average in June and -0.45 in. below average in July. Which month is closest to the average?

_____

R 10·3

Rational Numbers on a Number Line

Write < or > in the circle.

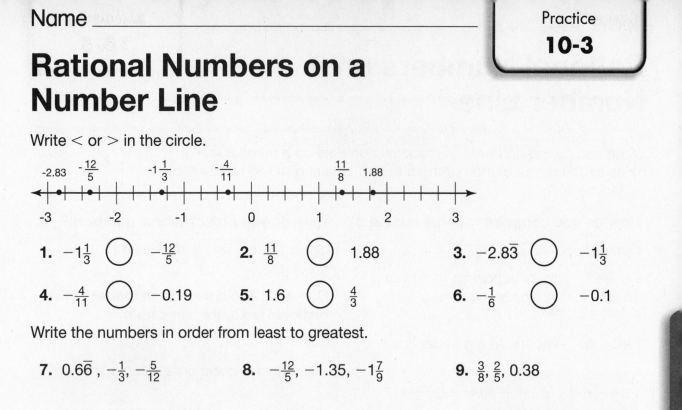

1. $-1\frac{1}{3}$ ◯ $-\frac{12}{5}$ **2.** $\frac{11}{8}$ ◯ 1.88   **3.** $-2.8\overline{3}$ ◯ $-1\frac{1}{3}$

4. $-\frac{4}{11}$ ◯ -0.19 **5.** 1.6 ◯ $\frac{4}{3}$ **6.** $-\frac{1}{6}$ ◯ -0.1

Write the numbers in order from least to greatest.

7. $0.6\overline{6}$, $-\frac{1}{3}$, $-\frac{5}{12}$ **8.** $-\frac{12}{5}$, -1.35, $-1\frac{7}{9}$ **9.** $\frac{3}{8}$, $\frac{2}{5}$, 0.38

_____   _____   _____

Use the table for **10** and **11**.

10. A scientist is testing lake water at different depths. Order the samples of lake water from greatest depth to least depth.

_____

Day	Feet Below the Lake Surface
Monday	$-1\frac{3}{8}$
Tuesday	-0.4
Wednesday	-1.55
Thursday	$-\frac{9}{16}$

11. Number Sense At what depth could the scientist take a new sample that would be shallower than the shallowest sample?

_____

12. Which rational number is least?

   A $0.6\overline{6}$

   B $-\frac{4}{5}$

   C $-\frac{6}{7}$

   D -0.6

13. Writing to Explain Lauren says that $-3.\overline{36}$ is greater than $-3\frac{1}{3}$. Do you agree? Explain.

_____

Adding Integers

You can use a number line or rules to add integers. On a number line, start at 0. Move right to add a positive number. Move left to add a negative number.

Add two integers with different signs.

Find 3 + (−4).

Start at 0. Move 3 units to the right. Then move 4 units to the left.	Find the absolute value for each addend. $\|-4\| = 4$ and $\|3\| = 3$

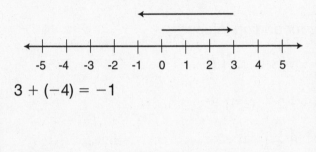

3 + (−4) = −1

Subtract the smaller absolute value from the greater: 4 − 3 = 1

Give the difference the same sign as the addend with the greater absolute value. Because +4 has the greater absolute value (4 > 3), this difference receives a negative sign.

3 + (−4) = −1

Add two integers with the same sign.

Find −1 + (−2).

Start at 0. Move 1 unit to the left. Then move 2 more units to the left.

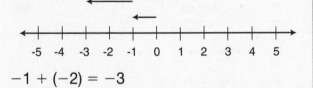

−1 + (−2) = −3

Find the absolute value for each addend. $\|-1\| = 1$ and $\|-2\| = 2$

Add the absolute values. 1 + 2 = 3

Give the sum the same sign as the addends.

−1 + (−2) = −3

Find each sum. Use the number line or rules.

-15 -14 -13 -12 -11 -10 -9 -8 -7 -6 -5 -4 -3 -2 -1 0 1 2 3 4 5 6 7 8 9 10 11 12 13 14 15

1. Find −5 + 7.
   Move *left* _____ spaces. Move *right* _____ spaces. So, −5 + 7 = _____

2. 8 + 4 = _____

3. 3 + (−5) = _____

4. −7 + (−8) = _____

5. −4 + (−4) = _____

6. −5 + 3 = _____

7. 7 + (−3) = _____

8. 10 + (−1) = _____

9. −8 + 6 = _____

10. 2 + (−3) = _____

11. 11 + 3 = _____

12. −9 + 6 = _____

13. −2 + 12 = _____

14. Algebra The rule is Add −5. The input is 10. What is the output? _____

R 10-4

Adding Integers

1. Draw a number line to find 3 + (−4).

Find each sum. Use a number line or the rules for adding integers.

2. 4 + (−12) = _____

3. −12 + (−14) = _____

4. 10 + (−1) = _____

5. −2 + (−1) = _____

6. −50 + (−1) = _____

7. 8 + (−4) = _____

8. −9 + 7 = _____

9. −3 + (−6) = _____

Algebra Use the rule to complete each table.

10. **Rule: Add -6**

Input	Output
5	
3	
−1	

11. **Rule: Add 2**

Input	Output
−7	
−4	
0	

12. Which is the sum of −6 + (−9) + (−9)?

A −24

B −12

C −6

D 24

13. **Writing to Explain** Explain how you would solve −4 + 4 + 5.

_____

_____

Subtracting Integers

You can use this rule to subtract integers.

Rule: To subtract an integer, add its opposite.

Examples:

Find: $8 - (-3)$
The opposite of -3 is 3.
Add: $8 + 3 = 11$
So, $8 - (-3) = 11$

Find: $-6 - 7$
The opposite of 7 is -7.
Add: $-6 + (-7) = -13$
So, $-6 - 7 = -13$

Find: $-3 - (-9)$
The opposite of -9 is 9.
Add: $-3 + 9 = 6$
So, $-3 - (-9) = 6$

Find each difference.

1. $5 - (-1)$
   The opposite of -1 is 1

   Add: $5 +$ ____ $=$ ____

2. $-10 - 3$
   The opposite of 3 is ____

   Add: $-10 +$ ____ $=$ ____

3. $-7 - (-2)$

   _____

4. $-9 - 4$

   _____

5. $6 - (-10)$

   _____

6. $-1 - (-3)$

   _____

7. **Writing to Explain** Without computing, how do you know that the answer to $7 - (-15)$ is positive?

   _____

   _____

   _____

8. **Draw a Picture** In one football game the Wildcats gained 5 yards on one play, lost 8 yards on the next play, and gained 6 yards the next play. In all, how many yards did they gain or lose?

   _____

Subtracting Integers

For **1** through **3** use the number line below to find each difference.

-10 -9 -8 -7 -6 -5 -4 -3 -2 -1 0 1 2 3 4 5 6 7 8 9 10

1. $5 - 10$ **2.** $-4 - 4$ **3.** $6 - (-3)$

_____   _____   _____

For **4** through **9**, use a number line or the rules for adding integers to find each difference.

4. $-6 - (-1)$ **5.** $-12 - 10$ **6.** $25 - (-5)$

_____   _____   _____

7. $14 - 22$ **8.** $7 - |-6|$ **9.** $|-2| - |2|$

_____   _____   _____

For **10** through **12**, evaluate each expression for $m = -5$.

10. $52 - m$ **11.** $m - (-15)$ **12.** $18 - |-3| - m$

_____   _____   _____

13. Writing to Explain Explain when you use the word "minus" and when you use the word "negative." Give an example.

_____

_____

14. Number Sense Ben's first score on a video game was 12. His second score was -15. Which expression can he use to find how many more points he got in the first game?

A $-12 + 15$

B $12 - 15$

C $12 + -15$

D $12 - (-15)$

Multiplying Integers

To multiply integers, remember these rules:

• The product of two positive integers is positive. $4 \times 5 = 20$
• The product of two negative integers is positive. $(-4) \times (-5) = 20$
• The product of one positive integer and one negative integer is negative. $(-4) \times 5 = (-20)$ $4 \times (-5) = (-20)$

A simple multiplication sentence will have two negative terms or no negative terms. If you see one negative term, look to find the other negative term.

Multiply.

1. $6 \times 3 =$ _____

2. $5 \times (-6) =$ _____

3. $-4 \times 0 =$ _____

4. $12 \times (-5) =$ _____

5. $-4 \times (+9) =$ _____

6. $22 \times 4 =$ _____

7. $(-1)(-37) =$ _____

8. $(-7)(-7) =$ _____

9. $(2)(4)(-3) =$ _____

10. $(-8)(-7) =$ _____

11. $(-3)(-5)(-3) =$ _____

12. $(5)(-3)(2) =$ _____

Evaluate each expression for $d = -3$.

13. $-4d =$ _____

14. $d \times (-6) =$ _____

15. $-10d - 3 =$ _____

16. $9 + (-2d) =$ _____

17. $5d + 38 =$ _____

18. $(2d)(-4)(-2) =$ _____

19. Number Sense Is the product of four negative integers positive or negative? Explain.

_____

_____

Multiplying Integers

1. $(-8)(-2) =$ _____

2. $7 \times (-10) =$ _____

3. $5 \times 3 =$ _____

4. $(-9)(-6) =$ _____

5. $(-6)(-3) =$ _____

6. $3 \times (-18) =$ _____

7. $-9 \times -41 =$ _____

8. $(-6)(-21) =$ _____

Number Sense Use order of operations to evaluate each expression.

9. $(-3) + 5 + 4 - 9 \times 3 =$ _____

10. $(-6) - 4 \times 8 + 11 \times 2 =$ _____

Algebra Evaluate each expression when $r = 8$.

11. $-12r - 120 =$ _____

12. $7r + -5 =$ _____

13. $(-4r)(-30) - (-8) =$ _____

14. $(-2r)(8) + (-25) =$ _____

15. From 1950 to 1970, some glaciers thinned by an average of 1.7 ft per year. What was the change in glacier thickness during this period? _____

16. From 1995 to 2000, the glaciers thinned by 6 ft per year. What was the change in glacier thickness during this period? _____

17. Which is the product of $(-4)(-12)$?

    A -48

    B -36

    C 36

    D 48

18. Writing to Explain Explain how to evaluate $5p + (-6)$ when $p = -4$.

_____

_____

_____

_____

Dividing Integers

Rules for dividing integers:

• The quotient of two integers with the same sign is positive.

• The quotient of two integers with different signs is negative.

$54 \div (-6)$	$-36 \div (-3)$
$54 \div 6 = 9$	$36 \div 3 = 12$
Because the signs of the two integers in the original problem are different, the sign of the quotient is negative.	Because the signs of the two integers in the original problem are the same, the sign of the quotient is positive.
So, $54 \div (-6) = -9$.	So, $-36 \div (-3) = 12$.

Find each quotient.

1. $-18 \div (-3)$ _____

2. $-28 \div 4$ _____

3. $-50 \div (-5)$ _____

4. $-24 \div 6$ _____

5. $30 \div 6$ _____

6. $48 \div (-8)$ _____

Use order of operations to evaluate each expression for $n = -4$.

7. $-40 \div n$ _____

8. $n \div 4$ _____

9. $76 \div n$ _____

10. $8n \div 2$ _____

11. $14 + (n \div 2)$ _____

12. $-3n \div (-3)$ _____

13. Nathan and Haley went scuba diving. It took 3 minutes to dive 18 meters. What was the average descent rate of their dive? Find $-18 \div 3$.

_____

14. Reasoning Without computing the answer, how do you know if the quotient $-232 \div 11$ is negative or positive?

_____

15. Algebra Write the next two integers in the pattern $-48, -24, -12,$ ____, ____

_____

Dividing Integers

Find each quotient.

1. $80 \div (-8)$

2. $-75 \div (-5)$

3. $-49 \div 7$

_____

_____

_____

4. $-45 \div (-9)$

5. $0 \div (-14)$

6. $-81 \div (-3)$

_____

_____

_____

Use order of operations to evaluate each expression for $c = -8$.

7. $-96 \div c$

8. $c \div 4$

9. $-144 \div c$

_____

_____

_____

10. $13 - (c \div 2)$

11. $(3c + 4) \div 5$

12. $c \div (-4) + 6$

_____

_____

_____

13. Reasoning Is $120 \div -6 \times -3$ positive or negative? Explain.

_____

_____

_____

14. Algebra A roller coaster dropped 224 feet in 2 seconds. What was the rate of change in height per second? Find $-224 \div 2$.

_____

15. What is the quotient of $-162 \div (-9)$?

A -18

B -16

C 16

D 18

16. Writing to Explain Jill says that the rules for multiplying and dividing integers are alike. Do you agree? Explain.

_____

_____

_____

Absolute Value

The absolute value of a number is its distance from 0 on a number line. You can use a number line to help you compare and order the absolute values of numbers.

Order the values from *least* to *greatest*: $|-4|, |-1|, |3|$.

Plot each number on the number line, and then look at each point's distance from 0.

Since -1 is the point closest to 0, $|-1|$ is the least value.

Since 3 is the next closest point to 0, $|3|$ is the next greater value.

Since -4 is the point farthest from 0, $|-4|$ is the greatest value.

The order of the values from least to greatest is $|-1|, |3|, |-4|$.

For **1** through **6**, use $<$ or $>$ to compare. You can use the number line to help you.

1. $|3| \bigcirc |-4|$

2. $|-5| \bigcirc |0|$

3. $|1| \bigcirc |-2|$

4. $|13| \bigcirc |-12|$

5. $|-10| \bigcirc |-9|$

6. $|6| \bigcirc |-14|$

For **7** through **12**, order the values from *least* to *greatest*. You can use the number line to help you.

7. $|-4|, |-2|, |11|$

8. $|-9|, |0|, |-2|$

9. $|4|, |-5|, |-7|$

_____

_____

_____

10. $|-1|, |-8|, |2|$

11. $|-14|, |0|, |-6|$

12. $|8|, |-11|, |-6|$

_____

_____

_____

13. Writing to Explain How do you know that $|8|$ and $|-8|$ are the same distance from 0? Do they have the same absolute value? Explain.

_____

_____

14. Number Sense Name two numbers that are not located the same distance from 0. What are their absolute values?

_____

R 10·8

Absolute Value

For **1** through **6**, use < or > to compare.

1. $|{-22}|$ ◯ $|{-12}|$

2. $|45|$ ◯ $|{-46}|$

3. $|13|$ ◯ $|{-2}|$

4. $|48|$ ◯ $|{-39}|$

5. $|{-55.5}|$ ◯ $|55|$

6. $|21\frac{1}{3}|$ ◯ $|{-21\frac{1}{2}}|$

For **7** through **12**, order the values from *greatest* to *least*.

7. $|{-6}|, |{-4}|, |11|, |0|$

8. $|{-20}|, |16|, |{-2}|, |37|$

9. $|41|, |{-42}|, |{-63}|, |11|$

_____

_____

_____

10. $|4|, |{-3}|, |{-18}|, |{-3.18}|$

11. $|0|, |{-27}|, |{-32}|, |6|$

12. $|{-\frac{1}{2}}|, |{-\frac{2}{3}}|, |{-\frac{1}{10}}|, |0|$

_____

_____

_____

13. Which pair of numbers are located the same distance from 0 on the number line?

A 5 and −4

B 0 and 1

C −3 and 3

D −2 and −4

14. A stock's price gained 3% in April and 5% in May, and then lost 4% in June and 1% in July. During which month did the stock's price change the most?

_____

15. Max starts on the 20th floor of a building and takes the elevator 4 floors down. Then he takes the elevator up 3 floors, and then down another 5 floors. Write the absolute value of the greatest change in floors that Max made.

_____

16. **Writing to Explain** The table shows the daily change in high temperature for several days. Explain how you can order the days from least to greatest amount of temperature change.

Day	Temperature Change
Monday	+3°F
Tuesday	−4°F
Wednesday	−1°F
Thursday	+2°F

_____

_____

_____

Graphing Points on a Coordinate Plane

Parts of a coordinate plane:

x-axis: a horizontal number line
y-axis: a vertical number line
origin: the place where the two number lines meet
quadrants: the four sections created by the two
          number lines

A point in a coordinate plane is represented by
an **ordered pair.**   (4, −3)

                  ↑   ↑
       x-coordinate y-coordinate

To locate point (4, −3), start at the origin.
Move to 4 on the x-axis. Then move to −3 on the y-axis.

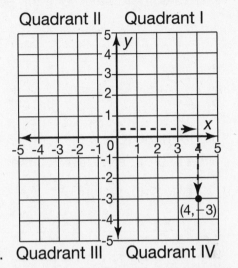

Quadrant II   Quadrant I

Quadrant III   Quadrant IV

Graph and label these points on the coordinate plane.

1. (4, 1)

2. (−3, 3)

3. (2, 0)

4. (4, −2)

5. (−2, 4)

6. (−3, −4)

Write the ordered pair for each point.

7. A _____

8. B _____

9. D _____

10. E _____

11. Geometry If you join points *BCDE* in order, what
shape is the figure?

_____

12. Reasoning In what quadrant will a point with a
negative x-coordinate and a positive y-coordinate
(negative number, positive number) be located?

_____

Graphing Points on a Coordinate Plane

Write the ordered pair for each point.

1. F _____

2. G _____

3. H _____

4. I _____

5. J _____

6. K _____

For **7** through **9**, graph the ordered pairs. Connect the points in order and describe the figure you drew.

7. (1,0), (5,0), (5, 4), (1,4)

_____

8. (0, 0), (2,−4), (−2, −4)

9. (−4, −2), (−2, −2), (−2, 5), (−4, 5)

_____   _____

10. Writing to Explain A point is located in Quadrant IV. What do you know about the signs of the coordinates for the point? Explain.

_____

_____

11. Critical Thinking Draw three lines that are parallel to the x-axis. Read the ordered pairs for points on each line. What generalization can you make about the ordered pairs for lines parallel to the x-axis?

_____

_____

12. Geometry Which set of ordered pairs can be connected in order to form a right triangle?

   A (−1, 3), (−1, −1), (2, −1)

   B (−4, 0), (0, 1), (1, −2)

   C (2, 2), (2, −2), (−2, −2), (−2, 2)

   D (0, 5), (−3, 3), (3, −3)

P 10·9

Problem Solving: Use Reasoning

After he bought a meal for $7.72 and a new DVD for $22.95,
Eric had $13.84 in his pocket. How much money did he start with?

You can solve the problem by using reasoning.

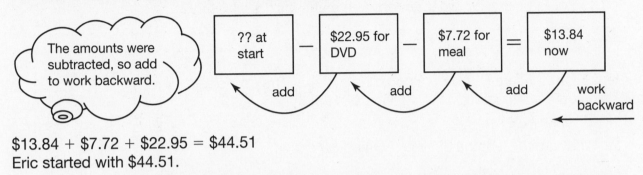

The amounts were subtracted, so add to work backward.

| ?? at start | − | $22.95 for DVD | − | $7.72 for meal | = | $13.84 now |

add   add   add   work backward

$13.84 + $7.72 + $22.95 = $44.51
Eric started with $44.51.

1. Elana spent 45 minutes at the library, half an hour at the grocery store, 20 minutes visiting a friend, and arrived home at 4:10 P.M. What time did she leave home?

    _____

2. The football team gained 13 yards, lost 5 yards, gained 8 yards, and gained another 11 yards to end on their 47-yard line. At what yard line did they start?

    _____

3. Scott has $82.50 in his checking account after he wrote checks to pay bills for $37.96, $52.00, $12.26, and $97.36. How much was in his checking account before he paid his bills?

    _____

4. Vince helped the Pep Club make sandwiches to raise money. He put two sandwiches in each of 30 bags and 5 sandwiches in 26 family bags, and he has 17 sandwiches left over. How many sandwiches did they make to start with?

    _____

5. Kimo divided a number by 3, subtracted 6, multiplied by 3.6 and added 12 to get 282. What number did he start with?

    _____

Problem Solving: Use Reasoning

1. The delivery person stopped on the 14ᵗʰ floor to talk to a friend. Before stopping, he had just made a delivery 4 floors above. Before that he made a delivery 6 floors below. Before that he had made a delivery 9 floors above. Before that he had made a delivery 15 floors below. On what floor did he make his first delivery?

_____

Elena plotted figure *FGHJ* on a coordinate plane. The corners of the figure are located at *F*(1, 3), *G*(1, 6), *H*(3, 6) and *J*(3, 3). Draw Elena's figure.

2. What are the lengths of sides *FG* and *HJ*?

_____

3. What are the lengths of sides *GH* and *JF*?

_____

4. What is the perimeter of the figure?

_____

5. At the end of the day, Brooke had $138.75 in her checking account. She had made a deposit of $115.07 and written checks totaling $176.94. How much did she have in her checking account at the beginning of the day?

   A –$76.88   C $200.62

   B $76.88   D $430.76

6. **Writing to Explain** The football team gained 7 yards, gained 4 yards, lost 5 yards, gained 21 yards, lost 2 yards, and gained 4 yards to their 43 yard line. Explain how you solved this problem. Then find the yard line where the team began.

_____

_____

_____

Basic Geometric Ideas

A **point** is an exact location.	•
A **line** is a straight path of points that goes on forever in two directions.	←————————→
A **ray** is a part of a line. A ray has one endpoint and goes on forever in one direction.	•————————→
A line **segment** is a part of a line with two endpoints.	•————————•
Congruent line segments are line segments that have the same length.	
The **midpoint** of a line segment is halfway between the endpoints of a line segment.	•————•————•
A **plane** is a flat surface that extends forever in all directions.	

Intersecting lines meet at exactly one point.	Parallel lines never meet. They are always the same distance apart.	Perpendicular lines form a 90° angle.

Use the diagram at the right. Name the following.

1. Three line segments

_____

2. Two parallel lines

_____

3. Two lines that intersect $\overleftrightarrow{PS}$

_____

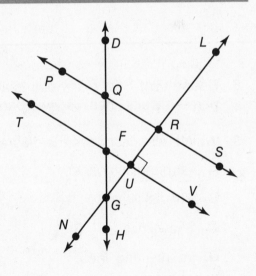

4. Draw a Diagram Draw a diagram in which the midpoint of $\overline{CD}$ is also the endpoint of $\overrightarrow{EF}$, which is perpendicular to $\overline{CD}$.

R 11·1

Basic Geometric Ideas

Use the diagram at the right. Name the following.

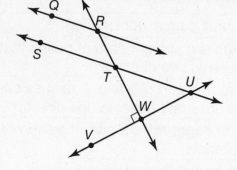

1. Two perpendicular lines

_____

2. Two rays

_____

3. Two parallel lines

_____

4. Four line segments

_____

5. Two lines that intersect

_____

Draw a diagram to illustrate each situation.

6. $\overline{XY}$ with midpoint R

7. $\overline{JK}$ perpendicular to $\overline{LM}$

8. Reasoning How many points are shared by two
perpendicular lines? By two parallel lines?

_____

9. Which best describes the diagram?

A Perpendicular lines

B Parallel lines

C Skew lines

D. Intersecting lines

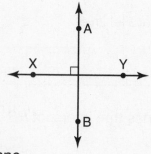

10. Writing to Explain In your own words, describe a plane.

_____

Measuring and Drawing Angles

How to measure an angle:

Step 1 Place the protractor's center on the angle's vertex.

Step 2 Place the 0° mark on one side of the angle.

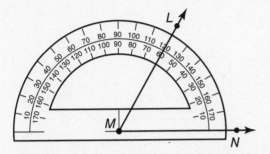

Step 3 Use the scale beginning with the 0° mark to read the measurement where the other side of the angle crosses the protractor.

∠LMN = 60°

How to draw an angle:

Draw an angle of 52°.

Step 1 Draw a ray.

Step 2 Place the protractor's center on the endpoint. Line up the ray with the 0° mark.

Step 3 Using the scale with the 0° mark, place a point at 52°.

Step 4 Draw the other ray.

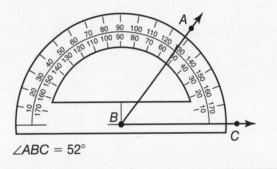

∠ABC = 52°

Classify each angle as acute, right, obtuse, or straight. Then measure the angle.

1.

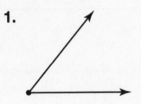

_____

2.

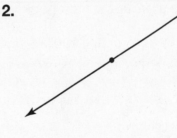

_____

Draw an angle with each measure.

3. 45°

4. 120°

Measuring and Drawing Angles

Classify each angle as acute, right, obtuse, or straight. Then measure the angle.

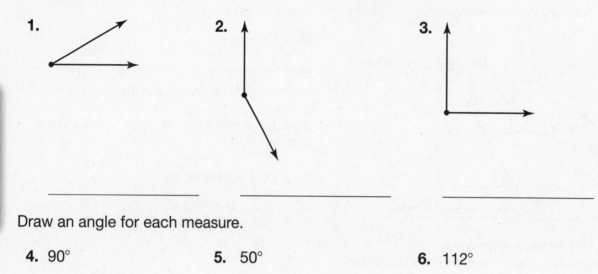

1.

2.

3.

_____   _____   _____

Draw an angle for each measure.

4. 90°

5. 50°

6. 112°

Estimation Without a protractor, try to sketch an angle with the given measure. Then use a protractor to check your estimate.

7. 120°

8. 100°

9. 10°

10. Which is a measure of an acute angle?

   A 40°   **B** 90°   **C** 120°   **D** 180°

11. Writing to Explain Explain the steps you use to measure an angle using a protractor.

_____

_____

_____

Angle Pairs

Vertical angles are pairs of congruent angles created when two lines intersect.

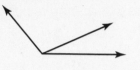

Complementary angles are pairs of angles that together form a right angle.

Their sum is 90°.

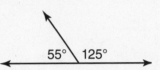

Adjacent angles are pairs of angles that share a common ray.

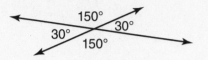

Supplementary angles are pairs of angles that together form a straight angle.

Their sum is 180°.

55°   125°

For **1** through **3**, find x.

1.

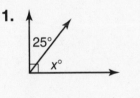

90° − 25° = _____

2.

110° $x°$

180° − _____ = _____

3.

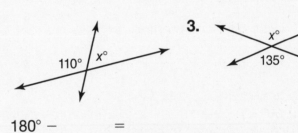

$x°$
135°

_____

For **4** and **5,** find the measure of an angle that is complementary to an angle with each measure.

4. 15°   **5.** 80°

For **6** and **7,** find the measure of an angle that is supplementary to an angle with each measure.

6. 5°   **7.** 100°

_____   _____   _____   _____

8. Critical Thinking Which pair of angles are NOT adjacent?

   A w and x

   B x and y

   C w and y

   D z and w

Angle Pairs

For **1** through **3**, find *x*.

1.

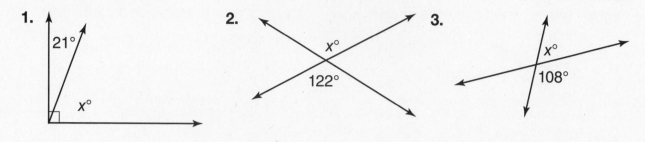

21°

x°

2.

x°

122°

3.

x°

108°

_____   _____   _____

For **4** and **5**, find the measure of an angle that is complementary to an angle with each measure.

For **6** and **7**, find the measure of an angle that is supplementary to an angle with each measure.

4. 43°   **5.** 72°

6. 54°   **7.** 119°

_____   _____   _____   _____

Use the diagram for **8** through **10.**

8. Name two pairs of supplementary angles.

_____

9. Name two angles adjacent to *DAE.*

_____

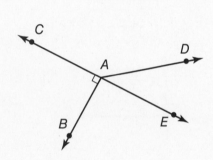

C

D

A

B

E

10. Writing to Explain How could you draw an angle complementary to ∠*DAE* without using a protractor? Tell why your method works.

_____

_____

_____

11. Critical Thinking Which statement is **NOT** true for a pair of intersecting lines?

A They form two pairs of congruent angles.

B They form four pairs of complementary angles.

C They form four pairs of supplementary angles.

D They form two pairs of vertical angles.

Triangles

Triangles can be classified by their angles or their sides.

Classified by angles

Acute triangle
All three angles are
acute angles.

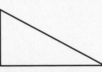

Right triangle
One angle is a right
angle.

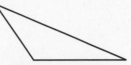

Obtuse triangle
One angle is an
obtuse angle.

Classified by sides

Equilateral triangle
All sides are
congruent.

Isosceles triangle
At least two sides
are congruent.

Scalene triangle
No sides are
congruent.

How to find angle measures in a triangle:

Find the measure of angle x.

Remember, when you add up all three
of the angles, the sum must be 180°.

$$x + 110 + 40 = 180$$

$$x + 150 = 180$$

$$x = 30$$

Find the missing angle measure. Then classify the triangle by its angles and by its sides.

1.

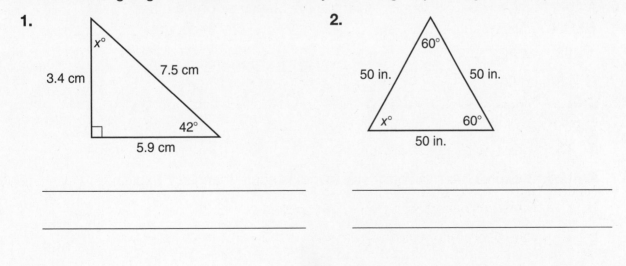

2.

_____   _____

_____   _____

Triangles

Find the missing angle measure. Then classify the triangle by its angles and by its sides.

1.

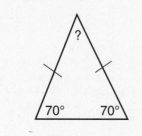

70°   70°

_____

2.

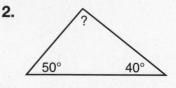

50°   40°

_____

Draw the described triangle.

3. An obtuse scalene triangle

4. A triangle with a 2–inch side between two 50° angles

5. Reasoning Can a scalene triangle have two congruent angles? Why or why not?

_____

_____

_____

6. A right triangle has a 28° angle. What are the measures of the other angles?

A 28° and 62°

B 28° and 90°

C 62° and 90°

D 62° and 118°

7. Writing to Explain Are all equilateral triangles acute triangles? Explain.

_____

Quadrilaterals

Classifying quadrilaterals

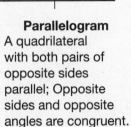

Trapezoid	**Parallelogram**	**Rhombus**	**Rectangle**	**Square**
A quadrilateral with only one pair of parallel sides	A quadrilateral with both pairs of opposite sides parallel; Opposite sides and opposite angles are congruent.	A parallelogram with all sides congruent	A parallelogram with four right angles	A rectangle with all sides congruent; A square is also a rhombus.

Finding the missing measure of a quadrilateral:

The measures of three angles of a quadrilateral are 115°, 68°, and 45°. Find the measure of the fourth angle.

Remember, the sum of all four angles must be 360°.

$$115 + 68 + 45 + x = 360$$

$$228 + x = 360$$

$$x = 132$$

The measure of the fourth angle is 132°.

Classify each polygon in as many ways as possible.

1.

2.

_____

_____

_____

The measures of three angles of a quadrilateral are given. Find the measure of the fourth angle.

3. 90°, 90°, 90° _____

4. 80°, 60°, 120° _____

5. 70°, 120°, 120° _____

6. 130°, 40°, 50° _____

Quadrilaterals

Classify each polygon in as many ways as possible.

1.

2.

3.

_____   _____   _____

_____   _____   _____

_____   _____   _____

The measures of three angles of a quadrilateral are given. Find the measure of the fourth angle and classify each quadrilateral according to its angles.

4. 125°, 55°, 125°   **5.** 110°, 100°, 80°   **6.** 90°, 70°, 150°

_____   _____   _____

_____   _____   _____

7. Draw a quadrilateral with one pair of parallel sides. One side is 1.5 in. The other side is 0.5 in. The bottom right and top right angles are 90°. The bottom left angle is 40°. Label the sides and angles.

8. A rhombus has one 65° angle and a 5 cm side. Is this enough information to find the remaining angles and side lengths? Explain.

_____

_____

9. Which pair of angles would be side-by-side in a parallelogram?

A 40°, 40°   **B** 40°, 140°   **C** 60°, 110°   **D** 65°, 105°

10. Writing to Explain What characteristics help you classify a quadrilateral as a parallelogram and not a rectangle? Explain.

_____

_____

Circles

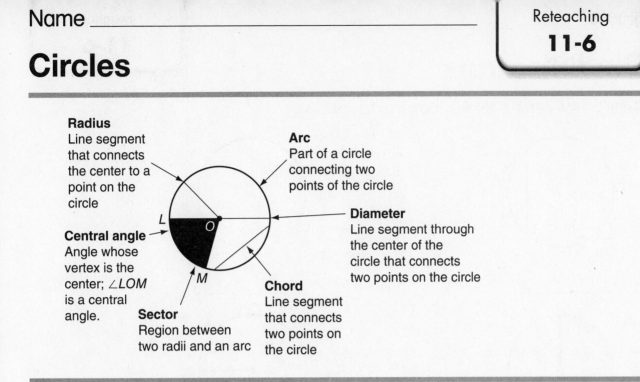

Radius
Line segment that connects the center to a point on the circle

Arc
Part of a circle connecting two points of the circle

Central angle
Angle whose vertex is the center; ∠LOM is a central angle.

Diameter
Line segment through the center of the circle that connects two points on the circle

Sector
Region between two radii and an arc

Chord
Line segment that connects two points on the circle

Identify the figure or portion of the figure that is drawn in each circle.

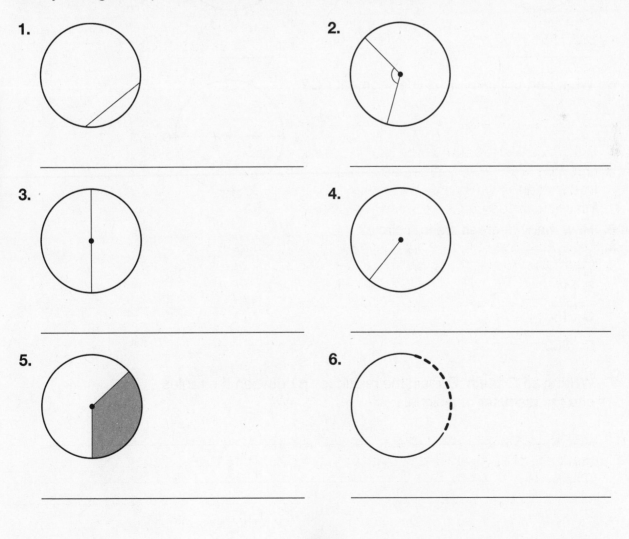

1.

2.

3.

4.

5.

6.

Circles

Identify the figure shown in bold.

1.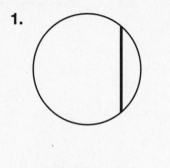

_____

2.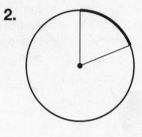

_____

3.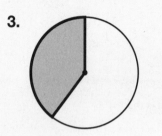

_____

4.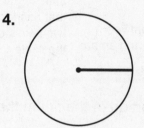

_____

5. What part of the circle is line segment *FG*?

_____

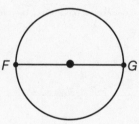

6. How many degrees are in a circle?

A 90°

B 120°

C 180°

D 360°

7. Writing to Explain Explain the relationship between the radius and the diameter of a circle.

_____

_____

Transformations and Congruence

Congruent figures have the same size and shape. In congruent shapes, corresponding angles and corresponding sides are congruent. You can use this relationship to find the measures of different angles and different sides. The symbol for congruence is ≅.

The figures at the right are congruent.

$\angle ABC \cong \angle QRS$, so $\angle QRS = 55°$
$\angle BCD \cong \angle RST$, so $\angle RST = 125°$
$\overline{BC} \cong \overline{RS}$, so $\overline{RS} = 9$ cm
$\overline{CD} \cong \overline{ST}$, so $\overline{ST} = 4$ cm

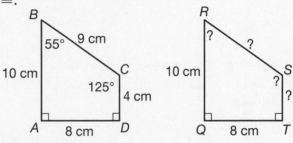

A transformation moves a figure to a new position without changing its size or shape.

A **translation** moves a figure in a straight direction.	A **reflection** gives a figure its mirror image over a line.	A **rotation** moves a figure about a point.	A **glide reflection** is a translation followed by a reflection.

These figures are congruent. Find the angle and side measures.

1.

2.

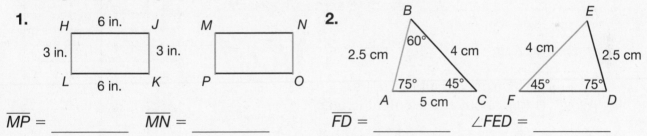

$\overline{MP} =$ _____ $\overline{MN} =$ _____

$\overline{FD} =$ _____ $\angle FED =$ _____

Tell whether the figures in each pair are related by a translation, a reflection, a glide reflection, or a rotation.

3.

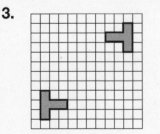

4.

_____   _____

5. Writing to Explain Describe the relationship between the two triangles in Item 2.

_____

R 11·7

Transformations and Congruence

1. These parallelograms are congruent.
   Find $\overline{CD}$, $\overline{GH}$, and $m\angle D$.

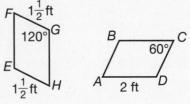

$\overline{CD} =$ _____ $\overline{GH} =$ _____

$m\angle D$ _____

Tell whether the figures in each pair are related by a translation, a refection, a glide reflection, or a rotation. If the relationship is a rotation, describe it.

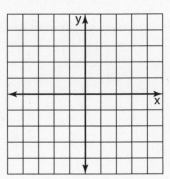

2. _____   3. _____   4. _____

5. Use the grid. Draw a semi-circle to the left of the y-axis. Then show the semi-circle reflected across the y-axis.

_____

6. Cole drew two congruent polygons.
   Which is true about *all* congruent figures?

   A Corresponding angles are congruent.

   B Corresponding angles are complementary.

   C Corresponding angles are supplementary.

   D There are no corresponding angles.

7. **Writing to Explain** Draw a figure. Use different transformations of your figure to make a pattern. Show three repetitions. Then explain which transformations are used in your pattern.

_____

Symmetry

A figure has **reflection symmetry** if it can be reflected onto itself. The line of reflection is called the **line of symmetry**. Some figures have more than one line of symmetry.

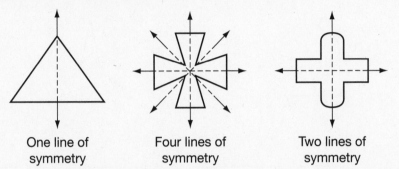

One line of symmetry

Four lines of symmetry

Two lines of symmetry

A figure has **rotational symmetry** when it rotates onto itself less than one full turn.

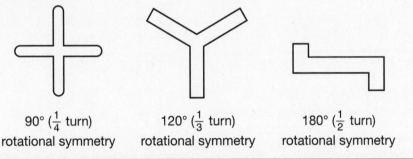

$90°$ ($\frac{1}{4}$ turn)
rotational symmetry

$120°$ ($\frac{1}{3}$ turn)
rotational symmetry

$180°$ ($\frac{1}{2}$ turn)
rotational symmetry

Tell if each figure has reflection symmetry, rotational symmetry, or both. If it has reflection symmetry, how many lines of symmetry are there? If it has rotational symmetry, what is the smallest turn that will rotate the figure onto itself?

1. _____

_____

_____

2. _____

_____

_____

3. _____

_____

_____

4. _____

_____

_____

R 11·8

Symmetry

Tell if each figure has reflection symmetry, rotational symmetry, or both. If it has reflection symmetry, how many lines of symmetry are there? If it has rotational symmetry, what is the smallest turn that will rotate the figure onto itself?

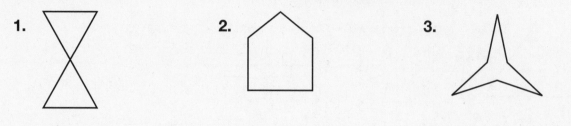

1.

2.

3.

_____   _____   _____

4. **Reasoning** Describe the symmetry of an equilateral triangle.

_____

_____

5. 808 is an example of a number with reflection symmetry. Write another number that has reflection symmetry.

_____

6. Which does the figure have?

   A Rotational symmetry

   B Reflection symmetry

   C Neither

   D Both

7. **Writing to Explain** Draw a figure with reflection symmetry, and draw the line of symmetry.

Name _____

Problem Solving: Make a Table and Look for a Pattern

How could you explain the pattern shown by the blocks? How many blocks will there be in the 10th element of the pattern?

Make a table to show the number of blocks in each element.

Element number	1	2	3	4	5	6	7	8	9	10
Number of blocks	1	3	5	7						

The pattern: Each element has 2 more blocks than the element before it.

Write a mathematical expression you can use to find the number of blocks in any element.

$x(2) - 1$, where x is the element number

Evaluate for the 10th element:

$10(2) - 1 = 20 - 1 = 19$

The 10th element will have 19 blocks.

1   2   3   4
Element

---

1. What is the pattern in this table? Write this as an expression.

Row a	1	2	3	4	5
Row b	4	7	10	13	16

_____

_____

2. The table shows the sum of the interior angles of several polygons. What is the sum of the interior angles in a regular polygon with 14 sides?

Number of sides	3	4	5	6	7	8
Sum of angles	180°	360°	540°			

_____

3. A quarry charges $56.00 per ton of gravel. A discount of $3.00 is given for buying 2 tons, $6.00 for buying 3 tons, and so on. What would the discount be for buying 12 tons of gravel?

_____

4. The first square in a pattern is 1 cm in a side. Each square after that adds 1 cm to each side. What is the area of the 7th square?

_____

Problem Solving: Make a Table and Look for a Pattern

1. Find the next three numbers in each row. Write a formula to find any number in row B.

_____

A	2	4	6			
B	2	8	14			

2. A company offers a 2% discount if you buy 1–5 of their products. If you buy 6–10 of their products, you earn a 3.5% discount. Buying 11–15 products will earn you a 5% discount. If the pattern continues, what discount would be offered for buying 33 products?

_____

3. Explain the pattern. Draw the next eleven shapes.

○□○△○□□○△△○□□□○△△△○□□□□○△

_____

_____

4. In a contest, the first place team gets $\frac{1}{2}$ of the million-dollar prize. The second place team gets $\frac{1}{2}$ of the remaining money. Each team after that gets $\frac{1}{2}$ of the remaining money. How much will the sixth place team get?

_____

5. An advertising sign lights up for 5 seconds then goes out for 2 seconds. For how many seconds will the sign be off in the first minute after the sign is turned on?

A 46 seconds **B** 30 seconds **C** 16 seconds **D** 2 seconds

6. **Writing to Explain** Explain your thinking as you find how many triangles would be in the 8th row of the pattern

_____

_____

_____

Understanding Ratios

A ratio is a pair of numbers that compares two quantities.

Count to find the ratio of squares to circles.

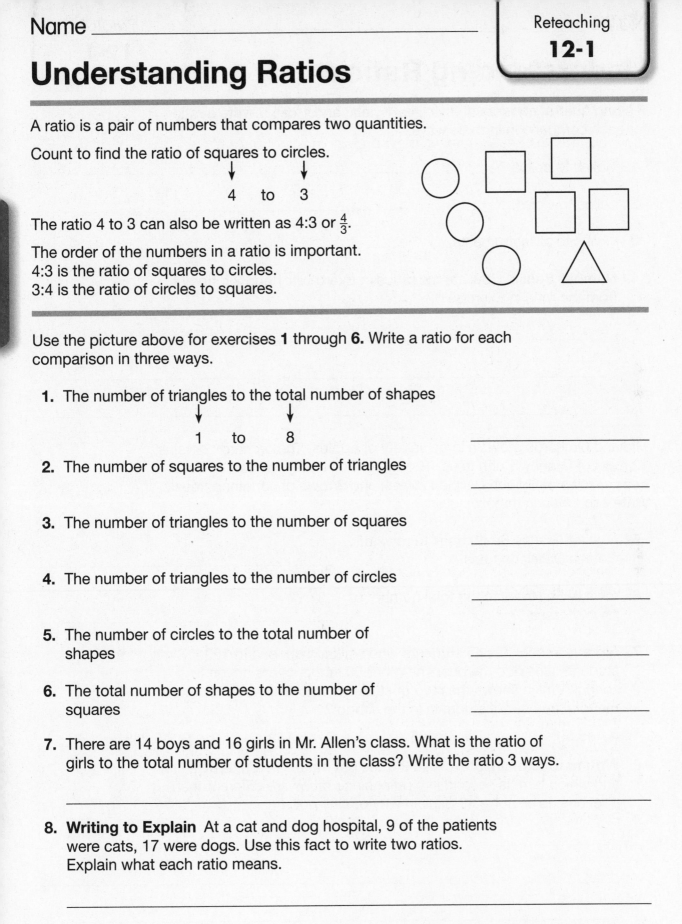

4   to   3

The ratio 4 to 3 can also be written as 4:3 or $\frac{4}{3}$.

The order of the numbers in a ratio is important.
4:3 is the ratio of squares to circles.
3:4 is the ratio of circles to squares.

Use the picture above for exercises **1** through **6.** Write a ratio for each comparison in three ways.

1. The number of triangles to the total number of shapes

    1   to   8

    _____

2. The number of squares to the number of triangles

    _____

3. The number of triangles to the number of squares

    _____

4. The number of triangles to the number of circles

    _____

5. The number of circles to the total number of
   shapes

    _____

6. The total number of shapes to the number of
   squares

    _____

7. There are 14 boys and 16 girls in Mr. Allen's class. What is the ratio of girls to the total number of students in the class? Write the ratio 3 ways.

   _____

8. **Writing to Explain** At a cat and dog hospital, 9 of the patients were cats, 17 were dogs. Use this fact to write two ratios. Explain what each ratio means.

   _____

Understanding Ratios

A string quartet consists of 2 violins, 1 viola, and 1 cello. Write a ratio for each comparison in three ways.

1. violins to cellos

_____

2. cellos to violas

_____

3. violins to all instruments

_____

4. Number Sense How are the ratios in Exercises 1 and 2 different from the ratio in Exercise 3?

_____

_____

_____

Midland Orchards grows a large variety of apples. The orchard contains 12 rows of Granny Smith trees, 10 rows of Fuji trees, 15 rows of Gala trees, 2 rows of Golden Delicious trees, and 2 rows of Jonathan trees. Write each ratio in three ways.

5. rows of Granny Smith trees to rows of
Golden Delicious trees

_____

6. rows of Fuji trees to the total number of
rows of trees

_____

7. A grade school has 45 students who walk to school and 150 students who ride the bus. The other 50 students are driven to school. Which shows the ratio of students who walk to school to the total number of students in the school?

A 45:50   **B** 45:195   **C** 45:150   **D** 45:245

8. Writing to Explain Steve said it does not matter which term is first and which term is second in a ratio, since ratios are different than fractions. Is he correct? Explain why or why not.

_____

_____

_____

P 12·1

Equal Ratios and Proportions

You can find equal ratios just like you find equivalent fractions.

Find ratios equal to $\frac{30}{40}$.

Multiply both terms by the same number.

$$\frac{30 \times 2}{40 \times 2} = \frac{60}{80}$$

Divide both terms by the same number. To find the simplest form ratio, divide by the greatest common factor (GCF) of the two numbers.

The GCF of 30 and 40 is 10.

$$\frac{30 \div 10}{40 \div 10} = \frac{3}{4}$$

Two equal ratios form a proportion. The units must be the same in both ratios.

Do the ratios 24 ft:16 seconds and 36 ft:24 seconds form a proportion?

First check the units.

Both ratios compare feet to seconds, so the units are the same.

Then write each ratio in simplest form.

$$\frac{24 \text{ ft}}{16 \text{ seconds}} = \frac{3 \text{ ft}}{2 \text{ seconds}}$$

$$\frac{36 \text{ ft}}{24 \text{ seconds}} = \frac{3 \text{ ft}}{2 \text{ seconds}}$$

Compare the simplest form ratios. They are the same, so the ratios form a proportion.

Write three ratios that are equal to the ratio given.

1. $\frac{3}{5}$ _____

2. $\frac{4}{8}$ _____

3. $\frac{6}{18}$ _____

4. 8:10 _____

5. 6:8 _____

6. 10:12 _____

7. 12 to 18

8. 16 to 18

9. 5 to 25

_____   _____   _____

Write the ratios in simplest form.

10. $\frac{10}{15}$ _____

11. 21 to 14 _____

12. 15:25 _____

Write = if the ratios form a proportion; if they do not form a proportion, write ≠.

13. $\frac{15}{18}$ ∣ $\frac{10}{12}$ _____

14. 20:24 ∣ 24:30 _____

15. 16 to 20 ∣ 28 to 35 _____

16. Number Sense Dale says that the ratios 3:5 and 2:10 are equal. Is he correct? Explain.

_____

Equal Ratios and Proportions

Write three ratios that are equal to the ratio given.

1. $\frac{8}{10}$ _____

2. $\frac{2}{3}$ _____

3. $\frac{3}{4}$ _____

4. 21 to 18 _____

5. 5 to 4 _____

6. 1 to 3 _____

7. 14:16 _____

8. 2:4 _____

9. 2:5 _____

Write = if the ratios form a proportion; if they do not form a proportion, write ≠.

10. 3:12 | 6:24 _____

11. $\frac{14}{16}$ | $\frac{7}{4}$ _____

12. 4 to 20 | 1 to 4 _____

Find the number that makes the ratios equivalent.

13. $\frac{8}{9}$ = _____ /36

14. 15:18 = 5: _____

15. _____ to 7 = 9 to 21

Write the ratios in simplest form.

16. $\frac{42}{28}$ _____

17. 21 to 36 _____

18. 15:45 _____

19. $\frac{35}{25}$ _____

20. 60 to 30 _____

21. 10:40 _____

22. **Writing to Explain** Tell why you cannot multiply or divide by zero to find equal ratios.

_____

23. **Geometry** Is the ratio of length to width for these two rectangles proportional? Tell how you know.

14 in. 7 in.

21 in. 15 in.

_____

24. **Algebra** Which value for x would make the ratios equivalent?
$\frac{3}{8} = \frac{x}{32}$

A $x = 4$

B $x = 6$

C $x = 8$

D $x = 12$

Understanding Rates and Unit Rates

A rate is a ratio in which the two terms are measured in different units.

Example: 18 bracelets for 3 girls.

18 bracelets
——————
3 girls

In a unit rate, the second number is 1.

Example: 6 bracelets for 1 girl.

6 bracelets
——————
1 girl

Remember that the fraction bar shows division.
If you know a rate, you can divide to find the unit rate.

Example: 17 goals in 5 games is written as $\frac{17 \text{ goals}}{5 \text{ games}}$.

$\begin{array}{r} 3.4 \\ 5\overline{)17.0} \end{array}$ The unit rate is 3.4 goals per game. (Per means "for each".)

Write the rate and the unit rate.

1. 25 flowers for 5 vases

_____

2. 32 games in 8 weeks

_____

3. 144 pencils in 12 packages

_____

4. 252 students in 9 classes

_____

5. $13.20 for 6 pounds

_____

6. 34 minutes for 8 pages

_____

7. Number Sense If a car travels 350 miles in 7 hours, what is its rate per hour?

_____

8. Estimation Bare root plum trees are on sale at 3 for $40. To the nearest dollar, what is the cost per tree?

_____

Understanding Rates and Unit Rates

Write the rate and the unit rate.

1. 42 bricks laid in 2 hours

_____

2. 15 points scored in 4 quarters

_____

3. 225 chairs in 15 rows

_____

4. 24 trees pruned in 5 days

_____

5. 480 miles in 12 hours

_____

6. $6.50 for 10 pounds

_____

7. 72 plants in 9 square feet

_____

8. 357 miles on 14 gallons

_____

9. Estimation Over 5 days, 8,208 people visited an amusement park. About how many people visited the park per day?

_____

10. Writing to Explain Explain how you could convert a rate of 18,000 miles per hour to miles per second.

_____

_____

11. Critical Thinking Matt makes 5 bookcases in 8 days. What is his unit rate?

_____

12. A space shuttle orbits Earth 1 time in 90 minutes. How many times does it orbit Earth in 6 hours?

_____

13. Which is the unit rate for 39 people in 3 vans?

A 39 people per van

B 13 vans per person

C 13 people per van

D 3 people per van

Comparing Rates

Use unit rates to compare two rates that have the same units of measurement.

Daniel painted 9 planks in 6 minutes. Meredith painted 22 planks in 11 minutes. Who painted at a faster rate?

Write each rate as a unit rate.

Daniel's Rate: $\frac{9\ planks}{6\ min}$

Meredith's Rate: $\frac{22\ planks}{11\ min}$

$= \dfrac{9\ planks \div 6}{6\ min \div 6}$ $= \frac{1.5\ planks}{1\ min}$

$= \dfrac{22\ planks \div 11}{11\ minutes \div 11}$ $= \frac{2\ planks}{1\ min}$

Since 2 is greater than 1.5, Meredith is the faster painter. The faster rate is 22 planks in 11 min.

Find each unit rate and determine which rate is greater.

1. 51 hits on Jon's website in 3 h or 96 hits on Shana's website in 6 h

_____

_____

2. 330 mi on 15 gal or 240 mi on 10 gal

_____

3. 90 breaths in 6 min or 112 breaths in 8 min

_____

Find each unit price and determine which is a better buy.

4. 20 gallons of gas for $66.00 or 25 gallons of gas for $81.25

_____

5. Writing to Explain Earl and Mia danced in a charity fundraiser. Earl raised $275 when he danced for 5 hours. Mia raised $376 when she danced for 8 hours. Which dancer earned more for each hour danced? Explain how you found your answer.

_____

_____

Comparing Rates

Find each unit rate and determine which rate is greater.

1. 250 mi per 10 gal or 460 mi per 20 gal

_____

2. 1,000 words in 20 min or 2,475 words in 45 min

_____

3. 6 in. of rain in 4 h or 8 in. of rain in 5 h

_____

Find each unit price and determine which is a better buy.

4. 1 lb of apples for $2.15 or 3 lb of apples for $5.76

_____

5. 8 bungee cords for $10.00 or 20 bungee cords for $22.00

_____

6. 5 oz of insect repellant for $6.95 or 14 oz of insect repellant for $19.60

_____

7. Fritz earns $75.60 for each 7-h shift that he works. Which shift pays a higher hourly wage than the wage Fritz earns?

   A $60.30 for a 6-h shift

   B $80.00 for an 8-h shift

   C $36.30 for a 3-h shift

   D $40.40 for a 4-h shift

8. Writing to Explain Shaunda said that buying 4 towels for $17 was a better buy than buying 2 towels for $9. She found her answer by doubling the terms in the ratio $\frac{9}{2}$ and comparing the first terms in the ratios. Is she correct? Use unit prices to support your answer.

_____

Distance, Rate, and Time

The formula $d = r \times t$ uses symbols to relate the quantities for distance (*d*), average rate of speed (*r*), and time (*t*).

Example 1

How long will it take a car moving at 50 mph to travel 70 mi?

Substitute what you know into the formula $d = r \times t$.

Solve the equation.

$70 \text{ mi} = 50 \text{ mph} \times t$

$$\frac{70 \text{ mi}}{50 \text{ mph}} = \frac{50 \text{ mph} \times t}{50 \text{ mph}}$$

$1.4 \text{ h} = t$

It will take 1.4 h to travel 70 mi at 50 mph.

- -

Example 2

A car travels 325 mi in 5 h. What is its rate of speed?

Substitute what you know into the formula $d = r \times t$.

Solve the equation.

$325 \text{ mi} = r \times 5 \text{ h}$

$$\frac{325 \text{ mi}}{5 \text{ h}} = \frac{r = 5 \text{ h}}{5 \text{ h}}$$

$65 \text{ mph} = r$

The rate of speed of a car that travels 325 mi in 5 h is 65 mph.

1. An airplane flies at 250 mph. How far will it travel in 5 h at that rate of speed?

Substitute the information you know into the formula $d = r \times t$:	Solve the equation.	Write the answer with the correct units.

$d =$ _____   _____   _____

Find the missing variable.

2. Distance = 60 km   time = 4 h   rate = _____

3. Distance = 24 cm   time = 12 sec   rate = _____

4. Distance = 56 yd   time = _____   rate = 8 yd/min

5. Distance = _____   time = 25 d   rate = 160 m/d

6. **Writing to Explain** A storm is 15 mi from Lodi. If the storm travels at 6 mph towards the city, how many hours will it take for the storm to get to Lodi? Show your work.

_____

R 12·5

Distance, Rate, and Time

Find the missing variable.

1. Distance = 15 mi   time = 2h   rate = _____

2. Distance = 56 km   time = 4 h   rate = _____

3. Distance = 72 yd   time = _____   rate = $\frac{12 \text{ yd}}{\text{min}}$

4. Distance = 27 cm   time = _____   rate = $\frac{3 \text{ cm}}{\text{sec}}$

5. Distance = _____   time = 2 d   rate = $\frac{5,000 \text{ m}}{\text{d}}$

6. Distance = _____   time = 6 wk   rate = $\frac{80 \text{ ft}}{\text{wk}}$

7. The California Speedway hosts automobile races. Which rate of speed is higher: a car completing a 500-mi race in about $3\frac{1}{3}$ h or a car completing a 300-mi race in about $2\frac{1}{2}$ h? _____

8. A train traveled 250 mi in 2 h. If it traveled at the same rate of speed, how long would it take the train to travel 600 mi? _____

9. The space shuttle travels 4,375 mi in 15 min as it orbits the earth. Estimate its average rate of speed during that time to the nearest hundred.

    A About 400 mi per min

    B About 300 mi per min

    C About 60,000 mi per min

    D About 70,000 mi per min

10. **Writing to Explain** Kevin drove his scooter 62 km in 2 h. Explain how to find how far he drives if he drives at the same rate for 3 h.

_____

_____

_____

Problem Solving:
Draw a Picture

Veronica is celebrating her birthday by having a skating party. As part of a birthday special, Veronica paid for 10 tickets and 2 guests received free admission. What fraction of the people at Veronica's party were not charged for admission?

Read and Understand

What do you know? There were 10 paid admissions and 2 free admissions.
What are you trying to find? The fraction of people attending Veronica's party that were admitted at no charge.

Plan and Solve

What strategy will you use? Draw a picture to show the 10 paid admissions and the 2 free admissions.
Count the boxes. There were 12 people admitted. Since 2 of the 12 people were admitted at no charge, the fraction is $\frac{2}{12}$, or $\frac{1}{6}$ in simplest form.

Paid admission										
Free admission										

Look Back and Check

Is your answer reasonable? Yes. The picture shows 2 out of 12 boxes, which is $\frac{2}{12}$, or $\frac{1}{6}$.

Draw or use a picture to solve each problem.

One afternoon, the ratio of black shirts sold to white shirts sold at The Clothes Horse was 2:1. Complete the picture to show the ratio.

Black shirts sold									
White shirts sold									

1. How many boxes are shaded in all? _____

2. What fraction of the shirts sold were black? _____

3. The Clothes Horse sold 12 shirts that afternoon. How many black shirts were sold? HINT: YOU CAN ADD TO THE PICTURE UNTIL THERE ARE 12 SHADED BOXES TO REPRESENT THE PROBLEM. _____

4. Ilene earns $20. She saves $2 for every $8 that she spends. How much of the $20 will she save? _____

Problem Solving:
Draw a Picture

Draw a picture to solve each problem.

For **1** through **3**, Pamela walks 1 mile and runs 4 miles during her daily workout.

1. What is the ratio of miles walked to miles ran during each of
   Pamela's workouts?   _____

2. What is the ratio of miles walked to total miles in each of
   Pamela's workouts?   _____

3. Pamela ran 20 miles last week. How many days did she workout? _____

4. There are 5 pens with blue ink, 3 pens with red ink,
   and 2 pens with purple ink in each package.
   What fraction of the pens has blue ink?

   A 5

   B $\frac{5}{5}$

   C $\frac{5}{8}$

   D $\frac{1}{2}$

5. There are 18 baseballs and basketballs in one gym storage locker.
   There are 3 baseballs for every 6 basketballs in the locker. How
   many basketballs are in the locker?   _____

6. **Writing to Explain** Rasheed takes photographs with a digital
   camera. He estimates that for each photograph he prints, he has
   5 photographs that he never prints. How many photographs has
   Rasheed taken if he makes 4 prints? Explain how drawing a picture
   can help you solve the problem. Then solve.

   _____

   _____

   _____

Using Ratio Tables

A ratio table showing equal ratios can be used to solve a proportion.

Ross uses 11 skeins of yarn to make 4 scarves. How many scarves can he make from 66 skeins of yarn?

Write a proportion. Use x for the number of scarves.

$$\frac{4 \text{ scarves}}{11 \text{ skeins}} = \frac{x \text{ scarves}}{66 \text{ skeins}}$$

Make a ratio table. Multiply or divide to find equal ratios. Find ratios equivalent to $\frac{4}{11}$ by multiplying both terms of the ratio by the same number until you find 66 skeins.

Number of scarves	4	8	12	16	20	24
Number of skeins	11	22	33	44	55	66

$$\frac{4 \text{ scarves}}{11 \text{ skeins}} = \frac{24 \text{ scarves}}{66 \text{ skeins}}$$

So, Ross can make 24 scarves from 66 skeins of yarn.

Answer the question and complete each ratio table.

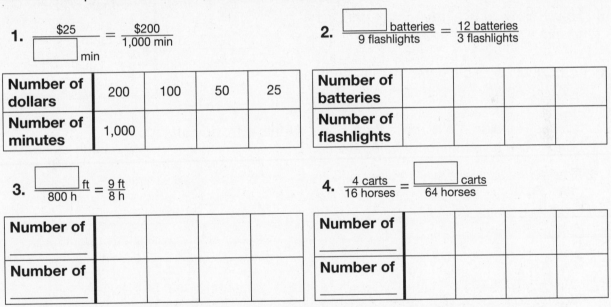

1. $\dfrac{\$25}{\boxed{} \text{ min}} = \dfrac{\$200}{1,000 \text{ min}}$

Number of dollars	200	100	50	25
Number of minutes	1,000			

2. $\dfrac{\boxed{} \text{ batteries}}{9 \text{ flashlights}} = \dfrac{12 \text{ batteries}}{3 \text{ flashlights}}$

Number of batteries				
Number of flashlights				

3. $\dfrac{\boxed{} \text{ ft}}{800 \text{ h}} = \dfrac{9 \text{ ft}}{8 \text{ h}}$

Number of _____				
Number of _____				

4. $\dfrac{4 \text{ carts}}{16 \text{ horses}} = \dfrac{\boxed{} \text{ carts}}{64 \text{ horses}}$

Number of _____				
Number of _____				

5. Laine was practicing her free throws. She shot nine times and made five baskets. At this rate, how many times will she need to shoot to make 35 baskets?

_____

6. Hiram said that he can use the same ratio table to solve the two proportions below. Do you agree or disagree with Hiram?

$\dfrac{8 \text{ cows}}{2 \text{ pigs}} = \dfrac{c \text{ cows}}{10 \text{ pigs}}$ $\qquad$ $\dfrac{2 \text{ pigs}}{8 \text{ cows}} = \dfrac{10 \text{ pigs}}{c \text{ cows}}$

_____

R 13-1

Using Ratio Tables

Complete the ratio table. Add columns if needed.

1. $\dfrac{3 \text{ hops}}{5 \text{ jumps}} = \dfrac{\boxed{} \text{ hops}}{15 \text{ jumps}}$

Number of hops		
Number of jumps		

_____

2. $\dfrac{\$60}{2 \text{ weeks}} = \dfrac{\$240}{\boxed{} \text{ weeks}}$

_____

3. $\dfrac{12 \text{ cans}}{7 \text{ bottles}} = \dfrac{60 \text{ cans}}{\boxed{} \text{ bottles}}$

_____

4. How many cups of loam are needed to make 66 c of potting soil?

_____

5. How many cups of humus are needed to make 11 c of potting soil?

_____

6. Sondra uses 78 c of loam to make potting soil. How many cups of humus did she use?

_____

Potting Soil for Ferns (Makes 22 c)
6 c sand
6 c loam
9 c peat moss
3 c humus
1 c dried cow manure

7. It takes Renaldo 8 h to make 7 carvings. At this rate, how many hours will it take him to make 63 carvings?

A $7\frac{7}{8}$ h

B 9 h

C 56 h

D 72 h

8. **Writing to Explain** Find three sets of values for *x* and *y* to make $\dfrac{x \text{ mi}}{y \text{ min}} = \dfrac{4 \text{ mi}}{32 \text{ min}}$ a proportion. Explain how you found the values.

_____

_____

Using Unit Rates

A unit rate is a special ratio that compares one quantity to one unit of another quantity. You can use unit rates to solve proportions.

Geraldo earns $100 for 4 hours of work. If he works 7 hours at the same rate of pay, how much will he earn?

Write a proportion. Use d for dollars earned. $\frac{\$100}{4\,h} = \frac{\$d}{7h}$

Find the unit rate. Divide the first term by the second term.

$\$100 \div 4 = \$25$

The unit rate is $\frac{\$25}{1\,h}$.

> Think: Find an equal ratio with 1 as the second term.
>
> $\frac{100 \div 4}{4 \div 4} = \frac{25}{1}$

Multiply by the unit rate. $\frac{\$25}{h} \times 7h = \$175$

> Think: Find an equal ratio.
>
> $\frac{25 \times 7}{1 \times 7} = \frac{175}{7}$

So, $\frac{\$100}{4\,h} = \frac{\$175}{7\,h}$. Geraldo will earn $175 when he works 7 hours.

Use unit rates to solve each proportion. Estimate to check reasonableness.

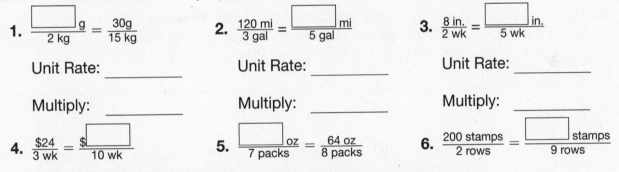

1. $\dfrac{\boxed{}\,g}{2\ kg} = \dfrac{30g}{15\ kg}$

 Unit Rate: _____

 Multiply: _____

2. $\dfrac{120\ mi}{3\ gal} = \dfrac{\boxed{}\,mi}{5\ gal}$

 Unit Rate: _____

 Multiply: _____

3. $\dfrac{8\ in.}{2\ wk} = \dfrac{\boxed{}\,in.}{5\ wk}$

 Unit Rate: _____

 Multiply: _____

4. $\dfrac{\$24}{3\ wk} = \dfrac{\$\boxed{}}{10\ wk}$

5. $\dfrac{\boxed{}\,oz}{7\ packs} = \dfrac{64\ oz}{8\ packs}$

6. $\dfrac{200\ stamps}{2\ rows} = \dfrac{\boxed{}\,stamps}{9\ rows}$

7. Wes used 49 quarts of oil when he changed the oil in 7 cars. Complete and solve the proportion to find how many quarts of oil he would use to change the oil in 20 cars, assuming that all cars need the same quantity of oil.

 $\dfrac{49\ quarts}{7\ cars} = $ _____

8. **Writing to Explain** A café served 180 pickles with 60 sandwiches. If the ratio of sandwiches to pickles is always constant, explain how you can use unit rates and proportions to find how many pickles are needed to serve 32 sandwiches.

_____

R 13·2

© Pearson Education, Inc. 6

Using Unit Rates

Use unit rates to solve each proportion. Estimate to check for
reasonableness.

1. $\dfrac{a \text{ ft}}{6 \text{ h}} = \dfrac{20 \text{ ft}}{4 \text{ h}}$ _____

2. $\dfrac{36 \text{ oz}}{6 \text{ lb}} = \dfrac{b \text{ oz}}{4 \text{ lb}}$ _____

3. $\dfrac{c \text{ players}}{10 \text{ teams}} = \dfrac{27 \text{ players}}{3 \text{ teams}}$ _____

4. $\dfrac{d \text{ c}}{20 \text{ tsp}} = \dfrac{60 \text{ c}}{12 \text{ tsp}}$ _____

5. $\dfrac{e \text{ m}}{12 \text{ cm}} = \dfrac{63 \text{ m}}{9 \text{ cm}}$ _____

6. $\dfrac{16 \text{ adults}}{2 \text{ children}} = \dfrac{f \text{ adults}}{5 \text{ children}}$ _____

7. $\dfrac{\$g}{30 \text{ lawns}} = \dfrac{\$200}{8 \text{ lawns}}$ _____

8. $\dfrac{12 \text{ mL}}{6 \text{ pt}} = \dfrac{h \text{ mL}}{40 \text{ pt}}$ _____

9. $\dfrac{33 \text{ meals}}{11 \text{ days}} = \dfrac{k \text{ meals}}{365 \text{ days}}$ _____

10. It takes DeShawn 30 min to paint 90 feet of fence. If he paints at
the same rate, how many feet of fence can he paint in 45 min?

_____

11. Inez types 280 words in 7 minutes. If she types at the same rate,
how many words will she type in 1 hour?

_____

12. **Algebra** Explain how you can tell that $\dfrac{20 \text{ pens}}{2 \text{ packages}} = \dfrac{30 \text{ pens}}{3 \text{ packages}}$ using
mental math?

_____

_____

13. Darryl was looking at the speeds of different airplanes. When he
wrote a proportion to compare the speeds, he forgot to write one
term. If the proportion is correct, which is the term he forgot?

$$\dfrac{45 \text{ mi}}{\boxed{}} = \dfrac{135 \text{ mi}}{12 \text{ min}}$$

A 4 mi

C 36 mi

B 4 min

D 36 min

14. **Writing to Explain** Jeanette estimates that she mails 2 letters
for every 50 e-mails that she sends. She has mailed 9 letters this
week. To find how many e-mails she has sent, Jeanette wrote the
proportion $\dfrac{2 \text{ letters}}{50 \text{ e-mails}} = \dfrac{9 \text{ letters}}{e \text{ e-mails}}$. Tell how she can use unit rates to
solve the proportion. Tell how many e-mails she received.

_____

_____

_____

_____

Applying Ratios

You can use a diagram to solve problems about ratios.

A zoo has 3 zebras for every 2 giraffes. How many giraffes does the zoo have if it has 12 zebras? Draw a diagram to solve the problem.

Draw rectangles to model the ratio 3 zebras to 2 giraffes.

Divide the number of zebras into 3 equal parts to find how many animals each part represents. $12 \div 3 = 4$

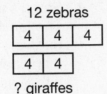

Then multiply the number of parts for the giraffes times 4 animals per part to find the number of giraffes.

$4 \times 2 = 8$

The zoo has 8 giraffes.

Draw a diagram to help you solve each problem.

1. One exhibit at the zoo has 7 birds for every 2 mammals. If there are 10 mammals in the exhibit, how many birds are there?

   _____

2. There are 5 children for every 3 adults who visit the zoo. If there are 30 children at the zoo, how many adults are there?

   _____

3. The monkeys get fed 6 buckets of vegetables for every 2 buckets of cereal. How many buckets of vegetables do the monkeys get fed if they get 8 buckets of cereal?

   _____

4. It takes 8 minutes for the train to fill 3 cars with people from the zoo. How long does it take the train to fill 18 cars of people from the zoo?

   _____

5. **Writing to Explain** Arlen buys 2 small cups of food for the animals for 5 tokens. Explain how to use a diagram to find how many cups of food Arlen could buy for 20 tokens.

   _____

   _____

Applying Ratios

In **1** through **8**, draw a diagram to solve the problem.

1. Sam puts 3 tulips and 4 lilacs in each vase. How many lilacs does Sam use if he puts 36 tulips into vases?

_____

2. Seven students ride the bus to school for every 2 students who walk. If there are 105 students who ride the bus, how many students walk?

_____

3. A golf store is having a special, giving away 10 free golf tees for every box of 3 golf balls a customer buys. If a customer buys 24 golf balls, how many golf tees does she get?

_____

4. Sarah's family has an apple orchard. The family sells 8 baskets of apples for every 3 jars of applesauce. How many baskets of apples do they sell if they sell 120 jars of applesauce?

_____

5. Martin enjoys hiking on rural trails near his home in Michigan. He can hike 6 miles in 2 hours. At this rate, how long would it take Martin to hike 24 miles?

_____

6. The coach mixes 15 scoops of powder with 2 gallons of water to make a sports drink for his team. How many scoops of powder does the coach need to mix with 10 gallons of water?

_____

7. A 4-pound bag of potatoes costs $3.16. At that rate, how much would 32 pounds of potatoes cost?

_____

8. Ali packs 54 cans into 3 boxes to ship. How many boxes of the same size will Ali need to ship 324 cans?

_____

9. Algebra Which value of p makes the ratios equal?

$$\frac{5}{7} = \frac{p}{56}$$

A 8   **B** 13   **C** 40   **D** 64

10. Writing to Explain There are 4 girls to every 3 boys on the school's track team. Explain how to use a diagram to find how many members are on the track team if there are 16 girls on the team.

_____

_____

Problem Solving:
Writing to Explain

In a chess club, 1 out of every 4 members is in sixth grade. There are 24 members in the chess club. How many members are in the sixth grade? Explain your solution.

Gerry's explanation:
    6 members are in the sixth grade.
    Use reasoning: I multiplied 4 members by 6 to get 24 members, so I multiplied 1 by 6 to get 6 members in the sixth grade.
    Then I checked to see if the ratios were proportional.

$$\frac{1 \text{ sixth grader}}{4 \text{ members}} = \frac{6 \text{ sixth graders}}{24 \text{ members}}$$

Since the ratios are proportional, the answer is correct.

- Use words, numbers, symbols, pictures, diagrams, or tables. If the problem includes pictures, diagrams, or tables that provide information or give details, refer to these.
- Describe the steps and operations you used. Show your work.

Explain your solution. Show your work.

1. Ms. Chin's class recorded the weather conditions for 14 days. The weather was cloudy 3 days out of every 7 days. Ms. Jensen's class recorded the weather for the next 10 days. The weather was cloudy 4 days out of every 5 days. Which class recorded more cloudy days?

_____

_____

_____

_____

_____

_____

2. Lynette earns $5 by delivering newspapers. She saves $3 and she spends the rest. If she saved $27 one month, how much did she spend?

_____

_____

Problem Solving: Writing to Explain

Explain your solution. Show your work.

1. A fundraiser is being held to raise money for a new school playground. Of every $20 raised, $16 will be spent on playground equipment. If the goal of the fundraiser is $320.00 for playground equipment, how much total money will it need to raise?

_____

_____

_____

_____

2. Stephan is planning a hiking trip at Kings Canyon National Park. He plans to hike 14 miles every 2 days. If he hikes 42 miles, how many days will he hike?

_____

_____

_____

_____

3. A rental store at the beach has 56 umbrellas and 24 surfboards. Which ratio describes the relationship of surfboards to umbrellas?

   A 56:24   **B** 7:3   **C** 3:8   **D** 3:7

4. **Writing to Explain** Kara can run 3 miles in 25.5 minutes. At this rate, how long would it take her to run 2 miles? *Diana's answer: If I subtract 1 mile from 3 miles, I get 2 miles, so if I subtract 1 minute from 25.5 minutes, I get 24.5 minutes. Kara takes 24.5 minutes to run 2 miles.* Is Diana's answer correct? Explain.

_____

_____

Ratios and Graphs

You can make or complete a table of equal ratios and graph the values on a coordinate grid.

Complete the table to show equal ratios for $\frac{3}{4}$.

3	6	9	12
4			

To complete the table, find fractions that are equal to $\frac{3}{4}$ that have numerators of 6, 9, and 12.

$$\frac{3 \times \mathbf{2}}{4 \times \mathbf{2}} = \frac{6}{8} \qquad \frac{3 \times \mathbf{3}}{4 \times \mathbf{3}} = \frac{9}{12} \qquad \frac{3 \times \mathbf{4}}{3 \times \mathbf{4}} = \frac{12}{16}$$

The missing values in the table are the denominators of the equal fractions. The values are: 8, 12, and 16.

Graph the equal ratios on a coordinate grid. Use an appropriate scale for the x and y axes.

Plot the points for each ratio, x to y. Draw a dashed line from (0, 0) through the points extending through the final point.

Complete the table to show equal ratios. Graph the set of equal ratios on a coordinate grid.

1.

2	4	6	8	10
3				

2.

1	2	3	4	5
2				

3.

3	6	9	12	15
5				

4.

2	6	12	18	24
7				

5.

4	12	16	48	60
12				

6.

6	18	24	36	48
9				

7.

5	15	25	35	45
8				

8.

1	5	8	10	15
7				

Ratios and Graphs

For **1** through **6**, complete the table to show equal ratios.

1.

4				
3	6	9	12	15

2.

4	2	8	12	16
6				

3.

10	20	30	40	70
7				

4.

3				
2	4	8	12	24

5.

6				
11	22	44	88	110

6.

12	4	24	36	48
3				

For **7** and **8**, complete the table to show equal ratios, and graph the pairs of values on the coordinate grid.

7.

5	10	15	25	40
4				

8.

5				
2	4	6	10	14

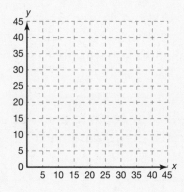

9. Writing to Explain How are the graphs of the ratios in Exercises 7 and 8 alike, and how are they different?

_____

_____

_____

10. A birdwatcher counted 7 robins for every 4 sparrows. Complete the table to show how many robins she counted if she counted 24 sparrows in a weekend. On a separate piece of graph paper, graph the values on a coordinate grid.

4	8	12	16	20	24
7					

Maps and Scale Drawings

On the drawing, the scale tells us that 1 cm = 2 ft.

For every 1 cm on the drawing, there are 2 ft in the kitchen.

What is the real length of the room?

Step 1: Set up a proportion.
Write the scale as the first ratio.
Use the information about the
kitchen for the second ratio.

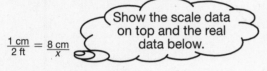

Show the scale data
on top and the real
data below.

$$\frac{1\text{ cm}}{2\text{ ft}} = \frac{8\text{ cm}}{x}$$

Step 2: Use cross multiplication
to solve the proportion.
$$\frac{1\text{ cm}}{2\text{ ft}} = \frac{8\text{ cm}}{x}$$
$$1x = 2 \times 8$$
$$x = 16$$

Scale: 1 cm = 2ft

The real room is 16 feet long.

Use the scale drawing to answer **1** through **3**.

1. What is the actual length of the
   living room?

   _____

2. What are the dimensions of the
   dining room?

   _____

3. What are the dimensions of
   the kitchen?

   _____

Living Room

Dining Room   Kitchen

Scale: 1 cm = 2.5 ft

4. **Reasoning** A room measures 12 ft by 15 ft. Find the scale that
   would allow the room to be shown as large as possible on a piece
   of paper 7 in. by 8 in. Explain your reasoning.

   _____

   _____

Maps and Scale Drawings

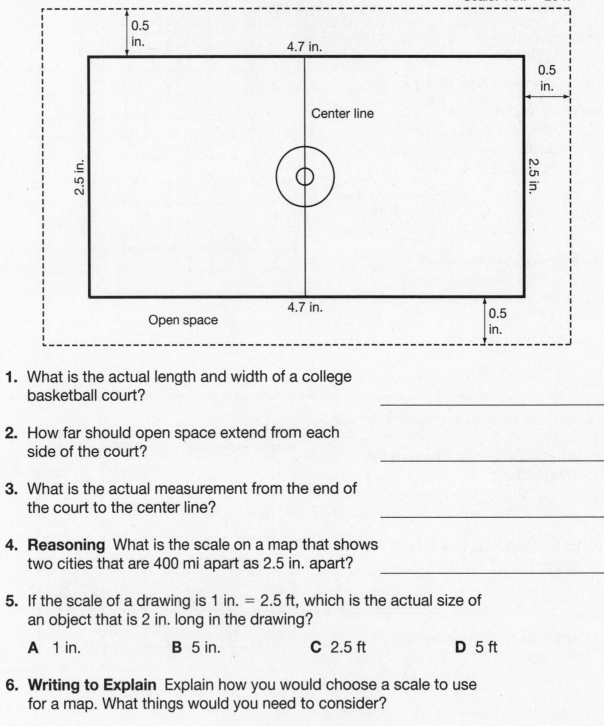

Scale: 1 in. = 20 ft

0.5 in.

4.7 in.

0.5 in.

Center line

2.5 in.

2.5 in.

4.7 in.

0.5 in.

Open space

0.5 in.

1. What is the actual length and width of a college basketball court? _____

2. How far should open space extend from each side of the court? _____

3. What is the actual measurement from the end of the court to the center line? _____

4. **Reasoning** What is the scale on a map that shows two cities that are 400 mi apart as 2.5 in. apart? _____

5. If the scale of a drawing is 1 in. = 2.5 ft, which is the actual size of an object that is 2 in. long in the drawing?

A 1 in.   **B** 5 in.   **C** 2.5 ft   **D** 5 ft

6. **Writing to Explain** Explain how you would choose a scale to use for a map. What things would you need to consider?

_____

_____

_____

Understanding Percent

A percent is a ratio that compares a part to a whole.
The second term in the ratio is always 100.
The whole is 100%.
The grid has 60 of 100 squares shaded.

$\frac{60}{100} = 60\%$

So, 60% of the grid is shaded.

When the second term of a ratio is not 100, you can write an equivalent
ratio with a denominator of 100 or use a proportion to find the percent
shown by the part.

$\frac{1}{10} = \frac{10}{100} = 10\%$ or $\frac{1}{10} = \frac{x}{100}$
$10x = 100$
$x = 10$

So, 10% of the circle is shaded.

The line segment
represents 100%.
What percent is
shown by Point *A*?

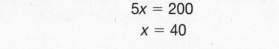

$\frac{2}{5} = \frac{40}{100} = 40\%$ or $\frac{2}{5} = \frac{x}{100}$
$5x = 200$
$x = 40$

So, 40% of the line segment is shaded.

Write the percent of each figure that is shaded.

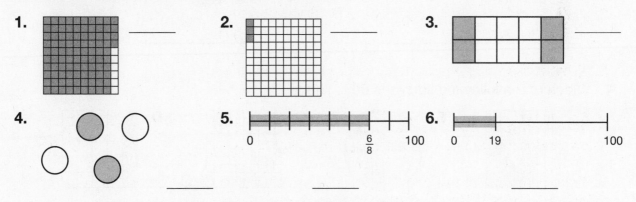

1. _____

2. _____

3. _____

4. _____   5. _____   6. _____

7. **Number Sense** Jana divided a sheet of paper into
5 equal sections and colored 2 of the sections red.
What percent of the paper did she color? _____

8. **Writing to Explain** Shade each model to show 100%. Explain how
you knew how many parts to shade.

_____

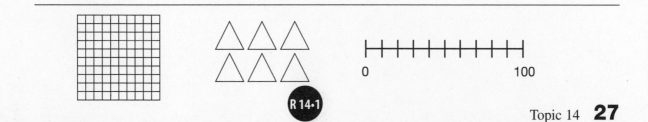

Understanding Percent

Write the percent of each figure that is shaded.

1.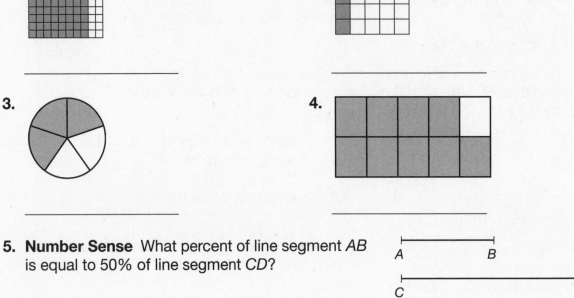

_____

2.

_____

3.

_____

4.

_____

5. Number Sense What percent of line segment *AB* is equal to 50% of line segment *CD*?

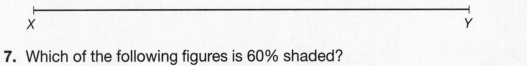

_____

6. The line segment below shows 100%. Show 25%, 50%, and 75% of the segment.

X ─────────────────────────────── Y

7. Which of the following figures is 60% shaded?

A   **B**   **C**   **D**

8. Writing to Explain You are thirsty, so a friend has offered to give you 50% of his water. What information must you have in order to find out how much water your friend will give you?

_____

_____

Fractions, Decimals, and Percents

Fractions, decimals, and percents all name parts of a whole.
Percent means per hundred, so 15% means 15 parts per hundred.
The grid to the right has 72 out of 100 squares shaded. The shaded part
can be represented with a fraction, $\frac{72}{100}$ ($\frac{18}{25}$ in simplest form), by a decimal,
0.72, and by a percent, 72%.

Write 36% as a fraction in simplest form and as a decimal.

$36\% = \frac{36}{100} = 0.36$

Simplify the fraction:

$\frac{36}{100} = \frac{36 \div 4}{100 \div 4} = \frac{9}{25}$

So, $36\% = \frac{9}{25} = 0.36$.

Write 0.47 as a fraction in simplest form and as a percent.

$0.47 = \frac{47}{100} = 47\%$

Write $\frac{3}{4}$ as a decimal and as a percent.

You can use a proportion or divide to help you.

Use a proportion:

$\frac{3}{4} = \frac{n}{100}$

$4n = 300$

$n = 75$

Use division:

$$\begin{array}{r} 0.75 \\ 4\overline{)3.00} \\ \underline{2\ 8} \\ 20 \\ \underline{20} \\ 0 \end{array}$$

So, $\frac{3}{4} = \frac{75}{100} = 0.75 = 75\%$.

Write each number in two other ways. Write fractions in simplest form.

1. $\frac{2}{100}$ _____ ; _____

2. $\frac{71}{100}$ _____ ; _____

3. $\frac{9}{10}$ _____ ; _____

4. 17% _____ ; _____

5. 48% _____ ; _____

6. 60% _____ ; _____

7. 0.04 _____ ; _____

8. 0.22 _____ ; _____

9. Writing to Explain Jamal said that he could write a percent as
a decimal by moving the decimal point two places to the left and
deleting the percent sign. Is he correct? How do you know?

_____

10. Number Sense Two stores sell their goods at
the manufacturers' suggested retail prices, so
their prices are the same. Which store has the
greatest markdown from their original prices?

GOODS 2 GO	BUY AND BYE
$\frac{1}{4}$ off original prices!	30% off original prices!

_____

_____

Fractions, Decimals, and Percents

Describe the shaded portion of each as a fraction, decimal, and percent.

1.

2.

_____

_____

Write each in two other ways.

3. 64%

4. 0.09

5. $\frac{12}{50}$

6. 37%

_____

_____

_____

_____

7. $\frac{4}{250}$

8. 0.023

_____

_____

The table at the right shows the number of states in the United States at different times in history. There are currently 50 states in the United States. Use the information to answer the questions.

Year	States
1792	15
1817	20
1836	25
1848	30
1863	35
1889	40
1896	45
1959	50

9. In what year were there 0.5 as many states as today?

_____

10. What percent of the current number of states had joined the United States by the year 1863?

_____

11. In what year were there about $\frac{2}{3}$ as many states as in 1896? _____

12. Which of the following is equivalent to 98%?

A 0.49

B $\frac{100}{98}$

C 0.98

D $\frac{49}{100}$

13. Writing to Explain Explain how you would write $\frac{5}{6}$ as a percent.

_____

Percents Greater Than 100 and Less Than 1

All percents can be written as fractions in simplest form and as decimals. Percents greater than 100% represent amounts greater than one whole and can be written as improper fractions and as decimals greater than 1. Percents less than 1% represent amounts less than $\frac{1}{100}$ of the whole.

Write 275% as a fraction in simplest form and as a decimal.

Since percent is parts per hundred, write the
percent as a fraction with a denominator of 100.

$\frac{275}{100}$

Simplify the fraction.

$\frac{275}{100} = \frac{275 \div 25}{100 \div 25} = \frac{11}{4} = 2\frac{3}{4}$

To write the number as a decimal, divide the numerator
by the denominator.
So, 275% = $2\frac{3}{4}$ = 2.75

$275 \div 100 = 2.75$

Write $\frac{1}{5}$% as a fraction in simplest form and as a decimal.

Write the fraction in the percent as a decimal.

$\frac{1}{5}\% = 0.2\%$

Write the percent as a fraction with a denominator of 100.

$\frac{0.2}{100}$

Write the numerator as a whole number.

$\frac{0.2}{100} = \frac{0.2 \times 10}{100 \times 10} = \frac{2}{1,000}$

Simplify the fraction.

$\frac{2}{1,000} = \frac{2 \div 2}{1,000 \div 2} = \frac{1}{500}$

Divide the fraction to write the number as a decimal.

$\frac{1}{500} = 0.002$

So, $\frac{1}{5}\% = \frac{1}{500} = 0.002$.

Write each percent as a fraction and as a decimal. Write fractions in simplest form.

1. 137% _____ ; _____

2. 115% _____ ; _____

3. 222% _____ ; _____

4. 500% _____ ; _____

5. 182% _____ ; _____

6. 450% _____ ; _____

7. 0.4% $= \dfrac{\boxed{}}{100} = \dfrac{\boxed{}}{100 \times 10} \times 10 = \dfrac{\boxed{}}{\boxed{}}$; Simplify: $\dfrac{\boxed{}}{\boxed{}}$; Decimal: _____

8. $\frac{3}{4}$% $= \dfrac{0.75}{100} = \dfrac{\boxed{}}{100 \times 100} \times 100 = \dfrac{\boxed{}}{\boxed{}}$ Simplify: $\dfrac{\boxed{}}{\boxed{}}$; Decimal: _____

9. **Writing to Explain** Caryn and Alfonso bought school supplies. Caryn spent 130% of the amount Alfonso spent. She said that she spent 1.3 times the amount that Alfonso spent. Is Caryn correct? Explain.

_____

Percents Greater Than 100 and Less Than 1

Write a fraction in simplest form, a decimal, and a percent to name each shaded part.

1.

2.

_____   _____

Write each percent as a fraction and as a decimal. Write fractions in simplest form.

3. 188% _____ ; _____   **4.** 145% _____ ; _____

5. 261% _____ ; _____   **6.** 350% _____ ; _____

7. 275% _____ ; _____   **8.** 420% _____ ; _____

9. 400% _____ ; _____   **10.** $\frac{1}{5}$% _____ ; _____

11. 0.7% _____ ; _____   **12.** $\frac{1}{3}$% _____ ; _____

13. The land area of Yosemite National Park is 3079 km^2. This is about 189% of the land area of Sequoia National Park. Write 189% as a fraction in simplest form and as a decimal.

A $\frac{100}{189}$, 0.53 (rounded)   **C** $\frac{189}{100}$, 18.9

B $\frac{189}{100}$, 1.89   **D** $\frac{3079}{189}$, 16.29

14. Writing to Explain Nathan wanted to save $400 for a new bicycle. He saved 110% of his goal amount. Write 110% as a fraction in simplest form and as a decimal. Has he saved enough money to buy the bicycle? Explain how you know.

_____

_____

_____

_____

Estimating Percent

Estimate 8% of 300,000.	**Estimate 27% of 297.**
Round the percent. 8% ≈ 10%	Round both numbers. 27% ≈ 30% 297 ≈ 300
Think of the equivalent decimal. 10% = 0.1	Think of an equivalent decimal. 30% = 0.3
Multiply. 0.1 × 300,000 = 30,000	Multiply. 0.3 × 300 = 90

To multiply by 0.1, move the decimal point one place to the left.

 0.1 × 50 = 5 　　 0.1 × 4700 = 470 　　 0.1 × 3,659 = 365.9

To multiply by a multiple of 0.1, such as 0.3, break apart the number.
 0.3 = 0.1 × 3

Multiply one step at a time.
 0.1 × 300 = 30 　　 30 × 3 = 90

Round each percent, then write the equivalent decimal.

1. 41% _____ **2.** 88% _____ **3.** 76% _____

4. 22% _____ **5.** 37% _____ **6.** 59% _____

Break apart each decimal so the numbers are easier to multiply.

7. 0.4 _____ **8.** 0.9 _____ **9.** 0.6 _____

Estimate each percent.

10. 9% of 20 _____ **11.** 21% of 31 _____ **12.** 31% of 37 _____

13. 38% of 49 _____ **14.** 49% of 101 _____ **15.** 61% of 19 _____

16. 59% of 304 _____ **17.** 70% of 471 _____ **18.** 84% of 149 _____

19. Number Sense What is another way to estimate 51% of 42?

_____

20. Reasoning If 10% of a number is 100, what is 15% of that number? Explain how you determined your answer.

_____

_____

Estimating Percent

Estimate.

1. 35% of 102 _____   2. 42% of 307 _____   3. 79% of 13 _____

4. 84% of 897 _____   5. 13% of 97 _____   6. 28% of 95 _____

7. 61% of 211 _____   8. 19% of 489 _____   9. 48% of 641 _____

10. 21% of 411 _____   11. 77% of 164 _____   12. 51% of 894 _____

13. 39% of 306 _____   14. 62% of 522 _____   15. 48% of 341 _____

16. **Number Sense** Which would you need to estimate to find an answer, 45% of 200 or 46% of 97?   _____

17. The school store sold 48 items on Monday. Of those items, 60% were pens. About how many pens were sold on Monday?   _____

18. The school cafeteria workers cooked 52 lb of pasta on Thursday. Of that, 90% was sold on Thursday, and 10% was stored in the refrigerator. About how much pasta was stored in the refrigerator?   _____

19. On a rainy day, 76% of the students in the school brought umbrellas. There are 600 students in the school. About how many students brought umbrellas?   _____

20. Which of the following is the best estimate for 68% of 251?

    A 150

    B 175

    C 204

    D 210

21. **Writing to Explain** Explain how you would estimate 79% of 389.

    _____

    _____

    _____

    _____

Finding the Percent of a Number

Find 77% of 240.

First estimate.
$$77\% \approx 75\% = \frac{3}{4}$$
$$\frac{3}{4} \times 240 = 180$$

Use a decimal.
Change the percent to a decimal.
$$77\% = 0.77$$

Multiply.
$$0.77 \times 240 = 184.8$$

The answer 184.8 is close to the estimate 180.

Use a proportion.

Write the percent as a fraction.
$$77\% = \frac{77}{100}$$

Write the proportion and solve.
$$\frac{x}{240} = \frac{77}{100}$$
$$100x = 18,480$$
$$\frac{100x}{100} = \frac{18,480}{100}$$
$$x = 184.8$$

Find the percent of each number.

1. 25% of 24 _____

2. 50% of 72 _____

3. 72% of 88 _____

4. 18% of 97 _____

5. 66% of 843 _____

6. 46% of 388 _____

7. 89% of 111 _____

8. 0.7% of 392 _____

9. 110% of 640 _____

10. Geometry Ava's aquarium is 10 in. tall, 15 in. long, and 8 in. wide. The aquarium is 95% filled with water. How many cubic inches of water are in the aquarium?

_____

11. DeWayne used his music club membership card to get 15% off the cost of a CD. If the regular price of the CD was $15.95, how much did DeWayne pay?

_____

12. Marla bought a dress priced at $89.99. She used a 20% off coupon. How much did she pay for the dress?

_____

13. Writing to Explain Tell how you could use a proportion to find 125% of 500. Why is the solution greater than the original number?

_____

Finding the Percent of a Number

Find the percent of each number.

1. 42% of 800 _____ **2.** 5.6% of 425 _____ **3.** 85% of 15 _____

4. $33\frac{1}{3}$% of 678 _____ **5.** 12% of 65 _____ **6.** 58% of 324 _____

7. 98% of 422 _____ **8.** 32% of 813.5 _____ **9.** 78% of 219 _____

10. 13% of 104 _____ **11.** 24% of 529 _____ **12.** 4.5% of 82 _____

13. 64% of 912 _____ **14.** 128% of 256 _____ **15.** 63% of 1,368 _____

16. About 42% of the flag of the United States is red. On a flag that is 9 feet tall and 15 feet wide, how many square feet are red?

_____

17. Estimation Estimate 68% of 32, then find the actual answer. Which is greater?

_____

For **18** and **19**, round your answer to the nearest whole number.

18. An adult has 206 bones. Of those, approximately 2.9% are found in the inner ear. About how many bones in the human body are found in the inner ear?

_____

19. Approximately 12.6% of the bones are vertebrae in the human back. About how many bones in the human body are vertebrae?

_____

20. 45 is 12% of which number?

A 540 **B** 450 **C** 375 **D** 5.4

21. Writing to Explain Without calculating, tell which is greater, 52% of 3,400 or 98% of 1,500. Explain.

_____

Applying Percents: Finding the Whole

You can draw a number line model to help you solve this problem:

> Darlene spent 10% of her allowance and saved the rest. The amount she spent was 50 cents. How much is Darlene's allowance?

In the problem, 50 cents is the part and 10% is the percent. You need to find Darlene's allowance, *a*.

The model shows 10% as the percent, 50 cents as the part, and *a*, the whole you are trying to find.

A proportion can also help you find the whole.

$$\frac{10}{100} = \frac{50}{a}$$

$a = 500$

Think: 10 times what number equals 50?
Since $10 \times 5 = 50$, then
multiply 100×5 to get 500.

500 cents = $5.00

Darlene's allowance is $5.00.

For **1** through **3**, draw a number line model to help you solve the problem.

1. Li rode her bike 25% of the way to school. She rode 5 blocks. How many blocks does Li live from school?

_____

2. Bob brought 40% of the collected canned goods to the food pantry. If Bob brought 160 cans to the pantry, how many cans were collected?

_____

3. Sid memorized 60% of his lines for the class play. He memorized 60 lines. How many lines long was Sid's part in the play?

_____

Applying Percents: Finding the Whole

In **1** through **4**, use the number lines and write a proportion to solve.

1. 10% of what number is 30?

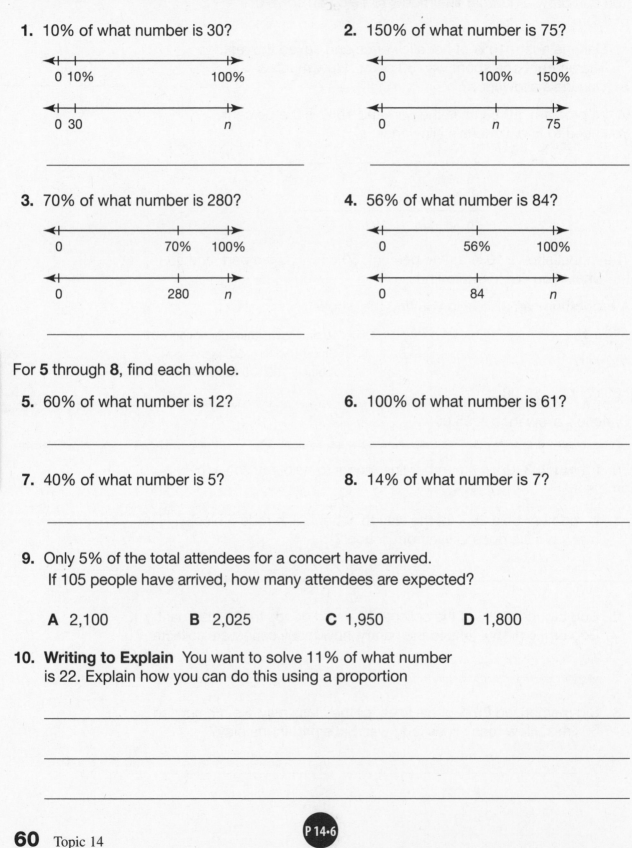

2. 150% of what number is 75?

_____

3. 70% of what number is 280?

_____

4. 56% of what number is 84?

_____

For **5** through **8**, find each whole.

5. 60% of what number is 12?

_____

6. 100% of what number is 61?

_____

7. 40% of what number is 5?

_____

8. 14% of what number is 7?

_____

9. Only 5% of the total attendees for a concert have arrived.
If 105 people have arrived, how many attendees are expected?

A 2,100   **B** 2,025   **C** 1,950   **D** 1,800

10. Writing to Explain You want to solve 11% of what number
is 22. Explain how you can do this using a proportion

_____

_____

_____

Problem Solving: Reasonableness

After solving a problem, look back and check that your answer is reasonable and that you answered the correct question.

Terrell bought a skateboard on sale for 20% off the original price. He also had a coupon for 10% off. The original price was $80. How much did Terrell pay for the skateboard before tax?

Answer: Terrell paid $24 for the skateboard.

Is my answer reasonable?

Since the discount is about 30% off, Terrell will pay about 70% of the original cost of the skateboard.

70% of $80 is $56.

The answer is not reasonable because the price of the skateboard should be about 70% of the original price, or $56.

Did I answer the correct question?

Yes. The question asks for the sale price of the skateboard.

Ask yourself:

Did I use the correct operation(s) to solve the problem?

Is all of my work correct?

Is the actual answer close to my estimate?

Ask yourself:

What am I asked to find?

Look back and check. Tell if the answer given is reasonable. Explain why or why not.

1. Marita bought some toys for her cat at the pet store. The pet store is having a storewide discount of 15% on all pet toys. How much will Marita pay for the toys if the total price before the discount is $42? *Answer: The discount price is $35.70.*

_____

_____

2. Frankie paid a total of $53.50 for some fish for his aquarium. The price includes a coupon for 7% off. What was the cost of the fish? *Answer: The fish cost $50.00.*

_____

_____

Problem Solving: Reasonableness

Look back and check. Tell if the answer given is reasonable.
Explain why or why not.

1. A shipment of 200 games is 20% video games, 50% board games, and 30% puzzles. How many board games are chess if 25% of the board games are chess?
Answer: The number of chess games is 50.

_____

_____

2. A DVD player costs $199. How much will it cost if it is 15% off?
Answer: The cost of the DVD player will be $169.15.

_____

_____

3. Write a Problem An ad in the newspaper is offering 25% off ski lift tickets at Big Bear. The original tickets cost $60. Write a problem using the information from the ad. Then give an answer for someone to look back and check for reasonableness.

_____

_____

4. Students at Warm Springs Middle School are going on a field trip to Orange County. If 60% of the 120 students signed up for the field trip are girls, and 25% of the girls are in sixth grade, how many sixth grade girls are going on the field trip?

A 18　　　　　　**B** 25　　　　　　**C** 43　　　　　　**D** 102

5. Writing to Explain Bailey paid $42 for a backpack that was 40% off the original price. Is $56 a reasonable price for the original cost of the backpack? Explain.

_____

_____

Equations with More Than One Operation

Some equations require more than one operation to solve. When you solve an equation with more than one step, undo the operations in this order:

> • First undo addition or subtraction.
> • Then undo multiplication or division.

Solve $5x - 10 = 95$.	
Step 1: Undo subtraction. Add 10 to both sides.	$5x - 10 = 95$ $5x - 10 + 10 = 95 + 10$ $5x = 105$
Step 2: Undo multiplication. Divide both sides by 5.	$\frac{5x}{5} = \frac{105}{5}$ $x = 21$
Step 3: Check by substitution.	$5x - 10 = 95$ $5(21) - 10 = 95$ $105 - 10 = 95$ $95 = 95$ ✔
Solve $10 = \frac{n}{5} + 6$	
Step 1: Undo addition. Subtract 6 from both sides.	$10 = \frac{n}{5} + 6$ $10 - 6 = \frac{n}{5} + 6 - 6$ $4 = \frac{n}{5}$
Step 2: Undo division. Multiply both sides by 5.	$4 \times 5 = \frac{5 \times n}{5}$ $20 = n$
Step 3: Check by substitution.	$10 = \frac{n}{5} + 6$ $10 = \frac{20}{5} + 6$ $10 = 4 + 6$ $10 = 10$ ✔

Solve each equation and check your solution.

1. $8b + 16 = 64$ _____

2. $2y - 4 = 24$ _____

3. $\frac{q}{10} + 5 = 10$ _____

4. $\frac{m}{3} + 2 = 17$ _____

5. $\frac{p}{4} + 13 = 21$ _____

6. $5b - 8 = 17$ _____

7. $\frac{a}{3} - 17 = 14$ _____

8. $3d + 17 = 24.5$ _____

9. Number Sense Would you expect the solution of $4x + 12 = 36$ to be greater than or less than 36? Explain.

Equations with More Than One Operation

1. $12a + 24 = 48$ _____

2. $4z - 8 = 32$ _____

3. $\frac{x}{5} - 10 = 2$ _____

4. $\frac{p}{3} + 6 = 42$ _____

5. $5b + 15 = 30$ _____

6. $7n + 14 = 21$ _____

7. $\frac{c}{4} + 3 = 5$ _____

8. $\frac{q}{2} - 4 = 18$ _____

9. $17 + 3y = 38$ _____

10. $\frac{m}{4} - 17 = 4$ _____

11. $\frac{c}{12} + 12 = 21$ _____

12. $8z - 13 = 7$ _____

For **13** and **14**, write and solve an equation.

13. Yoshi's age is twice Bart's age plus 3. Yoshi is 13 years old. How old is Bart?

_____

14. Caleb and Winona both travel by car to their friend's home. The distance Winona traveled was 124 miles less than twice the distance Caleb traveled. If Winona traveled 628 miles, how far did Caleb travel?

_____

15. Critical Thinking Explain the mistake in this solution and find the correct solution.

$$6x + 15 = 69$$
$$6x = 84$$
$$x = 14$$

_____

_____

16. Number Sense Which is the value of n when $4n + 16 = 64$?

A $n = 4$ **B** $n = 8$ **C** $n = 12$ **D** $n = 16$

17. Writing to Explain Explain how to solve the equation $6x - 3 = 39$.

_____

_____

Patterns and Equations

Write a rule and an equation for the pattern in the table.

x	1	4	7	8	9
y	3	12	21	24	27

Think: How can I get to the value of *y* if I start at the value of *x*?
Think: 3 is 1 × 3   12 is 4 × 3
State a theory: It seems that 3 × *x* is equal to *y*.
Test the other pairs: 7 × 3 = 21 ✔   8 × 3 = 24 ✔   9 × 3 = 27 ✔
Write a rule: The value of *y* is the value of *x* times 3.
Write an equation: $y = x \times 3$, or $y = 3x$

Write a rule and an equation for the pattern in each table.

1.

x	3	6	11	13	15
y	5	8	13	15	17

_____

_____

2.

x	2	5	6	8	9
y	6	15	18	24	27

_____

_____

3.

x	4	12	20	36	40
y	1	3	5	9	10

_____

_____

4.

x	5	7	9	10	12
y	0	2	4	5	7

_____

_____

5. Write a Problem Complete the table to show a pattern. Then write
a rule and an equation for the pattern.

_____

x					
y					

_____

6. Writing to Explain Explain how you would find the pattern in this
table, and how you would write a rule and an equation for the pattern.

x	4	5	7	10	12
y	0	1	3	6	8

_____

Patterns and Equations

Write a rule and an equation to fit the pattern in each table in **1** through **6**.

1.

x	0	1	2	3	4
y	5	6	7	8	9

_____

_____

2.

x	12	18	21	24	36
y	4	6	7	8	12

_____

_____

3.

x	11	14	18	21	25
y	3	6	10	13	17

_____

_____

4.

x	0	1	2	4	6
y	0	4	8	16	24

_____

_____

5.

x	3	9	13	22	27
y	10	16	20	29	34

_____

_____

6.

x	0	1	2	3	4
y	0	3	6	9	12

_____

_____

7. The Gadget Factory sells winkydiddles in different quantities, as shown by the table. How much would ten winkydiddles cost?

Number of Winkydiddles	7	12	26	31
Cost	$24.50	$42.00	$91.00	$108.50

_____

8. Which equation best describes the pattern in the table?

x	4	9	12	16	19
y	2	4.5	6	8	9.5

A $y = 2x$ **B** $y = x - 1$ **C** $y = \frac{x}{2}$ **D** $y = x + 1$

9. Writing to Explain All the values of x in a table are greater than the corresponding values of y. If x is a positive integer, what operation(s) and circumstance(s) could explain this pattern?

_____

_____

More Patterns and Equations

The entry fee to a carnival is $3. Each ride ticket is $2. The cost of going to the carnival equals the entry fee plus two times the number of tickets purchased, $c = 3 + 2t$.

You can substitute numbers into the equation to make a table showing the cost compared to the number of tickets purchased.

$c = 3 + 2t$.

Tickets t	$3 + 2t$	Cost c
0	3 + 2(0)	$3
2	3 + 2(2)	$7
4	3 + 2(4)	$11
6	3 + 2(6)	$15

In **1** through **4**, use the equation to complete each table.

1. $y = 3x + 7$

x	0	1	2	3
y				

2. $y = 4x - 4$

x	2	4	6	8
y				

3. $y = 2x + 7$

x	1	3	5	7
y				

4. $y = \frac{1}{4}x + 5$

x	0	4	8	12
y				

5. Reasoning For the equation $y = 1x - 25$, will the value of y increase or decrease as x increases?

_____

6. Algebra Write an equation in words and in symbols to represent this situation:
Grace has $100. She is buying charms for her bracelet that cost $5 each. Write an equation showing the relationship between the number of charms (c) she buys and the amount of money she has left (l).

_____

_____

7. Number Sense How many charms can Grace buy before she runs out of money?

_____

R 15·3

More Patterns and Equations

In **1** through **4**, use the equation given to complete each table.

1. $y = 2x + 4$

x	0	1	2	3
y				

2. $y = 4x - 3$

x	5	6	7	8
y				

3. $y = 100 - 4x$

x	2	4	6	8
y				

4. $y = \frac{1}{3}x + 1$

x	0	3	6	9
y				

5. Writing to Explain Complete the table and write an equation for the pattern. Tell how you do it.

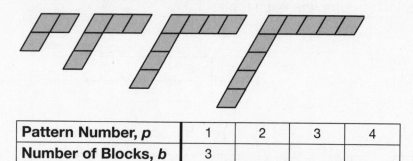

Pattern Number, p	1	2	3	4
Number of Blocks, b	3			

_____

_____

6. Algebra How many blocks are needed to make the 10th figure in the pattern above?

A 11 **B** 20 **C** 21 **D** 22

7. Reasoning Justin used 35 blocks to make a figure for the pattern above. What was the pattern number for the figure? _____

8. Write a Problem Write a problem that can be represented by this equation and table.

$y = 20x + 5$

x	1	2	3	4
y	25	45	65	85

_____

Graphing Equations

How to graph equations:

Graph the equation $y = x - 3$.

First make a T-table like the one at the right.

Use at least 3 values for x.

x	y
3	0
4	1
5	2

Graph each ordered pair onto the coordinate plane, then draw a line connecting the points. Every point on this line meets the condition that $y = x - 3$.

Because the graph of this equation is a straight line, it is called a linear equation.

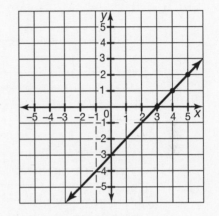

Complete each T-table. Then graph each equation.

1. $y = x + 1$

x	y
1	
2	
3	

2. $y = 3 - x$

x	y
0	
2	
3	

Graphing Equations

For **1** and **2,** make a T-table. Then graph each equation.

1. $y = x - 3$

2. $y = 2x$

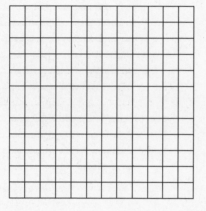

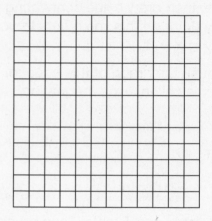

3. Reasoning Is the point (5, 6) on the graph for the equation $y = 2x + 5$?

_____

4. Which point is on the graph for the equation $y = x + 14$?

   A (2, 17)

   B (5, 20)

   C (10, 24)

   D (7, 23)

5. Writing to Explain Explain how making a T-table helps you graph an equation.

_____

_____

Graphing Equations with More Than One Operation

Use the same steps to graph an equation with more than one operation as you used to graph an equation with only one operation.
Graph $y = 2x - 4$.

Step 1: Make a T-table. Use at least three number pairs in the table.

x	y	Ordered Pairs
2	0	→ (2, 0)
3	2	→ (3, 2)
4	4	→ (4, 4)

Step 2: Graph each ordered pair on a coordinate plane. Connect the points.

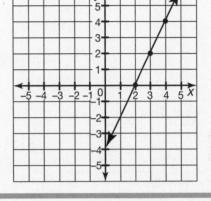

1. Complete the T-table and graph the equation.
   $y = 4x - 8$

x	y	Ordered Pairs
2		
3		
4		

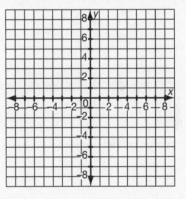

Graph $y = 6 - 2x$ at the right. Use it to answer **2** through **4**.

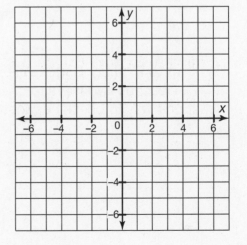

2. At what point does the equation
   $y = 6 - 2x$ cross the y-axis? _____

3. If $x = 2$, what is the value of y? _____

4. **Writing to Explain** Plot point (0, 4) on the grid.
   Is (0, 4) a solution to $y = 6 - 2x$? Explain.

   _____

Graphing Equations with More Than One Operation

For **1** and **2,** make a T-table and graph each equation.

1. $y = 3x - 5$

x	y

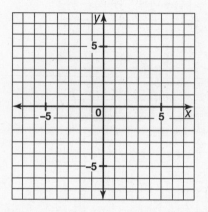

2. $y = 2x + 2$

x	y

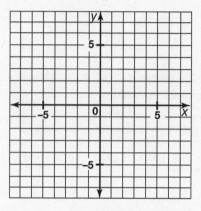

3. Which equation is shown by the graph?

A $y = 2x - 1$

B $y = x - 1$

C $y = 2x + 1$

D $y = x + 1$

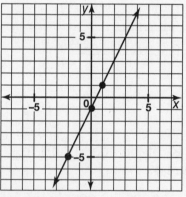

4. Writing to Explain Carrie says that one solution to $y = 3x - 5$ is (4, 7). Describe two ways to check if her statement is true. Use at least one way to check her answer.

_____

_____

Understanding Inequalities

An equation shows when expressions are equal. Equations use equal signs (=). An inequality is a statement that uses the greater-than symbol (>), the less-than symbol (<), the greater-than-or-equal-to symbol (≥), or the less-than-or-equal-to symbol (≤).

Variables can be used with inequalities. A variable in an inequality stands for all numbers that make the inequality true.

For example, in the inequality $x < 3$, the x stands for all numbers less than 3. So x can be 0, 1, or 2.

The inequality $13 \leq y + 5$ can have solutions $y = 8$, 9, and 10, since $8 + 5 = 13$, $9 + 5 = 14$, and $10 + 5 = 15$.

To graph $x < 3$, first draw an open circle on the number line above 3. Shade a line from the open circle to the left through the arrow. This represents all numbers that are less than 3.

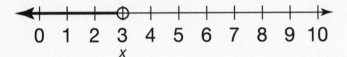

To graph x is greater than or equal to 5, first draw a closed circle on the number line at 5. Then shade a line from the closed circle to the right through the arrow.

1. Is 0 a solution of $x > 2$? _____

2. Is 5 a solution of $y \leq 10$? _____

3. Name 3 solutions for $z > 5$. _____

4. Name 3 solutions for $x \geq 4$. _____

5. Graph the inequality $x < 7$ on the number line below.

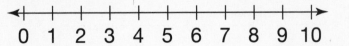

6. Graph the inequality $x \geq 4$ on the number line below.

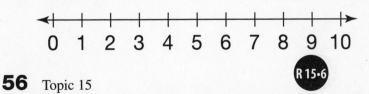

R 15·6

Understanding Inequalities

Give 3 values that solve the inequality for Exercises **1** through **16**.

1. $x > 0$ **2.** $y > 5$ **3.** $z \leq 10$ **4.** $z < 3$

_____   _____   _____   _____

5. $x > 4$ **6.** $x < 4$ **7.** $x > 170$ **8.** $x > 1$

_____   _____   _____   _____

9. $x < 9$ **10.** $x < 6$ **11.** $y > 2$ **12.** $y \geq 100$

_____   _____   _____   _____

13. $z < 8$ **14.** $x \geq 77$ **15.** $u > 10.9$ **16.** $u \leq 13.99$

_____   _____   _____   _____

17. Draw the inequality $x < 7$ on a number line.

18. Draw the inequality $x \geq 7$ on a number line.

19. Which is NOT a solution to $x > 18$?

    A 18   **B** 18.000001   **C** 19   **D** 30

20. **Writing to Explain** Is 0 a solution to $x > 0$? Why or why not?

_____

_____

Problem Solving: Act It Out and Use Reasoning

You can use counters, tables, ordered pairs, and graphs to act out a problem and show your reasoning.

Jenna is creating a display of photographs at her school for shark-awareness week. She has 24 photographs that she can display on 4 walls and 4 bulletin boards. She wants to put the same number of photographs on each wall and the same number of photographs on each bulletin board. How many different ways can Jenna display the photographs on the walls and bulletin boards?

Make a Table
Use walls and bulletin boards as the labels in the table.

Use counters to find the possible ways.

Walls	0	1	2	3	4	5	6
Bulletin Boards	6	5	4	3	2	1	0

Write Ordered Pairs
(walls, bulletin boards)

(0, 6), (1, 5), (2, 4), (3, 3), (4, 2), (5, 1), (6, 0)

Make a Graph
You can use the table or ordered pairs to graph the different ways.

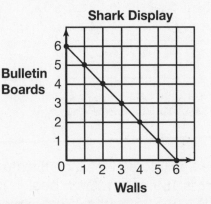

Shark Display

So, Jenna can display the shark photographs in 7 different ways on the walls and bulletin boards.

1. Cory is arranging 12 baseball caps on 2 shelves. He wants at least 2 caps on each shelf and the number of caps on each shelf to be even. How many possible ways can he arrange the caps on 2 shelves? Show your answer as ordered pairs.

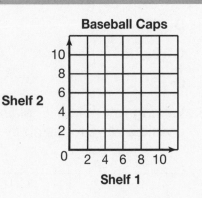

Baseball Caps

_____

2. Graph the solution for the above problem.

R 15·7

Problem Solving: Act It Out and Use Reasoning

1. A ranch owner has 18 bales of hay to distribute in 3 cow pastures and 3 horse pastures. He wants each cow pasture to have the same number of bales of hay and each horse pasture to have the same number of bales of hay. He wants at least 1 bale of hay in each pasture. How many different ways can hay be distributed among the pastures? Make a table to show your reasoning.

_____

2. A nursery has 10 tree seedlings to give out at 2 workshops. It wants to give out a minimum of 2 seedlings at each workshop. How many different ways can the nursery give out seedlings? Show your answer as ordered pairs.

_____

_____

3. Graph the solution to the tree seedling problem above.

4. A reading club at a bookstore gives a certificate for one free book after the reader earns 150 points. Each book a person reads is worth 3 points. Sonja has 96 points. What is the least number of books she needs to read to get the certificate?

   A 18

   B 23

   C 23

   D 54

5. **Writing to Explain** Explain how you know you found all of the possible ways to distribute the bales of hay in Problem 1.

_____

_____

_____

Converting Customary Measures

Units of Length

1 foot (ft)	= 12 in.
1 yard (yd)	= 3 ft
	= 36 in.
1 mile (mi)	= 5,280 ft
	= 1,760 yd

Units of Capacity

1 cup (c)	= 8 fluid ounces (oz)
1 pint (pt)	= 2 c
1 quart (qt)	= 2 pt
1 gallon (gal)	= 4 qt

Units of Weight

| 16 ounces (oz) | = 1 pound (lb) |
| 2,000 pounds | = 1 ton (T) |

How to change from one unit of measurement to another:

To change from larger units to smaller units, you have to multiply.

120 yd = _____ ft
1 yd = 3 ft
120 × 3 = 360
120 yd = 360 ft

To change from smaller units to larger ones, you have to divide.

256 oz = _____ c
1 c = 8 oz
256 ÷ 8 = 32
256 oz = 32 c

Complete.

1. 36 in. = _____ ft

2. 4 qt = _____ c

3. 5 lb = _____ oz

4. 39 ft = _____ yd

5. 1.5 mi = _____ ft

6. 3.5 gal = _____ qt

7. 2 T = _____ lb

8. 16 pt = _____ qt

9. 64 oz = _____ lb

10. 3 yd = _____ in.

11. 4 gal = _____ pt

12. 55 yd = _____ ft

13. 6.5 lb = _____ oz

14. 20 pt = _____ gal

15. 4.5 qt = _____ c

16. 205 yd = _____ ft

17. Reasoning A vendor at a festival sells soup for $1.25 per cup or $3.75 per quart. Which is the better buy?

_____

Converting Customary Measures

Complete.

1. 3.5 ft = _____ in.   **2.** 17 yd = _____ ft

3. 1.5 gal = _____ c   **4.** 4 mi = _____ ft

5. 160 fl oz = _____ qt   **6.** 72 in. = _____ ft

7. 3 mi = _____ yd   **8.** 12 pt = _____ qt

9. 180 ft = _____ yd   **10.** 2 gal = _____ fl oz

11. How many tons are in 35,000 lb? _____

12. Number Sense Brian pole vaulted over a bar that was 189 in.
high. How many more inches would he need to vault to go over
a bar that was 16 ft high?

_____

A paving company was hired to make a 4 mile section of the highway.
They need 700 tons of concrete to complete the job.

13. How many yards of highway do they need to repave?

_____

14. How many pounds of concrete will they need to repave the highway?

_____

15. Gary's cat weighs 11 lb. How many ounces is that?

A 132   **B** 144   **C** 164   **D** 176

16. Writing to Explain The average car manufactured in the United
States in 2001 could drive 24.5 mi on 1 gal of gas. Explain how to
find the number of yards the car can travel on 1 gal of gas.

_____

_____

_____

Converting Metric Measures

Changing from one metric unit to another:

To change from a larger unit to a smaller unit, multiply by a power of ten.

3.8 L = _____ mL

A liter is a larger unit than a milliliter. To change from liters to milliliters, multiply.

1 L = 1,000 mL

3.8 × 1,000 = 3,800

3.8 L = 3,800 mL

To change from a smaller unit to a larger unit, divide by a power of ten.

100 m = _____ km

The meter is a smaller unit than the kilometer. To change from meters to kilometers, divide.

1,000 m = 1 km

100 ÷ 1000 = 0.1

100 m = 0.1 km

Name the most appropriate metric unit for each measurement.

1. mass of a cow

_____

2. length of a carrot

_____

3. capacity of a thimble

_____

Complete.

4. 45 g = _____ mg

5. 3450 mL = _____ L

6. 4.5 m = _____ mm

7. 1.68 L = _____ mL

8. 28 cm = _____ mm

9. 7,658 g = _____ kg

10. 600 cm = _____ m

11. 5,000 mg = _____ g

12. 5.1 km = _____ m

13. 1.780 L = _____ mL

14. 0.780 L = _____ mL

15. 4,300 m = _____ km

16. 9,000 cm = _____ m

17. 8,000 mg = _____ g

18. Reasoning It is recommended that people have 1 g of calcium each day. How many milligrams of calcium is that?

_____

Converting Metric Measures

Name the most appropriate metric unit for each measurement.

1. mass of a paperclip _____

2. capacity of a water cooler _____

3. width of a sheet of paper _____

Complete.

4. 2.7 m = _____ cm

5. 1.6 kg = _____ g

6. 9 L = _____ mL

7. 14 m = _____ mm

8. 1.6 cm = _____ mm

9. 5,400 g = _____ kg

10. 1,840 mL = _____ L

11. 32 km = _____ m

12. **Number Sense** The chemist needs 2,220 mL of potassium chloride to complete an experiment. He has 2 L. Does he have enough to complete the experiment? Explain.

_____

13. A computer floppy disk has a mass of 20 g. How many would you need to have a total mass of 1 kg? _____

14. A battery is 5 cm long. How many batteries would you need to line up to get 3 m? _____

15. Which would you do to convert 25 cm to millimeters?

   A Divide by 10

   C Multiply by 10

   B Divide by 100

   D Multiply by 100

16. **Writing to Explain** A banana has a mass of 122 g. Explain how to find the mass of the banana in milligrams.

_____

_____

_____

Units of Measure and Precision

All measurements are approximations. The smaller unit of measure will be more precise than the larger unit of measure.

- ounce is more precise than pint
- $\frac{1}{8}$ inch is more precise than $\frac{1}{2}$ inch
- 0.001 kilogram is more precise than 0.01 kilogram

A pencil can be measured as 5 inches, $5\frac{1}{4}$ inches, $5\frac{3}{8}$ inches, or $5\frac{5}{16}$ inches.

Since $\frac{1}{16}$ is the smallest unit of measure, $5\frac{5}{16}$ is the most precise measurement.

Measure each line segment to the nearest $\frac{1}{8}$ inch and to the nearest centimeter.

1. _____

2. _____

Measure each line segment to the nearest $\frac{1}{16}$ inch and to the nearest millimeter.

3. _____

4. _____

5. _____

6. _____

7. **Geometry** Ed measured a piece of siding for his garage at 12 feet, $4\frac{3}{8}$ inches. Ed's father measured the same piece of siding at 12 feet, $4\frac{1}{4}$ inches. Which overall measurement is more precise? Why?

_____

8. **Writing to Explain** Abby measured the width of a doorway at 1 yd. Celia measured the same doorway at 3 ft 7 in. Which measurement is more precise? Explain.

_____

_____

R 16·3

Units of Measure and Precision

Measure each line to the nearest $\frac{1}{8}$ inch and to the nearest centimeter.

1. _____

2. _____

_____

3. _____

4. _____

_____

Measure each line segment to the nearest $\frac{1}{16}$ inch and to the nearest millimeter.

5. _____

6. _____

_____

7. _____

8. _____

_____

9. The mast of a sailboat was measured at 14.5 feet, 14.48 feet, and 14 feet $5\frac{3}{16}$ inches. Which is the most precise measurement? Why?

_____

10. A Maui's Dolphin is measured at 9.4 meters. Name three units of measure that would be more precise than the unit used to measure the dolphin.

_____

11. The doctor prescribed some powdered medicine in 3-centigram doses. The pharmacist prepared the medicine by measuring each dose in milligrams. Which measure is most precise? Why?

_____

12. You can buy soup measured in cups, fluid ounces, pints, or quarts. Which measure would give you the most precise measurement?

   A cups   **B** pints   **C** fluid ounces   **D** quarts

13. **Writing to Explain** Which would be a more precise unit of measure: 1 cm or 1 mm? Explain your reasoning.

_____

_____

Relating Customary and Metric Measures

You can convert between customary and metric measures using the table below.

Customary and Metric Unit Equivalents

Length	Weight/Mass	Capacity
1 in. = 2.54 cm	1 oz ≈ 28.35 g	1 L = 1.06 qt
1 m ≈ 39.37 in.	1 kg ≈ 2.2 lb	1 gal = 3.79 L
1 mi ≈ 1.61 km	1 metric ton (t) = 1.102 T	

You multiply to convert a larger unit to a smaller unit. For example, multiply when converting from inches to centimeters.

You divide to convert a smaller unit to a larger unit. For example, divide when converting from kilograms to pounds.

4 in. = _____ cm

An inch is larger than a centimeter. To convert from inches to centimeters, multiply.

1 in. = 2.54 cm

$4 \times 2.54 = 10.16$

4 in. = 10.16 cm

174 lb = _____ kg

A pound is a smaller unit than a kilogram. To convert from pounds to kilograms, divide.

1 kg ≈ 2.2 lb

$174 \div 2.2 \approx 79.09$

174 lb ≈ 79.09 kg

Complete. Round to the nearest tenth.

1. 12 gal ≈ _____ L

2. 35 lb ≈ _____ kg

3. 125 in. ≈ _____ m

4. 70 mi ≈ _____ km

5. 34 in. ≈ _____ cm

6. 20 kg ≈ _____ lb

7. 55 oz ≈ _____ g

8. 18 L ≈ _____ qt

9. Reasoning Which is a faster speed limit, 65 mi per hour or 100 km per hour?

_____

_____

Relating Customary and Metric Measures

Complete. Round to the nearest tenth.

1. 100 cm ≈ _____ in.

2. 16.5 gal ≈ _____ L

3. 24.8 kg ≈ _____ lb

4. 375 yd ≈ _____ m

5. 11.5 ft ≈ _____ cm

6. 24 oz ≈ _____ g

7. Estimation Use 1 t ≈ 1.1 T to estimate the
number of tons in 10 t.   _____

8. Reasoning If a recipe calls for 4 c of milk,
and you have 1 L of milk, would it be enough?   _____

Convert each. Round to the nearest tenth.

9. The number of feet in the 200 m race   _____

10. The number of miles in the 5,000 m race   _____

11. The number of miles in the 20 km race   _____

12. The phrase *800 lb gorilla* means you are facing a tough task.
How might you change this phrase to express it in metric terms?

_____

_____

13. Sarah has 2 L of milk. How many quarts of milk is this?

A 1.6   **B** 1.9   **C** 2.12   **D** 21.12

14. Writing to Explain Billy wants to ride the roller coaster. A sign
says he must be 138 cm tall. Explain how Billy can convert the
measurement to feet and inches.

Time

You can add or subtract units of time to find the elapsed time for an event, or to find the start or end of a period of elapsed time.

The movie started at 7:20 P.M. The theater showed 12 minutes of previews for upcoming movies and then began the main feature. The movie ended at 9:16 P.M. How long was the main feature?

Step 1: Add the time of the ads to the start time to find when the main feature started. Write the times in hours (h) and minutes (min).

Start time: 7 h   20 min

Time of ads   +   12 min
                  _____
                    7 h   32 min   The main feature began at 7:32 P.M.

Step 2: Subtract the time the movie started from the time it ended.

End time: 9 h 16 min   To subtract,   8 h 76 min
                                     regroup 1 hour
Start time: – 7 h 32 min   as 60 minutes,   – 7 h 32 min
                                                        _____
                                                         1 h 44 min

The movie was 1 hour 44 minutes long.

Find each elapsed time.

1. Start: 2:17 P.M.
   End: 7:28 P.M.

   _____

2. Start: 9:15 A.M.
   End: 11:08 A.M.

   _____

3. Start: 10:32 A.M.
   End: 1:56 P.M.

   _____

Find each start or end time.

4. Start: 4:13 P.M.
   Elapsed: 3 h 12 min

   _____

5. Start: 3:44 P.M.
   Elapsed: 8 h 2 min

   _____

6. End: 12:03 A.M.
   Elapsed: 5 h 52 min

   _____

7. Kari ran some errands for her mother. She left the house at 9:38 A.M. and returned at 11:14 A.M. How long did it take Kari to run the errands?

   _____

8. Gregg works the second shift at the factory. He reports to work at 2:45 P.M. and leaves at 11:00 P.M. During his shift he takes two 20-minute coffee breaks and one $\frac{1}{2}$ hour lunch break. How long does Gregg spend actually working?

   _____

Time

Find each elapsed time.

1. Start: 1:26 A.M.
End: 4:31 A.M.

_____

2. Start: 2:08 P.M.
End: 11:43 P.M.

_____

3. Start: 5:16 A.M.
End: 8:00 A.M.

_____

4. Start: 9:38 P.M.
End: 1:16 A.M.

_____

5. Start: 12:04 A.M.
End: 1:37 P.M.

_____

6. Start: 5:27 P.M.
End: 12:00 P.M.

_____

Find the start time or the end time using the given elapsed time.

7. Start: 4:58 P.M.
Elapsed: 2 h 37 min

_____

8. End: 6:31 A.M.
Elapsed: 3 h 40 min

_____

9. Start: 8:22 A.M.
Elapsed: 6 h 5 min

_____

10. End: 9:00 P.M.
Elapsed: 5 h 19 min

_____

11. Start: 11:42 A.M.
Elapsed: 4 h 45 min

_____

12. End: 12:22 A.M.
Elapsed: 7 h 51 min

_____

13. In 1990, Gary Stewart of California set a world record by
making 177,737 consecutive jumps on a pogo stick in 20 hours
20 minutes. If he began at 10:30 A.M. on Tuesday, at what time did
he stop?

_____

14. The play began at 7:30 P.M., and included two 20-minute
intermissions. If the play lasts 2 hours 35 minutes, at what
time did the play end?

A 9:45 P.M.   **B** 9:55 P.M.   **C** 10:25 P.M.   **D** 10:45 P.M.

15. Writing to Explain Sara leaves home for work at 6:55 A.M. She gets home after work
at 5:10 P.M. Explain what must be considered in finding how long she spends away
from home. Then solve the problem.

_____

_____

_____

Problem Solving: Use Reasoning

School Fair At the school fair, game winners could exchange their prizes for other prizes. The table shows some of the possible exchanges. Michael wants to find how many notebooks he would need to trade for one mug.

Prize Trade
10 pencils = 1 notebook
4 notebooks = 1 banner
4 banners = 1 t-shirt
2 mugs = 1 t-shirt

Read and Understand

What do you know?   Prize winners can exchange prizes using the equivalencies in the table.

What are you trying to find?   The number of notebooks that can be traded for one mug.

Plan and Solve

What strategy will you use?   Use reasoning.

You know that 2 mugs can be traded for 1 t-shirt. The table shows that 4 banners can also be traded for 1 t-shirt.

You know that 4 notebooks can be traded for 1 banner. You need 4 banners for 1 t-shirt. To get 4 banners you need 4×4, or 16 notebooks.

So, 16 notebooks can be traded for 1 t-shirt, which can be traded for 2 mugs. Michael wants 1 mug. He cannot cut a t-shirt in half, but he can divide the number of notebooks by 2: $16 \div 2 = 8$. Michael needs 8 notebooks to trade for 1 mug.

Look Back and Check

Is your answer reasonable?   Yes, 2 mugs can be traded for 4 banners, so 1 mug can be traded for 2 banners. Eight notebooks can also be traded for 2 banners.

Use the data in the Example to solve the problems.

1. How many banners are needed to trade for 8 t-shirts?

_____

2. How many pencils are needed to trade for a notebook and a banner?

_____

3. How many banners are needed to trade for 6 mugs? Explain.

_____

_____

Problem Solving:
Use Reasoning

Robert made a number line game with three sizes of jumps: small, medium, and large.

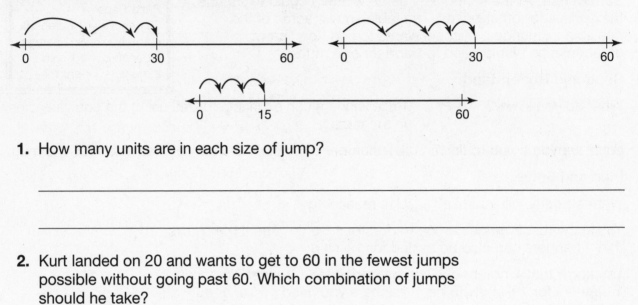

1. How many units are in each size of jump?

_____

_____

2. Kurt landed on 20 and wants to get to 60 in the fewest jumps possible without going past 60. Which combination of jumps should he take?

   A 8 small jumps

   B 3 medium jumps and 2 small jumps

   C 2 large jumps and 1 medium jump

   D 1 large jump, 2 medium jumps, and 1 small jump

3. Monique landed on 35. What are two ways she can get to 60 in exactly three jumps.

_____

4. How can you get from 0 to 60 in exactly seven jumps if you use at least one jump of each size?

_____

5. **Writing to Explain** Harvey has a 3-qt container and a 5-qt container. How can he measure exactly 4 qt of water?

_____

_____

_____

_____

Perimeter

Find the perimeter of the figure below.

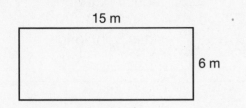

15 m

6 m

By using a formula:

There are two equal lengths and equal widths, so you can use the formula

$P = 2\ell + 2w$.

$P = 2(6) + 2(15)$

$= 12 + 30$

$= 42$

The perimeter is 42 m.

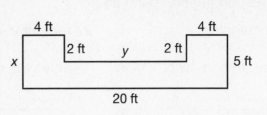

4 ft   4 ft

2 ft   y   2 ft

x   5 ft

20 ft

Sometimes you are not given the lengths of all the sides of a polygon.

Side x is the same size as the side parallel to it. So, side $x = 5$ ft.

You can figure out the length of side y by looking at the side parallel to it. That side is 20 ft.

4 ft + 4 ft + y ft = 20 ft

8 ft + y ft = 20 ft

8 ft + 12 ft = 20 ft

So, $y = 12$ ft.

Now you can add up all the sides to find the perimeter.

4 + 2 + 12 + 2 + 4 + 5 + 20 + 5 = 54

$P = 54$ ft

Find the perimeter of each figure.

1. rectangle, length 5.1 ft, width 7.4 ft

2. regular octagon, sides 4.6 cm long

_____

Find the length of each unknown side. Then find the perimeter.

3.

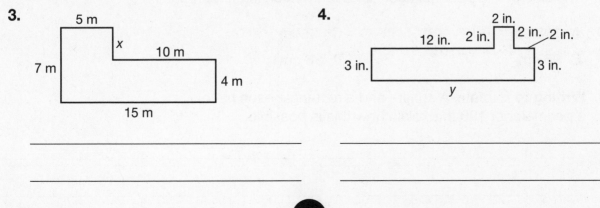

5 m

x

10 m

7 m

4 m

15 m

4.

2 in.

12 in.   2 in.   2 in. 2 in.

3 in.   3 in.

y

_____

R 17-1

Perimeter

Find the perimeter of each figure.

1. rectangle

length 6 in., width 14 in.

_____

2. regular pentagon

sides 3.3 cm long

_____

3. regular octagon

sides $8\frac{3}{4}$ in. long

_____

Estimate the perimeter of each figure. Then find the perimeter.

4. 11.97 m   8.21 m

5. 21.46 cm   16.03 cm   15.41 cm   18.9 cm

_____

_____

Find the length of each unknown side. Then find the perimeter.

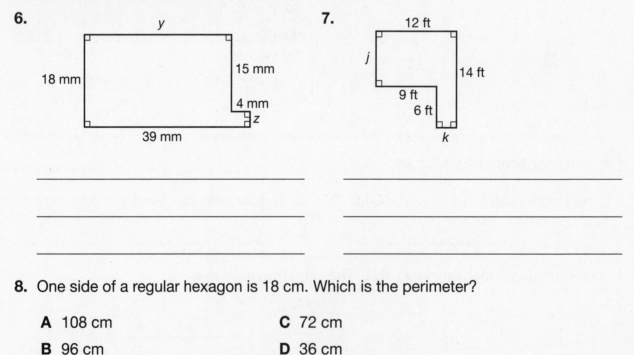

6. y   18 mm   15 mm   4 mm   z   39 mm

7. 12 ft   j   14 ft   9 ft   6 ft   k

_____

_____

_____

_____

_____

_____

8. One side of a regular hexagon is 18 cm. Which is the perimeter?

A 108 cm

B 96 cm

C 72 cm

D 36 cm

9. Writing to Explain A square and a rectangle each have a perimeter of 100 ft. Explain how this is possible.

_____

_____

Name _____

Area of Rectangles and Irregular Figures

Find the area of a rectangle that is 8 inches long and 3 inches wide.

Use Counting
Draw the rectangle on graph paper. Let each square represent 1 square inch.

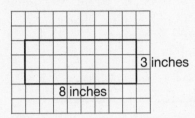

Count the squares inside the rectangle. There are 24 squares, so the area is 24 sq in.

Use a Formula
Use the formula for area. To find area, multiply length times width.

$A = \ell \times w$ ℓ = length, w = width
$A = 8 \times 3$ $\ell = 8, w = 3$
$A = 24$

The area of the rectangle is 24 sq in.

A path around a garden measures 8 ft by 7 ft. The garden measures 4 ft by 3 ft. What is the area of the path?

Use Counting
Draw the figure on graph paper. Let each square represent 1 square foot.

Count the squares in the path only. There are 44 squares, so the area is 44 sq ft.

Use a Formula
Find the total area of the path and then subtract the area of the garden.

Path: Display:
$A = \ell \times w$ $A = \ell \times w$
$A = 8 \times 7$ $A = 4 \times 3$
$A = 56$ sq ft $A = 12$ sq ft

$56 - 12 = 44$, so the area is 44 sq ft.

Find the area of each figure.

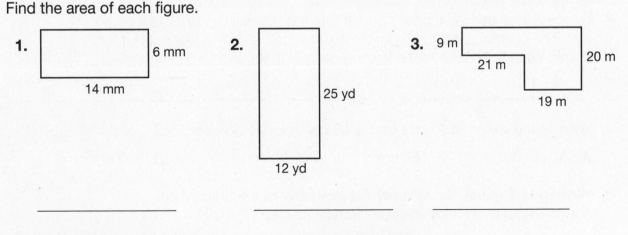

1. 6 mm   14 mm

2. 25 yd   12 yd

3. 9 m   21 m   20 m   19 m

_____   _____   _____

4. Suppose a rectangular path around a rectangular garden measures 4 meters by 7 meters. The garden measures 3 meters by 6 meters. What is the area of the path?   _____

R 17·2

Area of Rectangles and Irregular Figures

Find the area of each figure.

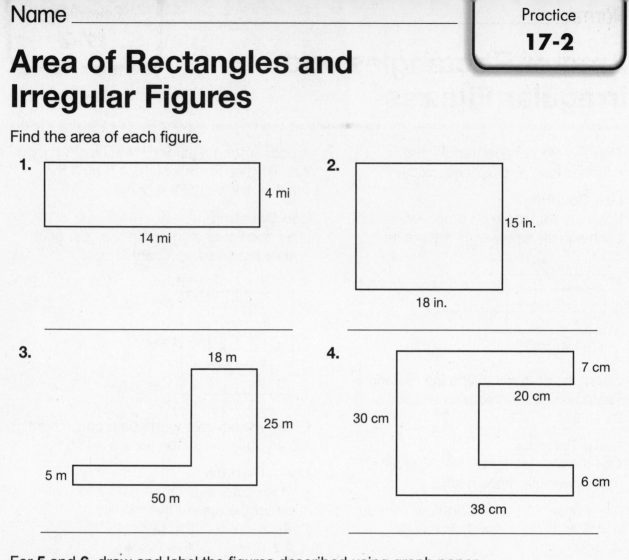

1.

4 mi

14 mi

_____

2.

15 in.

18 in.

_____

3.

18 m

25 m

5 m

50 m

_____

4.

7 cm

20 cm

30 cm

6 cm

38 cm

_____

For **5** and **6**, draw and label the figures described using graph paper.
Then calculate the area of each figure.

5. A rectangle that is 13 units by 9 units

_____

6. Carlos is laminating a kitchen counter that has dimensions of 12 feet by 3
feet. The counter has a hole with dimensions of 3 feet by 2 feet cut in it for
a sink. What is the area of the kitchen counter that Carlos will laminate?

_____

7. What is the area of a square that is 30 centimeters on one side?

A 60 cm²   **B** 120 cm²   **C** 300 cm²   **D** 900 cm²

8. Writing to Explain If you know the perimeter of a rectangle but
not its length or width, can you calculate its area? Explain.

_____

_____

Area of Parallelograms and Triangles

Find the area of this parallelogram.

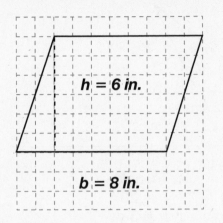

Use the formula $A = bh$.

$A = 8 \times 6$

$A = 48$ sq in.

The area of the parallelogram is 40 sq in.

Find the area of this triangle.

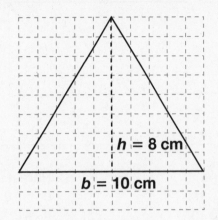

Use the formula $A = \frac{1}{2} bh$.

$A = \frac{1}{2} \times 10 \times 8$

$A = 5 \times 8$

$A = 40$ cm^2

The area of the triangle is 40 cm^2.

Find the area of each parallelogram or triangle.

1.

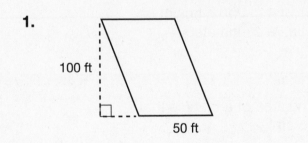

100 ft

50 ft

_____

2.

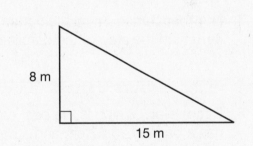

8 m

15 m

_____

3. Triangle: $b = 6$ ft, $h = 9$ ft

4. Parallelogram: $b = 18$ m, $h = 13$ m

5. Triangle: $b = 20$ in., $h = 9$ in.

6. Writing to Explain Tony says he does not have enough information to find the area of this parallelogram. Is he correct? Explain.

7.2 cm

14.5 cm

_____

Area of Parallelograms and Triangles

Find the area of each parallelogram or triangle.

1.

11 ft

14 ft

_____

2.

18 cm

12 cm

_____

3. Triangle
$b = 30$ m
$h = 15$ m

4. Parallelogram
$b = 18$ in.
$h = 2$ ft

5. Triangle
$b = 20$ ft
$h = 3$ yd

_____   _____   _____

6. Writing to Explain The area of a triangle is 42 square inches. The triangle's base is 6 inches. Find the height of the triangle. Explain how you do it.

_____

_____

7. Number Sense A parallelogram has a base of 4 m and a height of 3 m. Find the area of the parallelogram in square centimeters.

_____

8. Estimation Which is the best estimate of the area of a triangle that has a base of 23.62 cm and a height of 8.33 cm?

A 200 cm^2 **B** 160 cm^2 **C** 100 cm^2 **D** 50 cm^2

9. Reasoning The area of a figure is 36 cm^2. Give 4 possible shapes of the figure. Where possible give 3 possible sets of dimensions for each possible shape.

_____

_____

_____

P 17·3

Circumference

Find the circumference. Use 3.14 or $\frac{22}{7}$ for π.

Use the formula $C = 2\pi r$.

$C = 2\pi r$
$C = 2 \times 3.14 \times 8$
$C = 6.28 \times 8$
$C = 50.24$ m

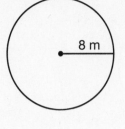

Find the diameter and the radius of a circle with a circumference of 65.94 in.

Divide by π to find the diameter.

$65.94 \div \pi = d$
$65.94 \div 3.14 = 21$
$d = 21$ in.

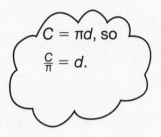

$C = \pi d$, so
$\frac{C}{\pi} = d$.

To find the radius, divide the diameter by 2.

$21 \div 2 = 10.5$
$r = 10.5$ in.

Find each circumference. Use $\frac{22}{7}$ or 3.14 for π.

1.

9.5 m

2.

14.4 ft

3.

12.4 cm

_____   _____   _____

Find the missing measurements for each circle. Round to the nearest hundredth.

4. $C = 39.25$ ft.

$d =$ _____

5. $C = 63.3024$ m

$r =$ _____

6. $r = 5.95$ yd

$C =$ _____

7. Number Sense Which circle has the greater circumference: a circle with a diameter of 13.2 in., or a circle with a radius of 6.9 in.? Explain.

_____

_____

_____

R 17·4

Circumference

Find each circumference. Use 3.14 or $\frac{22}{7}$ for π.

1.

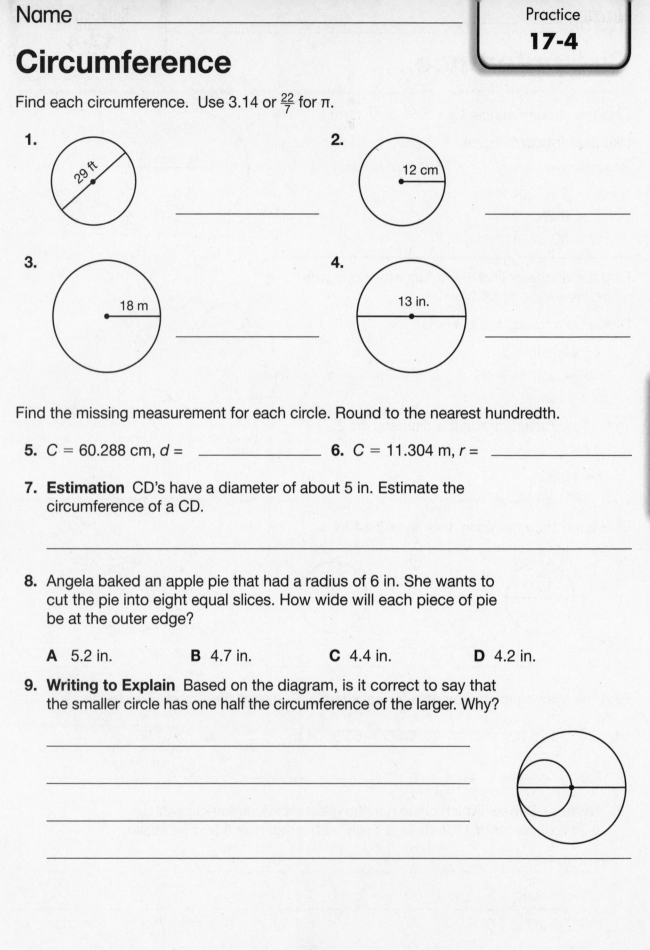

29 ft

_____

2.

12 cm

_____

3.

18 m

_____

4.

13 in.

_____

Find the missing measurement for each circle. Round to the nearest hundredth.

5. $C = 60.288$ cm, $d =$ _____

6. $C = 11.304$ m, $r =$ _____

7. Estimation CD's have a diameter of about 5 in. Estimate the circumference of a CD.

_____

8. Angela baked an apple pie that had a radius of 6 in. She wants to cut the pie into eight equal slices. How wide will each piece of pie be at the outer edge?

A 5.2 in.   **B** 4.7 in.   **C** 4.4 in.   **D** 4.2 in.

9. Writing to Explain Based on the diagram, is it correct to say that the smaller circle has one half the circumference of the larger. Why?

_____

_____

_____

Area of a Circle

A circular bucket has a radius of 6 in. Find the area of the bottom of the bucket. The formula for finding the area of a circle is $A = \pi r^2$.

One Way

Use 3.14 for π.

$A = \pi r^2$

$= 3.14 \times 6^2$

$= 3.14 \times 36$

$= 113.04$ in^2

Another Way

Use $\frac{22}{7}$ for π.

$A = \pi r^2$

$= \frac{22}{7} \times 6^2$

$= \frac{22}{7} \times 36$

$= \frac{22}{7} \times \frac{36}{1}$

$= \frac{792}{7}$

$= 113.14$ in^2

With a Calculator

Press: π × 6 x^2 =

Display: 113.09734

The bucket's area is about 113 in^2.

Find the area of each circle to the nearest whole number.
Use 3.14 or $\frac{22}{7}$ for π.

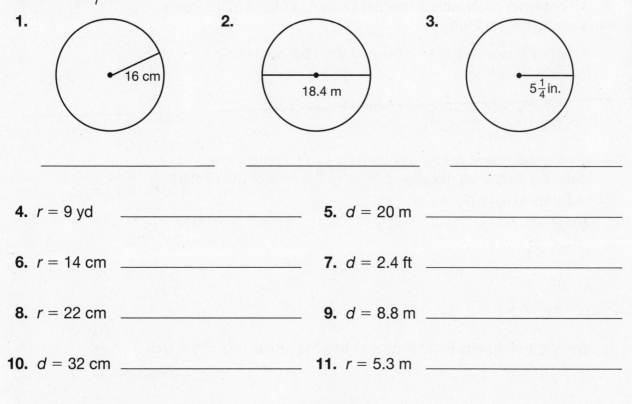

1. 16 cm

2. 18.4 m

3. $5\frac{1}{4}$ in.

_____   _____   _____

4. $r = 9$ yd _____   **5.** $d = 20$ m _____

6. $r = 14$ cm _____   **7.** $d = 2.4$ ft _____

8. $r = 22$ cm _____   **9.** $d = 8.8$ m _____

10. $d = 32$ cm _____   **11.** $r = 5.3$ m _____

12. Reasoning If the circumference of a circle is 18π, what is the area of the circle? _____

Area of a Circle

Find the area of each circle to the nearest whole number.
Use 3.14 or $\frac{22}{7}$ for π.

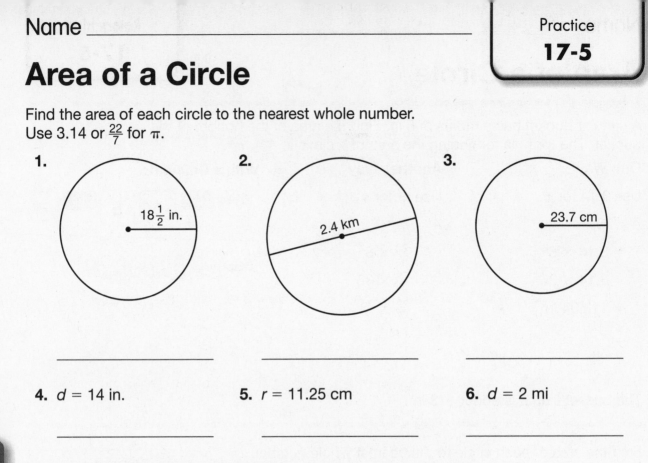

1. $18\frac{1}{2}$ in.

2. 2.4 km

3. 23.7 cm

_____   _____   _____

4. $d = 14$ in.   **5.** $r = 11.25$ cm   **6.** $d = 2$ mi

_____   _____   _____

Brian's dad wants to put a circular pool in their backyard. He can
choose between pools with diameters of 15 ft, 17 ft, or 22 ft. Round
to the nearest square foot.

7. How many more square feet would the 17 ft pool use
than the 15 ft pool?   _____

8. How many more square feet would the 22 ft pool
use than the 17 ft pool?   _____

9. On a water ride at the amusement park, a rotating valve sprays
water for 15 ft in all directions. What is the area of the circular
wet patch it creates?

A 30 ft^2

B 31.4 ft^2

C 94.2 ft^2

D 706.5 ft^2

10. Writing to Explain Explain how to find the radius of a circle with
an area of 50.24 mi.

_____

_____

_____

P 17·5

Problem Solving:
Use Objects

Pentomino Construction Company There are 12 different
pentominoes. Which two pentominoes can be used to make this
shape?

Read and Understand

What do you know? There are 12 different pentominoes.
Two pentominoes are used to construct this shape.

What are you trying to find? The two pentominoes used to make the shape.

Plan and Solve

What strategy will you use? Use objects, in this case pentominoes.

Study the shape and compare the corners and angles to the group of pentominoes.
Choose two pentominoes to make the figure.

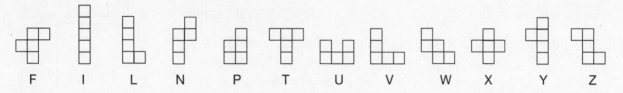

F I L N P T U V W X Y Z

Since the base is 5 units, try the I and the T pentominoes. If your first
choice does not work, try other pentominoes.

Look Back and Check

Is your answer reasonable? Yes. The two pentominoes make the same shape.

Fit two pentominoes together to create each shape. Draw the
pentominoes used in each figure.

1.

2.

3. Writing to Explain A figure is made from three pentominoes. What
is the area of the figure in square units? How did you find your answer?

_____

Problem Solving:
Use Objects

Fit two pentominoes together to create each shape. Draw the
pentominoes used in each figure.

1.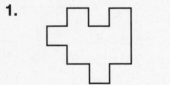

2.

3. What is the area in square units of each figure
you made in Problems 1 and 2? _____

4. Tessa used pentominoes to make this rectangle. The I pentomino
is shown. What is the area of the rectangle in square units?

   A 5 square units   **C** 20 square units

   B 6 square units   **D** 25 square units

5. Use nine pentominoes to make a figure that is three times the
size of the pentomino below. Two pentominoes have been
placed to get you started. Write the perimeter and the area
of both figures.

X

$A =$ _____ $P =$ _____ $A =$ _____ $P =$ _____

6. Writing to Explain Circle the pentominoes. Explain why any
figures are not pentominoes.

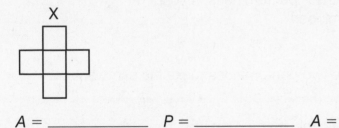

_____

_____

_____

_____

Solid Figures

Polyhedrons
Prisms

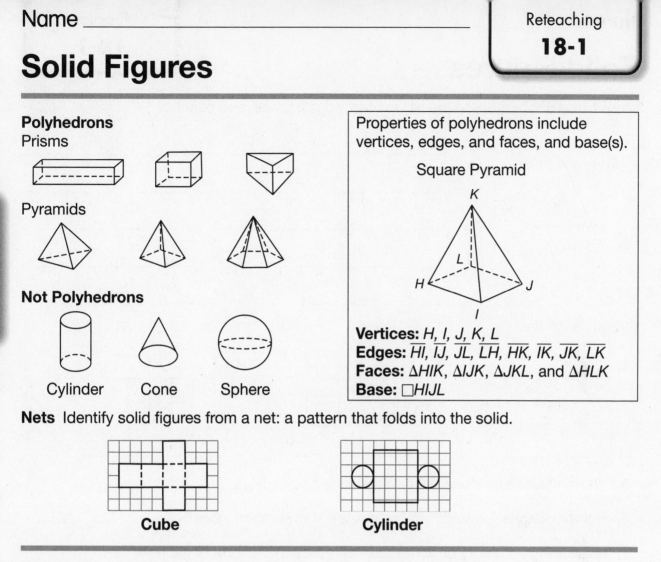

Pyramids

Not Polyhedrons

Cylinder   Cone   Sphere

Properties of polyhedrons include vertices, edges, and faces, and base(s).

Square Pyramid

Vertices: *H, I, J, K, L*
Edges: $\overline{HI}$, $\overline{IJ}$, $\overline{JL}$, $\overline{LH}$, $\overline{HK}$, $\overline{IK}$, $\overline{JK}$, $\overline{LK}$
Faces: $\triangle HIK$, $\triangle IJK$, $\triangle JKL$, and $\triangle HLK$
Base: $\square HIJL$

Nets Identify solid figures from a net: a pattern that folds into the solid.

Cube   **Cylinder**

Classify the polyhedron. Name all vertices, edges, faces, and bases.

1.

_____
_____
_____
_____
_____

In **2** through **4,** classify each figure.

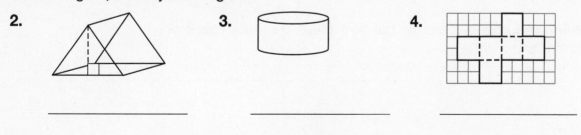

2.   **3.**   **4.**

_____   _____   _____

R 18·1

Solid Figures

Classify the polyhedron. Name all vertices, edges, faces, and bases.

1.

_____

_____

_____

_____

Classify each figure.

2.

3.

4.

_____ _____ _____

5. Which solid figure looks like a round cake?_____

6. **Number Sense** How many faces make up six number cubes? _____

7. **Reasoning** A factory buys the boxes it needs in the form of flat nets. What advantages might the factory have in doing this?

_____

_____

8. What is the name of the polyhedron shown below?

A Rectangular prism

B Hexagonal prism

C Pentagonal prism

D Octagonal prism

9. **Writing to Explain** Describe the similarities and differences of a cylinder and a cone.

_____

_____

Surface Area

You can use formulas to find the surface area of different solid figures.

Rectangular Prism

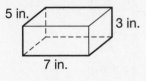

5 in. 3 in.

7 in.

$SA = 2\ell w + 2\ell h + 2wh$

$= 2(5 \times 7) + 2(5 \times 3) + 2(7 \times 3)$

$= 70 + 30 + 42$

$= 142$

The surface area is 142 in².

Triangular Prism

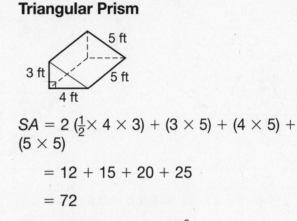

5 ft

3 ft 5 ft

4 ft

$SA = 2(\frac{1}{2} \times 4 \times 3) + (3 \times 5) + (4 \times 5) + (5 \times 5)$

$= 12 + 15 + 20 + 25$

$= 72$

The surface area is 72 ft².

Find the surface area of each figure.

1.

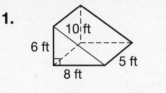

10 ft
6 ft
5 ft
8 ft

_____

2.

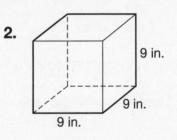

9 in.

9 in.

9 in.

_____

Find the surface area of each rectangular prism.

3. $\ell = 5.5$ cm, $w = 4.5$ cm, $h = 3.5$ cm

_____

4. $\ell = 15$ in., $w = 9$ in., $h = 3.8$ in.

_____

5. $\ell = 2$ yd, $w = 6$ yd, $h = 1.7$ yd

_____

6. Reasoning Write the dimensions of two different rectangular prisms that have the same surface area.

_____

_____

_____

Surface Area

Find the surface area of each figure.

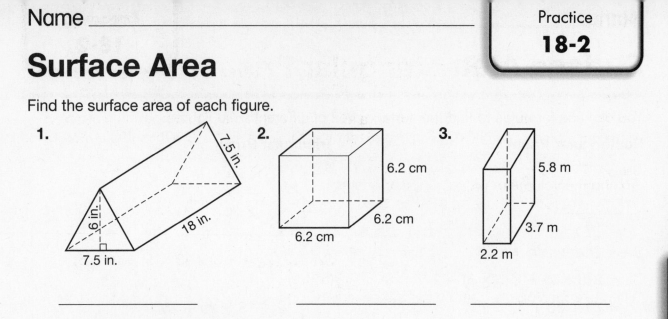

1. 7.5 in. 6 in. 18 in. 7.5 in.

2. 6.2 cm 6.2 cm 6.2 cm

3. 5.8 m 3.7 m 2.2 m

_____   _____   _____

Find the surface area of each rectangular prism.

4. ℓ = 6.9 mm, w = 8.2 mm, h = 14 mm   _____

5. ℓ = 3.4 cm, w = 12.7 cm, h = 16.5 cm   _____

6. ℓ = 5.7 yd, w = 9 yd, h = 12.9 yd   _____

7. Reasoning Margaret wants to cover a footrest in the shape of a
rectangular prism with cotton fabric. The footrest is 18 in. × 12 in. ×
10 in. She has 1 yd^2 of fabric. Can she completely cover the footrest?

_____

_____

_____

8. Which is the surface area of a rectangular prism with a length of
2.3 in., a width of 1.1 in., and a height of 3 in.?

A 26.48 in^2 **B** 25.46 in^2 **C** 24.58 in^2 **D** 21.5 in^2

9. Writing to Explain A square pyramid has 2 m sides on the base.
Each face is a triangle with a base of 2 m and a height of 1.5 m.
Explain how to find the surface area.

_____

_____

_____

Volume of Rectangular Prisms

Volume is the measure of space inside a solid figure. It is measured in cubic units. You can use a formula to find the volume of rectangular prisms: $V = B \times h$ where V stands for volume, B stands for the area of the base, and h stands for the height.

To find the volume of the rectangular prism at the right, first find the area of the base.

$B = \ell \times w$
$ = 4 \times 8$
$ = 32$ So the base is 32 sq in.

Then use the volume formula to find the volume.

$V = B \times h$
$ = 32 \times 5$
$ = 160$ So the volume is 160 sq in.

Find the volume of each rectangular prism. Don't forget to label the units.

1.

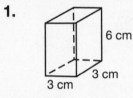

Area of Base ($B = \ell \times w$): _____

Volume ($V = B \times h$): _____

2.

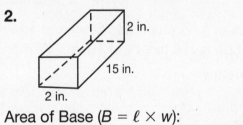

Area of Base ($B = \ell \times w$): _____

Volume ($V = B \times h$): _____

3.

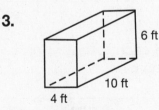

Area of Base ($B = \ell \times w$): _____

Volume ($V = B \times h$): _____

4.

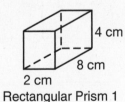

Area of Base ($B = \ell \times w$): _____

Volume ($V = B \times h$): _____

5. Find the volume of Rectangular Prism 1. How can you find the volume of Rectangular Prism 2 without using the volume formula?

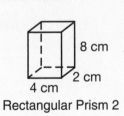

Rectangular Prism 1   Rectangular Prism 2

_____

_____

_____

Volume of Rectangular Prisms

Find the volume of each rectangular prism.

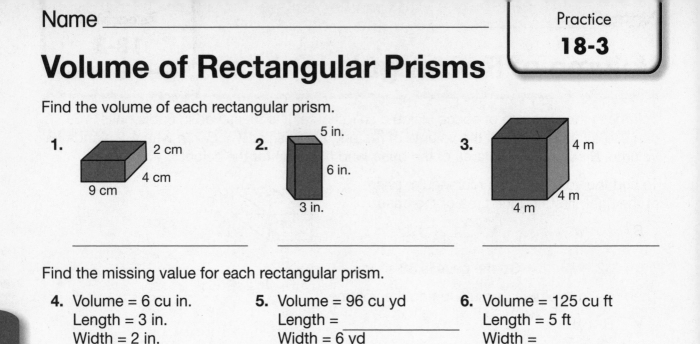

1.   2 cm
     4 cm
     9 cm

_____

2.   5 in.
     6 in.
     3 in.

_____

3.   4 m
     4 m
     4 m

_____

Find the missing value for each rectangular prism.

4. Volume = 6 cu in.
   Length = 3 in.
   Width = 2 in.
   Height = _____

5. Volume = 96 cu yd
   Length = _____
   Width = 6 yd
   Height = 8 yd

6. Volume = 125 cu ft
   Length = 5 ft
   Width = _____
   Height = 5 ft

7. **Number Sense** Suppose a box has a volume of 1 cu yd.
   What is its volume in cubic feet? _____

8. A rectangular prism has a base of 12 cm^2, a length of 3 cm, a width
   of 4 cm, and a height of 10 cm. Which is the volume of the prism?

   A 36 cm^3

   B 48 cm^3

   C 120 cm^3

   D 1,440 cm^3

9. **Writing to Explain** Find and compare the volumes of the two
   rectangular prisms below. How does doubling the measure of each
   dimension in a rectangular prism change the volume of the prism?

	Length	Width	Height	Volume
Rectangular Prism 1	5 ft	2 ft	10 ft	
Rectangular Prism 2	10 ft	4 ft	20 ft	

_____

_____

© Pearson Education, Inc. 6

Volume with Fractional Edge Lengths

When finding the volume of a rectangular prism with fractional edge lengths, you have to find the number of cubes with fractional edge lengths that can fill the prism. What is the volume of the rectangular prism shown below at the right?

Consider a $\frac{1}{2}$-inch cube. 8 half-inch cubes can fill a 1-inch cube.

Next, figure out how many $\frac{1}{2}$-inch cubes will fill the prism.
The prism can be filled with $5 \times 7 \times 3 = 105$ half-inch cubes.

Divide 105 by 8 because 8 half-inch cubes make up a
1-inch cube. $105 \div 8 = 13\frac{1}{8}$

The volume of this rectangular prism is $13\frac{1}{8}$ in^3.

For **1** through **4**, find the volume of each rectangular prism.

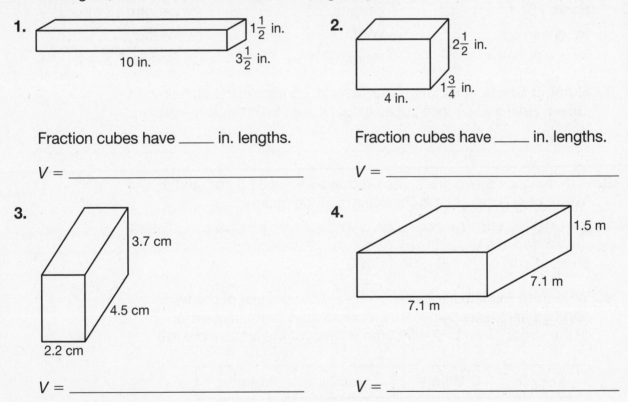

1.

10 in. $1\frac{1}{2}$ in. $3\frac{1}{2}$ in.

Fraction cubes have _____ in. lengths.

$V =$ _____

2.

$2\frac{1}{2}$ in. $1\frac{3}{4}$ in.   4 in.

Fraction cubes have _____ in. lengths.

$V =$ _____

3.

3.7 cm   4.5 cm   2.2 cm

$V =$ _____

4.

1.5 m   7.1 m   7.1 m

$V =$ _____

5. Writing to Explain How many $\frac{1}{2}$-inch cubes could fit inside the rectangular prism shown in Exercise 1? Explain how you know.

_____

_____

Volume with Fractional Edge Lengths

Find the volume of each rectangular prism.

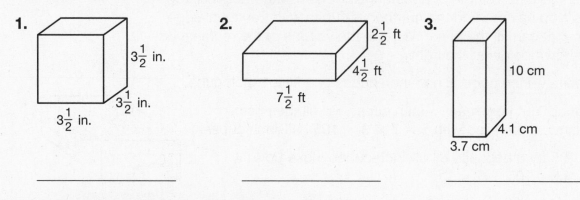

1. $3\frac{1}{2}$ in. $3\frac{1}{2}$ in. $3\frac{1}{2}$ in.

2. $2\frac{1}{2}$ ft $4\frac{1}{2}$ ft $7\frac{1}{2}$ ft

3. 10 cm 4.1 cm 3.7 cm

_____   _____   _____

Find the missing value for each rectangular prism.

4. Volume: $111\frac{3}{8}$ in^3
   Base: $20\frac{1}{4}$ in^2
   Height: _____

5. Volume: $8\frac{2}{3}$ ft^3
   Length: _____
   Width: $4\frac{1}{3}$ ft
   Height: $\frac{2}{3}$ ft

6. Volume: 758.16 mm^3
   Length: 13 mm
   Width: _____
   Height: 7.2 mm

7. **Number Sense** A rectangular prism can be filled with 210 half-inch cubes. How many $\frac{1}{4}$-inch cubes would it take to fill the same prism?

_____

8. A rectangular prism has a base with an area of 31.5 cm^2 and a height of 4.7 cm. What is the volume of the prism?

   A 36.2 cm^3 **C** 148.05 cm^3

   B 72.4 cm^3 **D** 296.1 cm^3

9. **Writing to Explain** Find and compare the volumes of the two rectangular prisms below. How does dividing each dimension of the larger prism by 2 affect the volume of the smaller prism?

Length	Width	Height	Volume
5 in.	$4\frac{1}{2}$ in.	6 in.	
$2\frac{1}{2}$ in.	$2\frac{1}{4}$ in.	3 in.	

_____

_____

Problem Solving:
Use Objects and Reasoning

Each cube has a volume of 1 cm³.

The area of one face of the cube is 1 cm².

The surface area of the cube is the sum of the area of each face of the cube.

To find the surface area of a figure of cubes, count only the faces that are exposed.

$V = 2(1 \times 1 \times 1) = 2$ cm³
$SA = 10(1 \text{ cm}^2) = 10$ cm²

The arrangement of cubes can affect the surface area, but the same number of cubes will always have the same volume.

1 cm
1 cm
1 cm
$V = 1 \times 1 \times 1 = 1$ cm³
$A(\text{face}) = 1 \times 1 = 1$ cm²
$SA = 6 \times 1 \text{ cm}^2 = 6$ cm²

$V = 4$ cm³
$SA = 18$ cm²

$V = 4$ cm³
$SA = 16$ cm²

1. Find the volume and surface area of the figure.

   _____

2. Make a figure of cubes that has a volume of 7 cm³ and a surface area of 26 cm². Draw your figure.

3. **Reasoning** Explain how you know how many cubes to use to make the figure in problem 2.

   _____

4. Find the volume and surface area of the figure.

   _____

5. **Geometry** If the cubes in problem 4 were increased to 3 cm on a side, how would the volume and surface area be affected?

   _____

   _____

Problem Solving:
Use Objects and Reasoning

Find the volume and surface area of each figure of centimeter cubes.

1.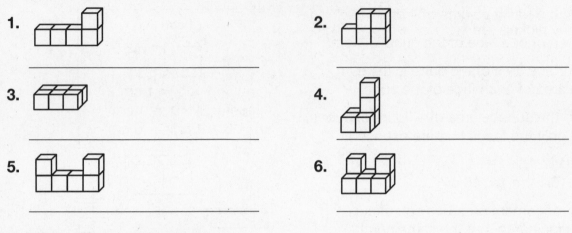
_____

2.
_____

3.
_____

4.
_____

5.
_____

6.
_____

7. Make a figure of cubes that has a
volume of 6 cm³ and a surface area
of 22 cm². Draw your figure.

8. **Critical Thinking** Without building a model, tell whether a long row of 8 cubes or
a cube made from 8 cubes would have a greater surface area. Explain.

_____

_____

9. Make a figure that has the same
volume as the diagram, but a greater
surface area. Draw your figure.

10. **Writing to Explain** Find the volume and surface area of these figures. Then describe
the pattern(s) you see. Can you determine the volume of the next element
in the pattern? The surface area? Explain.

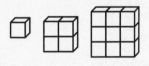

_____

_____

Practice 18-5

© Pearson Education, Inc. 6

Statistical Questions

To determine if a question you want to ask a group of people is statistical, ask yourself if it has several different answers.

How many nickels are in a dollar?　　**Not statistical**
How many nickels are in your bank?　　**Statistical**

A dot plot shows one way to display data collected from a statistical question.

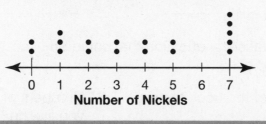

Number of Nickels in your Bank

Number of Nickels

For **1** through **6**, tell whether or not each question is statistical.

1. How many of the cards are baseball cards?

_____

2. When does summer break begin?

_____

3. Who is the current President of the United States?

_____

4. Who are the debate team members' favorite presidents?

_____

5. How long does it take sixth-grade students to eat lunch?

_____

6. Where are your classmates' favorite places to vacation?

_____

7. Writing to Explain Explain why *How many days did it rain in September this year?* is not a statistical question.

_____

8. Dean asked his class, *How many apples do you eat in a week?*
He got the following responses: 7, 5, 5, 5, 7, 3, 2, 1, 0, 0, 4, 3, 2, 1,
0, 7, 5, 6, 7, 0, 2, 2, 1, 4. Make a dot plot to display the data.

Statistical Questions

For **1** through **4**, tell whether or not each question is statistical.

1. What was the low temperature each day last month?

_____

2. What color shirt am I wearing?

_____

3. What size shoes do the students in your class wear?

_____

4. How long does it take students in a class to read a book?

_____

For **5** through **8**, write a statistical question that could be used to gather data on each topic.

5. Distances members of the track team jogged last week

_____

6. Numbers of letters in name of street you live on

_____

7. Cost of a restaurant dinner

_____

8. Numbers of cars of different colors in a parking lot

_____

9. The data shown are the responses to the question, *How tall, in centimeters, is each bean plant?* Make a dot plot to display the data.

| 8 | 6 | 7 | 5 | 8 | 6 | 8 | 7 | 9 | 4 |
| 5 | 2 | 8 | 6 | 9 | 5 | 7 | 6 | 7 | 7 |

10. What statistical question might Brittany have asked to get this data?

18 min, 20 min, 30 min, 16 min, 45 min

A How long did you spend on homework last night?

B How long do the directions say to cook the pie?

C At what time does school end?

D How many minutes does it take Eric to get to school?

11. Writing to Explain Wyatt says that statistical questions must involve numbers in the question. Do you agree with Wyatt? Explain.

_____

_____

Looking at Data Sets

You can describe a data distribution, or how data values are arranged, by looking at its overall shape, its center, and its least and greatest values.

By looking at this dot plot, you can describe the data distribution as being spread out to the right and not symmetric. The data is grouped between 50 and 51, and there is a gap between 55 and 60.

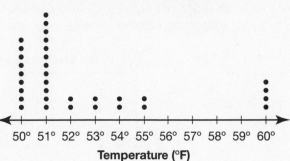

Temperatures in September

Temperature (°F)

The center of the data can be found by looking for the middle number in the largest group of data. A good estimate would be 50 or 51 because that is where most of the temperatures are plotted.

Use the dot plot to the right to answer the following questions.

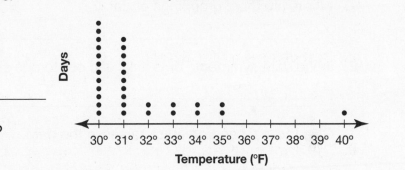

Temperatures in December

Days

Temperature (°F)

1. What is the least temperature? greatest temperature?

   _____

2. Are there any gaps in the data? If so, where?

   _____

3. What temperature would be considered an outlier?

   _____

4. Is the data symmetric or spread out to one side?

   _____

5. **Writing to Explain** Where do you think the center of the data is in the dot plot? Explain how you found your answer.

   _____

   _____

   _____

R 19·2

Looking at Data Sets

For **1** through **4**, use the dot plot.

Maria took a school survey to find out how many hours per week students watch television. Her results are in the dot plot below.

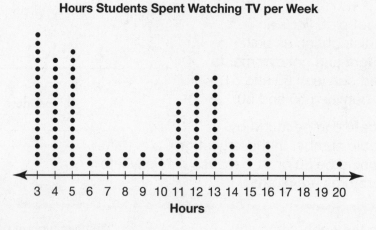

Hours Students Spent Watching TV per Week

Hours

1. Where are there groupings of data?

   _____

2. Is the data symmetric or is it spread out to one side?

   _____

3. Give the least and greatest values in the data.

   _____

4. **Writing to Explain** Using the dot plot for the hours students spend watching TV, where do you think the center of the data is? Explain how you found your answer.

   _____

   _____

For **5** and **6**, use the line plot.

5. Which is the best representation of the center of this data set?

   A 2 dogs   **B** 3 dogs

   C 4 dogs   **D** 5 dogs

6. Which best describes this data set?

   A Spread out to the left   **B** No noticeable shape

   C Spread out to the right   **D** Symmetric

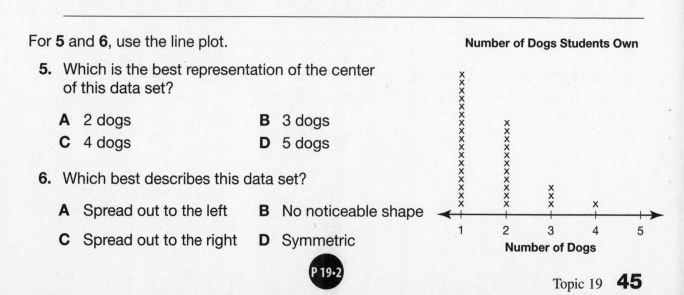

Number of Dogs Students Own

Number of Dogs

P 19·2

Mean

The mean is the sum of all the values in a set divided by the number of items in the set. The mean is also called the average.

How to find the mean of a set of data:

Eduardo surveyed 7 of his friends to find out how many books they read during the month. The frequency table hows the data. What is the average number of books read by Eduardo's friends?

Book Reading	
Friend	**Number of books read**
Jean	2
Raul	3
Sally	8
Jonathan	5
Haley	6
Kristen	3
Owen	1

1. Add the number of books read by each friend.

$2 + 3 + 8 + 5 + 6 + 3 + 1 = 28$

2. Divide the sum of by the number of friends.

$\frac{28}{7} = 4$

3. Use the average to answer the question.

Eduardo's friends read an average of 4 books during the month.

1. Find the mean of this set of data: 241, 563, 829, 755. _____

2. This frequency table shows the number of silver medals won by American athletes in Summer Olympic Games between 1972 and 2000. What is the mean of this set of data?

_____

3. **Estimation** What is the approximate average of these three numbers: 9, 18, and 31? _____

4. **Explain It** Explain how you would find the mean of this set of data: 4, 3, 5.

_____

_____

US Silver Medals Summer Olympics Games	
Year	**Medals**
2000	24
1996	32
1992	34
1988	31
1984	61
1980	0
1976	35
1972	31

Mean

Find the mean of each set of data.

1. 2, 5, 9, 4 _____

2. 44, 73, 63 _____

3. 11, 38, 65, 4, 67 _____

4. 3, 6, 3, 7, 8 _____

5. 120, 450, 630 _____

6. 4.2, 5.3, 7.1, 4.0, 11.9 _____

Gene's bowling scores were as follows: 8, 4, 10, 10, 9, 6, 9.

7. What was his average bowling score? _____

8. If Gene gets two more strikes (scores of 10),
what is his new average? _____

9. Reasoning Krishan wants his quiz average to be at least
90 so that he can get an A in the class. His current quiz scores
are: 80, 100, 85. What does he have to get on his
next quiz to have an average of 90?

A 85 **B** 90 **C** 92 **D** 95

10. Explain It Suppose Krishan's teacher says that he can drop one
of his test scores. Using his test scores of 80, 100, and 85, which
one should he drop, and why? What is his new average?

_____

_____

Median, Mode, and Range

The median, mode, and range are each numbers that describe a set of data.

Here is Eduardo's survey of how many books his friends read last month.

What are the median, mode, and range of Eduardo's survey?

Book Reading	
Friend	**Number of books read**
Jean	2
Raul	3
Sally	8
Jonathan	5
Haley	6
Kristen	3
Owen	1

Median: The median is the middle number in a set of data. To find it:

1. Arrange the data in order from least to greatest.

2. Locate the middle number.

1, 2, 3, 3, 5, 6, 8

↑ middle number = 3

The median number of books read is 3.

Mode: The mode is the data value that occurs most often. To find it:

1. List the data.   1, 2, 3, 3, 5, 6, 8

2. Find the number that occurs most.   3

The mode of the books read by Eduardo's friends is 3 books.

Range: The range is the difference between the greatest and least values. To find it:

1. Identify the greatest and least values.   8 and 1

2. Subtract the least from the greatest value. $8 - 1 = 7$

The range of the books read by Eduardo's friends is 7 books.

---

1. Find the median of this data set: 12, 18, 25, 32, 67.   _____

2. Find the mode of this data set: 123, 345, 654, 123, 452, 185.   _____

3. Find the range of this data set: 24, 32, 38, 31, 61, 35, 31.   _____

R 19-4

© Pearson Education, Inc. 6

Median, Mode, and Range

1. Find the range of this data set: 225 342 288 552 263.   _____

2. Find the median of this data set: 476 234 355 765 470.   _____

3. Find the mode of this data set:
   16 7 8 5 16 7 8 4 7 8 16 7.   _____

4. Find the range of this data set:
   64 76 46 88 88 43 99 50 55.   _____

5. **Reasoning** Would the mode change if a 76 were added
   to the data in Exercise 4?

   _____

   _____

The table below gives the math test scores for Mrs. Jung's
fifth-grade class.

76	54	92	88	76	88
75	93	92	68	88	76
76	88	80	70	88	72
Test Scores					

6. Find the mean of the data.   _____

7. Find the mode of the data.   _____

8. Find the median of the data.   _____

9. What is the range of the data set?   _____

10. Find the range of this data set: 247, 366, 785, 998.

    A 998   **B** 781   **C** 751   **D** 538

11. **Explain It** Will a set of data always have a mode?
    Explain your answer.

    _____

    _____

Frequency Tables and Histograms

Maya recorded the number of bags of popcorn she sold each day at the carnival, and then represented the data in a frequency table and histogram.

Bags of popcorn: 62, 65, 58, 31, 64, 58, 66, 68, 56, 67, 68, 51

Make a Frequency Table

Choose a Range: The range should cover all of the data. Divide the range into equal intervals or groups.

Range in popcorn data: 31 to 68, or 38 You can make intervals of 10 by using a range of 30 to 69.

Tally Marks: Record a tally mark for each value in the range.

Frequency: Count the tally marks and record.

Bags	Tally	Frequency
30–39	I	1
40–49		0
50–59	IIII	4
60–69	⧣Ⅱ	7

Make a Histogram

Choose a Title: Bags of Popcorn Sold
Choose a Scale for the Vertical Axis: Use frequency of the data for the scale.
List Intervals on Horizontal Axis

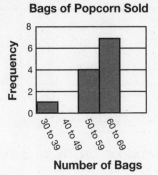

Use a Histogram
Look for clusters, gaps, and outliers.

Clusters: 50–69 for popcorn data
Gaps: 40–49; no bags sold in this interval
Outliers: 1 bag sold in 30–39 range

Use the information below for **1** through **3**.

Tickets Sold to Charity Ice-Skating Event							
72	81	88	51	90	89	85	74
87	100	80	99	87	96	99	84
84	86	94	88	91	85	78	90

1. Represent the data in the table in a histogram.
2. Where do most of the data in your histogram cluster?

_____

3. **Reasoning** Describe any outliers or gaps in the data.

_____

_____

_____

R 19•5

© Pearson Education, Inc. 6

Frequency Tables and Histograms

Conrad recorded the number of hours he spent on the Internet for two weeks. He made a frequency table of the data. Use the table for **1** through **2**.

| Hours on the Internet ||
Hours	Frequency
0–4	2
5–9	3
10–14	7
15–19	0
20–24	0
25–29	2

1. What is the mode of the data? Explain.

_____

_____

_____

2. How many days did Conrad spend 9 hours or less on the Internet? Explain.

_____

_____

Use the information below for **3** through **5**.

Ages of Players at Castle Miniature Golf				
14	7	6	24	15
9	19	25	10	17
51	8	21	48	12

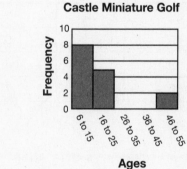

Ages of Players at Castle Miniature Golf

3. How many of the players are over 25? Explain.

_____

_____

4. Where do most of the data in the histogram cluster?

A 6–15   **C** 26–55

B 16–25   **D** Over 15

5. Writing to Explain Explain how you can tell whether a histogram has an outlier.

_____

_____

_____

Box Plots

To create a box plot for a data set, follow these steps:

Step 1: Check to see if the numbers are in order from least to greatest. If they are not, place them in that order. Draw a number line using an appropriate scale to include the numbers.

Step 2: Find the least value and greatest value. The least is the *minimum*. The greatest is the *maximum*.

Step 3: Find the number that is midway between the minimum and maximum. This value is the *median*.

Step 4: Find the value that is halfway between the minimum and the median. This is the *first quartile*.

Step 5: Find the value that is halfway between the median and the maximum. This is the *third quartile*.

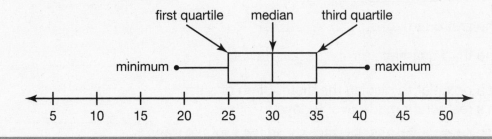

For **1** through **5**, use the five-step process for the following data:

8, 9, 3, 1, 2, 6, 5, 7, 4, 0, 10

1. Are the data in this set in order? If not, write them in order.

_____

2. What is the median? How can you tell?

_____

3. What is the minimum?   4. What is the first quartile?
   The maximum?   The third quartile?

   _____   _____

5. Draw a box plot for this data.

Box Plots

In **1** and **2** find the median, the first quartile, and third quartile.

1. In a bowling tournament, Sylvan got the following scores.

   167, 178, 193, 196, 199, 199, 203, 209, 217, 220, 221

   a. The median: _____

   b. The first quartile: _____

   c. The third quartile: _____

2. Sarina raised flowers. In a competition with other flower growers, she earned the following scores.

   7, 10, 10, 6, 7, 8, 8, 7, 9

   a. The median: _____

   b. The first quartile: _____

   c. The third quartile: _____

3. Make a box plot to display the distribution of sales Solon's restaurant made over 9 days:

   $1,074, $1,209, $1,315, $1,360, $1,391, $1,442, $1,482, $1,569, $1,601

4. Which describes how to find the first quartile in a data set?

   A Find the median of the data set.

   B Find the median of the upper half of the data.

   C Find the median of the lower half of the data.

   D Count 3 spaces to the right from the minimum.

5. **Writing to Explain** David wants to make a box plot showing his team's points for the year. The median score was 7, first quartile was 4, and third quartile was 10. The minimum was 2 and the maximum was 20. Explain how David can draw the box plot.

   _____

   _____

   _____

Measures of Variability

Variability describes how clustered or spread out data is. You might think of variability in terms of a game of horseshoes. The goal of the game is to get as many horseshoes as you can to "ring," or hook around, a post. Once a player has taken a turn, the horseshoes—or data—look something like this picture.

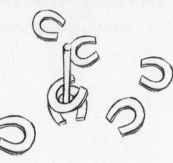

One way of measuring variability of data is by finding the *mean absolute deviation*.

Step 1. Find the mean of the data. To do this, you add the data values and divide by the number of values in the set. Suppose you have 20, 40, 60, 80, 100 as the data. The sum of these numbers 20 + 40 + 60 + 80 + 100 = 300. Since there are 5 items in the set, 300 ÷ 5 = 60.

Step 2. Find the absolute deviation for each value in the data set. To do this, find each absolute value of the difference between the mean and each number in the set. So, for the numbers in the set, you get:

$|60 - 20| = $ **40**

$|60 - 40| = $ **20**

$|60 - 60| = $ **0**

$|80 - 60| = $ **20**

$|100 - 60| = $ **40**

Step 3. Find the mean of the absolute deviations. You find the mean of the absolute deviations by adding 40 + 20 + 0 + 20 + 40 = 120. Then divide by the number of values, 5, which gives you 24. So the mean absolute deviation for 20, 40, 60, 80, 100 is 24.

Use the 3-step process to find the mean absolute deviation for each set of data. Give the mean of the original set, the sum of the absolute deviations, and the mean absolute deviation.

1. 10, 15, 20, 30, 50

_____

_____

2. 500; 1,000; 1,500; 2,000

_____

_____

Measures of Variability

For **1** through **6**, use the following data set: 12, 20, 16, 10, 17, 9, 23, 13

1. What is the mean of this set?

    _____

2. What is the absolute deviation from the mean for the following values:

    a. 12 _____

    b. 16 _____

    c. 20 _____

3. Which value in the original set has the greatest absolute deviation from the mean? Which has the least absolute deviation?

    _____

4. What is the mean absolute deviation for the set?

    _____

5. What is first quartile for the set? The third quartile?

    _____

6. What is the IQR for the set?

    _____

For **7** and **8**, use the following data set: 3, 7, 11, 15, 20, 31, 39, 42

7. **Writing to Explain** The data set shows the approximate hourly tides in feet recorded at a beach during an 8-hour period. What is the mean absolute deviation for the data set? Explain how you found it.

    _____

    _____

    _____

    _____

8. Which is the IQR for the set?

    A 26   **B** 28   **C** 35   **D** 36

Appropriate Use of Statistical Measures

Paige tracked the number of points scored so far this season by each member of her basketball team: 28, 30, 28, 30, 40, 30, 34, 32. Which measure of center and measure of variability best describe the typical number of points scored?

Make a dot plot to organize the data and identify any outliers.

The median and mode are 30. The mean is 31.5. There is a gap between 34 and 40, and 40 is an outlier.

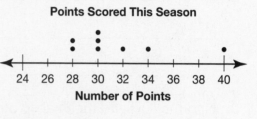

Points Scored This Season

Number of Points

Since the outlier, 40, affects the mean, the median is the best measure of center for the data. For measures of variability, use the mean absolute deviation when the mean is the appropriate measure of center. Use the interquartile range when the median is more appropriate. Since the median is the best measure of center, you would use the IQR to measure variability of this data.

1. Make a dot plot using this set of data:
   38, 68, 78, 88, 98

2. Which measure of center and measure of variability best describes this data set? Why?

   _____

   _____

   _____

3. Make a dot plot using this set of data:
   35, 38, 40, 35, 37, 38, 36, 40, 43

4. Find the mean, median, and mode of the data set.

   _____

5. Which measure of center best describes this data set? Why?

   _____

   _____

Appropriate Use of Statistical Measures

1. Find the mean, median, and mode of this data set:
   76, 74, 78, 72, 73, 80, 49, 72, 83

   _____

2. Which measure of center best describes the data set? Why?

   _____

   _____

3. Find the IQR and mean absolute deviation of the data set below.
   Round the mean absolute deviation to the nearest hundredth.
   13, 19, 17, 15, 11, 19, 18

   _____

4. Which measure of variability best describes the data set in Exercise 3? Why?

   _____

   _____

5. Find the mean, median, and mode of this data set:
   150, 138, 130, 127, 140, 108, 138

   _____

6. **Critical Thinking** What number could be added to the data set in
   Exercise 5, so that the mean, median, and mode are all the same?

   _____

7. **Writing to Explain** Ava found the mean, median, and mode of a
   data set. Then she discovered that she had not included a very
   high outlier in her calculations. How will the mean, median, and
   mode be affected by the inclusion of this outlier? Explain.

   _____

   _____

   _____

Summarizing Data Distributions

The box plot to the right displays data for the number of days the temperature was over 80°F for the month of July. Data in displays can be summarized.

Days above 80°F in July

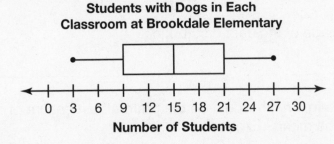

You can summarize this data set by choosing some ways to describe it. The data are spread out to the right. The median is 10, and it describes the center of the data. The first quartile is 3 and the third quartile is 22. The interquartile range or IQR describes the variability and it can be found by subtracting the first quartile (3) from the third quartile (22) to get 19.

Use the box plot to answer Questions **1** through **4**.

**Students with Dogs in Each
Classroom at Brookdale Elementary**

1. What is the greatest number of students in a classroom that have a dog? The least? _____

2. a. What is the median? _____

   b. What are the first and third quartiles? _____

   c. What is the interquartile range? _____

3. Describe the shape of the data distribution.

   _____

4. **Writing to Explain** If a dot plot was used to display the same data, make a prediction about how the data would look.

   _____

   _____

Summarizing Data Distributions

For **1** through **5** use the data set below.

Mr. Hansen's physical education class did a long jump competition.
Each person jumped 3 times, and wrote their best long jump (in inches).

84, 80, 80, 76, 79, 82, 89, 72, 76, 78,
80, 85, 110, 79, 77, 79, 81, 79, 80, 81, 72, 83

1. Make a box plot for the data.

2. **a** What is the mean? The median? _____

   b What are the first and third quartiles? _____

   c What is the interquartile range? _____

3. Describe the shape of the data distribution.

   _____

4. **Writing to Explain** Which would be the preferable measure of center,
   the median or the mean? Explain.

   _____

   _____

5. Would the median or the mean be more affected if a long jump of
   140 inches was added to the data? Explain how you know.

   _____

   _____

6. Which is the best representation of the
   center of this data set?

   A 2 fish   **C** 4 fish

   B 3 fish   **D** 5 fish

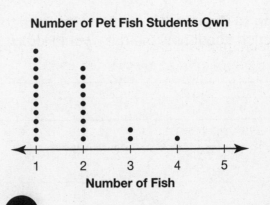

Number of Pet Fish Students Own

Number of Fish

Problem Solving:
Try, Check, and Revise

Audrey bowled 3 games. Her mean score was 148. Each score was different. Name three possible scores. Remember that the highest possible score in bowling is 300.

Use the problem solving plan.

Read and Understand:

What do you know?
Audrey bowled 3 games.
Her mean score was 148.

What are you trying to find?
Three scores that have a mean of 148.

Plan and Solve:

What strategy will you use?
Try, check, and revise.

Try 156, 140, 160. The mean is
$(156 + 140 + 160) \div 3 = 456 \div 3 = 152.$

The mean is too high by 4 points:
$152 - 148 = 4.$
Try subtracting 4 points from each score.
$156 - 4 = 152, 140 - 4 = 136,$
$160 - 4 = 156.$

Check:
Check to see if the mean is 148.

$(152 + 136 + 156) \div 3 = 444 \div 3 = 148$

1. The median time 5 people waited to ride on "The Whirl and Twirl" was 38 minutes. List 5 possible times they may have waited.

   _____

2. Ben checked the price of the camera he wants at 4 stores. Each price was different. The mean price was $238. What are 4 possible prices for the camera?

   _____

3. Five hamsters weighed between 12 and 20 ounces. The mode weight of the 5 hamsters is 18 ounces. List the possible weights of the hamsters.

   _____

4. The mean, median, and mode of a set of 4 numbers is 100. Name 4 numbers that could make up the set.

   _____

5. The mean and median of a set of 6 numbers is 140. Name 6 numbers that could make up the set.

   _____

R 19·10

Problem Solving:
Try, Check, and Revise

1. The mean number of passengers on a daily flight from Los Angeles to San Francisco is 82. The plane holds a maximum of 102 passengers. List the possible number of passengers on the flight over the past 5 days.

   _____

2. Four adult pandas weigh between 200 and 275 pounds. Their median weight is 240 pounds. List four possible weights for the pandas.

   _____

3. Over the past 7 years the median rainfall in West Berry has been 74 inches. The greatest rainfall was 102 inches. The least was 52 inches. List possible rainfall amounts for the 7 years.

   _____

4. The mean number of miles Mr. Austin drove in six days was 96. The mode was 82. The median was 97. What are possible distances Mr. Austin drove in the 6 days?

   _____

5. **Writing to Explain** The mode of the heights of 5 sunflowers is 70 inches. The median is 68 inches. What are some possible heights of the 5 sunflowers? Tell how you decide.

   _____

   _____

   _____

6. **Number Sense** Three consecutive odd integers have a sum of 195. What are the integers?

   _____

7. **Geometry** The area of a rectangle is 180 square inches. The perimeter is 58 inches. What are the dimensions of the rectangle?

   A 30 in. by 6 in.   **C** 14 in. by 16 in.

   B 20 in. by 9 in.   **D** 12 in. by 15 in.